PHILIP'S *Rea*

G000153762

ISLE OF WIGHT

www.philips-maps.co.uk
First published in 2004 by Philip's,
a division of Octopus Publishing Group Ltd
www.octopusbooks.co.uk
Endeavour House, 189 Shaftesbury Avenue
London WC2H 8JY
An Hachette UK Company
www.hachette.co.uk

Second edition 2010
Third impression 2014
IOWBA

978-1-84907-334-9

© Philip's 2010

ois Ordnance Survey®

This product includes mapping data licensed from
Ordnance Survey® with the permission of the
Controller of Her Majesty's Stationery Office.
© Crown copyright 2010. All rights reserved.
Licence number 100011710.

Photographic acknowledgements:
title page *Shellyrolo / iStockphoto.com*
XII top left *matphoto / iStockphoto.com*
XII top right *Amanda Lewis / iStockphoto.com*
XII centre *Chris Moncrief / Dreamstime.com*
XII bottom *rest / iStockphoto.com*
XIII left *Steve Stone / iStockphoto.com*
XIII right *Amanda Lewis / iStockphoto.com*
XIV *Biginfocus / Dreamstime.com*
XV top *Epphoto / Dreamstime.com*
XV bottom *Chris Steer / iStockphoto.com*

Printed in China

Contents

II	**Key to map pages**
IV	**Route planning**
XII	**Tourist information**
XVI	Major administrative and Postcode boundaries
1	**Key to map symbols**
2	**Street maps** at 2⅔ inches to 1 mile
54	**Street map** of Portsmouth at 5⅓ inches to 1 mile
55	**Index** of towns, villages, streets, hospitals, industrial estates, railway stations, schools, shopping centres, universities and places of interest

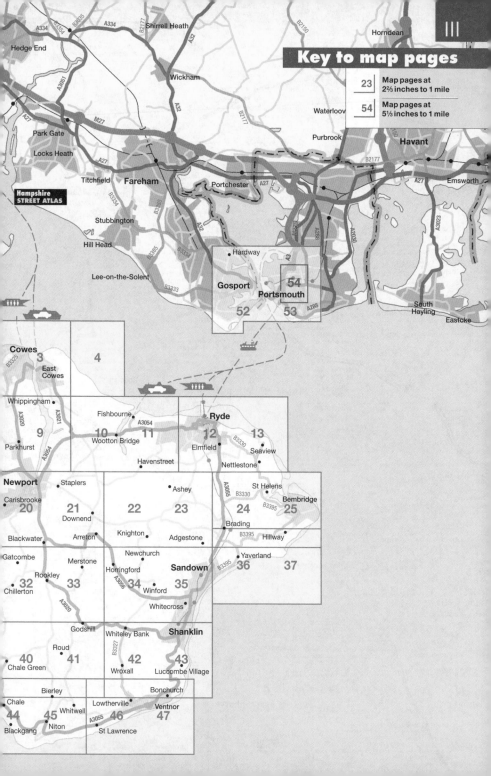

III

Hampshire
STREET ATLAS

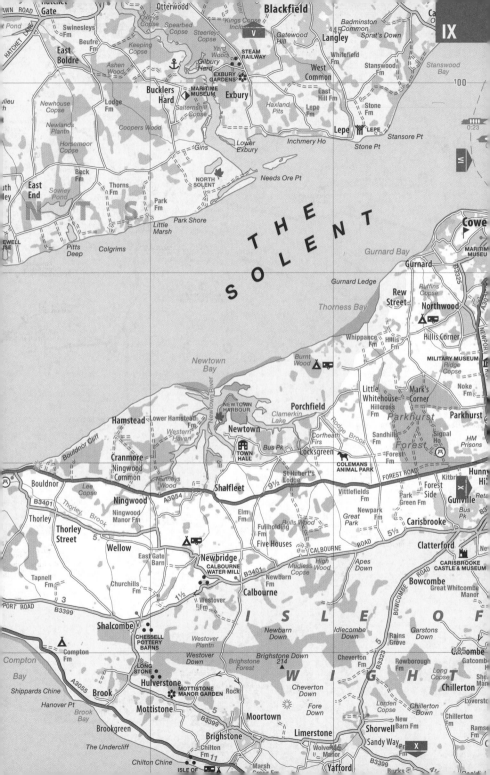

Tourist information

▲ Bembridge Windmill
◀ Ventnor
▶ St Catharine's Oratory
▶▶ St Boniface Church
◀ Carisbrook Castle
▼ Tennyson monument

Historic Buildings and Monuments

Afton Down Obelisk
A cliff-edge monument to a 15-year-old who fell to his death here in 1846, built as a warning to visitors. **Afton Down 27 E6**

Appuldurcombe House
A partially restored Baroque house built in the 18th century, with 11-acre grounds, including gardens designed by Capability Brown, a nature trail, and an Owl and Falconry Centre with daily flying displays. Special events include plays and military re-enactments. **Wroxall, near Ventnor** ✆ 01983 852484 · www.appuldurcombe.co.uk **42 A4**

Ashey Sea Mark
A solid white sea-mark constructed for sailors in 1735. **Ashey Down Summit 23 A4**

Bembridge Fort
An abandoned 1860s land fort. Guided tours only. **Between Culver Cliff and Brading** · www.nationaltrust.org.uk **24 E1**

Bembridge Windmill
The only surviving windmill on the island, built c.1700 and retaining its original wooden machinery. **Mill Road, Bembridge** · www.nationaltrust.org.uk ✆ 01983 873945 **25 B3**

Brading Roman Villa
A 1st-century AD Roman villa excavated in the 1880s, with important 4th-century mosaics. Visitor centre and exhibition. **Morton Old Road, Brading** · www.bradingromanvilla.org.uk ✆ 01983 406223 **23 F1**

Carisbrooke Castle
An imposing castle on a ridge, with a museum, a Donkey Centre, an 800-year-old Great Hall, a wellhouse with a treadwheel, and excellent views. **Carisbrooke, Newport** ✆ 01983 522107 · www.english-heritage.org.uk **20 B4**

Grays Monument
A memorial to a 9-year-old chimney sweep killed by his employer in 1822. **Church Litten, Newport 20 E6**

Hoy Monument
A tall stone column topped by a large finial sphere, erected in 1814 by local merchant Michael Hoy to commemorate a visit to Britain by Tsar Alexander I. **St Catherine's Down (near Blackgang) 44 F8**

Long Stone
Neolithic barrow (large grave) marker situated on tumuli and dated 3000–2000BC. **Mottistone Down, near Brighstone 29 D5**

Morton Manor
A manor house first built in 1249, augmented by a Tudor longhouse and largely rebuilt in 1680, with Georgian interiors and splendid gardens with rhododendrons, azaleas, magnolias and more. **Yarbridge, near Brading** ✆ 01983 406168 **36 A7**

Needles Old Battery
A dramatically sited 1862 coastal fort built to prevent invasion by the French, with an exhibition, the original gun barrels, a restored laboratory, searchlight position and position-finding cells, children's information boards and activity packs, and a 65m tunnel leading to a splendid viewpoint over the Needles (famous chalk pinnacles) and a tearoom. **West High Down, Alum Bay** ✆ 01983 754772 · www.nationaltrust.org.uk **26 B4**

Newport Roman Villa
The remains of a Roman farmhouse built c. AD280, with part of a bath and a hypocaust system, recreations of everyday scenes (and re-enactment days), and a Roman herb garden. **Cypress Road, Newport** ✆ 01983 529720 · www.iow.gov.uk **20 E6**

Nunwell House and Gardens
A handsome family residence built in 1522, with the Parlour Chamber where Sir John Oglander played host to Charles I on his last night of freedom. There are displays on the family's military connections, an Old Kitchen exhibition, and 5 acres of grounds, including a walled garden with views across the Solent. **Coach Lane, Brading** ✆ 01983 407240 · www.islandbreaks.co.uk **23 F3**

Old Town Hall, Newtown
A 17th-century hall, now containing an exhibition on local history, including 'Ferguson's Gang' of anonymous benefactors. **Newtown** ✆ 01983 531785 · www.nationaltrust.org.uk **6 E2**

Osborne House
Queen Victoria's imposing three-storey seaside retreat and the place where she died, built in 1848, given to the nation by Edward VII and managed by English Heritage. Interior highlights include the Indian Room, Victoria's bedroom and closet, and the royal nursery. The grounds include a late 18th-century walled kitchen garden and pleasure grounds that survived from the previous estate on the site, and the parterre gardens and terraces have been restored to their Victorian layout. **East Cowes** ✆ 01983 200022 · www.english-heritage.org.uk **3 F2**

St Catherine's Oratory (Pepper Pot)
An octagonal tower, built in 1328 as a penance for stealing property from a wreck. It is said to have been used as a lighthouse. **St Catherine's Down, Chale** · www.english-heritage.org.uk **44 E5**

Tennyson Monument
A marble Maltese cross erected in memory of Alfred Lord Tennyson after his death in 1892; the poet had

Ventnor Botanic Garden

A 22-acre botanic garden founded in 1970, with plants from around the world, a Visitor Centre with exhibitions and library, a coastal path, a picnic area and a playground. **Undercliff Drive, Ventnor** ☎01983 855397 •www.botanic.co.uk **46 D4**

Wayside Herbs and Flowers

A small herb and wildflower garden with Kune Kune pigs and Shetland and Jacob sheep, plus a programme of summer events. **Bamfurlong Chine Lane, Yafford** •www.waysideherbs.co.uk ☎01983 740787 **38 H8**

Places of Worship

All Saints (Church of the Lily Cross) A church on a 950-year-old site of Christian worship; the present (4th) church was built in the early 14th century, with two naves separated by a wooden screen, one for parishioners, the other for manorial workers. The 'Lily Cross' wall-painting was uncovered in the 19th century. **Godshill 41 D8**

Church of the Holy Cross Originally a Norman church retaining its old doorway with a sculpted grotesque, a 13th-century chancel, and a 15th-century bell thought to have come from nearby Quarr Abbey, now housed in a 1925 bellcote. The churchyard contains the tomb of Samuel Giant, said to have been the biggest man in the world, who died in 1844. **Binstead 11 F6**

St Andrew An isolated ancient church overlooking a treacherous stretch of coast, built in the 12th century but altered and enlarged several times, with a 15th-century tower. **Chale 44 C6**

St Boniface The island's second-smallest church, on a place of worship dating back as far as the Saxon occupation and dedicated to a Saxon saint. **Bonchurch 47 D7**

St George, Arreton A church on the site of a private chapel of the lords of the manor of Arreton, first recorded in AD901; the present building is mainly 11th century, with some late Saxon or early Norman elements and a 13th-century

tower. The churchyard contains the tomb of Elizabeth Wallbridge, heroine of bestselling story 'The Dairyman's Daughter'. **Arreton 21 E2**

St Mary the Virgin, Brading A church with a Norman nave containing a simple Jacobean table serving as an altar, beneath which Saxon remains were discovered, and a memorial to Reverend Leight Richmond, author of 'Annals of the Poor'. **24 B3**

St Mildred Built in the 1850s, this fanciful Gothic-inspired church was used by Queen Victoria when at Osborne House. As well as royal memorials and the queen's pew, it contains a beautiful bronze screen by Alfred Gilbert in the chancel arcade. **Beatrice Avenue, Whippingham 9 E8**

St Peter Originally a Norman building, the current grade-1 Perpendicular church mostly dates from the 15th century. It has an unusual layout, a pulpit that is entered through one of the piers, Jacobean benches and a 14th-century mural of St Christopher. **Shorwell 31 B2**

Museums and Galleries

See also Carisbrooke Castle

Bembridge Heritage Centre An exhibition of village life past and present, in a former Victorian school building. **Church Road, Bembridge** ☎01983 873606 **25 C5**

Brighstone Village Museum A small museum on Victorian

life. **North Street, Brighstone** ☎01983 740689 •www.nationaltrust.org.uk **30 B2**

Calbourne Water Mill and Rural Museum A working water mill first mentioned in the Domesday Book, with various small museums (including an old fire station and bakery), displays on renewable energy, punts and children's activities, and surrounded by ancient oak woodland providing a habitat for badgers, red squirrels and more. **Newport Rd, Calbourne** •www.calbournewatermill.co.uk ☎01983 521227 **17 E2**

Classic Boat Museum A collection of restored sailing and motor boats and boating memorabilia. **The Quay, Newport** •www.classicboatmuseum.co.uk ☎01983 583493 **20 E8**

Cowes Maritime Museum A small exhibition tracing local maritime history through models and paintings. **Library, Beckford Road, Cowes** ☎01983 823433 •www.iwight.com **3 B4**

Dimbola Lodge A photography museum and gallery in the one-time home of 19th-century photographer Julia Margaret Cameron, with displays of antique cameras and exhibitions of Cameron's and others' images, including contemporary work. **Terrace Lane, Freshwater Bay** ☎ 01983 756814 **27 C6**

East Cowes Heritage Centre Small museum on the history of East Cowes in permanent and temporary exhibits. **8 Clarence Road, East Cowes** ☎01983 280310 •www.eastcowesheritagecentre.org.uk **3 C3**

---

settled at Farringford in 1853. **Tennyson Down, Freshwater Bay**• www.isleofwightattractions.co.uk ☎01983 280111 **26 H5**

Yarmouth Castle

A Tudor castle, Henry VIII's last fortress, with exhibitions of local paintings and photographs of old Yarmouth, fine views over the Solent from its battlements and good picnic spots on its rampart lawns. **Yarmouth** • www.english-heritage.org.uk ☎01983 760678 **15 C6**

Gardens and Parks

See also Appuldurcombe House, Morton Manor and Nunwell House and Gardens (Historic Buildings)

Afton Park Beautifully sited 7-acre gardens with an orchard, a wildflower meadow, a plant nursery, farm shop and a café. **Newport Road, Freshwater** ☎01983 755774 • www.aftonpark.co.uk **27 D8**

Mottistone Manor Garden

A terraced garden with borders and a kitchen garden surrounding a medieval/Elizabethan manor house in a wooded valley with views of the Channel. **Hoxall Lane, Mottistone** ☎01983 741302 • www.nationaltrust.org.uk **29 D4**

Old Smithy Gardens

Landscaped gardens set around a former blacksmith's forge (now a retail complex), with a Model Village of local places of interest, an aviary, grottoes, and a cottage garden with unusual herbs. **High Street, Godshill** ☎01983 840364 •www.theoldsmithy.com **41 D8**

Fort Victoria Model Railway

The world's largest computer-controlled model railway. **Fort Victoria Country Park** ☎ 01983 761553 • www.fortvictoriamodelrailway.co.uk **14 F6**

Island Planetarium

An astronomy centre and planetarium theatre hosting multimedia shows, stargazing evenings and lectures. **Fort Victoria Country Park, near Yarmouth** • www.islandastronomy.co.uk ☎ 01983 761555 **14 F6**

Isle of Wight Bus Museum

A collection of island buses and coaches, plus an early-1900s Ryde Pier tram car, in a former grain warehouse. **The Quay, Newport** ☎ 01983 533352 • www.iowbusmuseum.org.uk **20 E8**

Isle of Wight Military Museum

A good selection of World War 2 and postwar armoured vehicles and other equipment, guided tours. Regular displays in summer includr rides round the tank course. **490 Newport Road, Cowes** www.isleofwight.com/militarymuseum ☎ 01983 527491 **9 A6**

Isle of Wight Model Railway

A miniature-railway centre with history displays, antique sets and track layouts. **The Parade, Cowes** ☎ 01983 280111 **3 B5**

Lilliput Antique Doll and Toy Museum

More than 2000 dolls and playthings dating from c.2000BC to 1945. **High Street, Brading** • www.lilliputmuseum.org.uk ☎ 01983 407231 **24 B3**

Museum of Island History

A museum charting the island's history from prehistoric times, with interactive exhibits, quizzes, games and more. **Guildhall, High Street, Newport** • www.iwight.com ☎ 01983 823433 **20 E7**

Quay Arts Centre

An art gallery and live events venue in a 19th-century brewery warehouse. **Sea Street, Newport Harbour** ☎ 01983 822490 **20 E7**

Shipwreck Centre and Maritime Museum

Local maritime heritage displays, including items recovered from shipwrecks, diving equipment, ships' models, and exhibits about the lifeboat services. **Arreton Barns Craft Village, Arreton** ☎ 01983 533709 **21 E2**

Smuggling Museum

An exhibition on smuggling history and methods from the 13th century onward. **Ventnor Botanic Garden (see xiii)** ☎ 01983 853677 **46 D4**

Nature and Animals

See also Appuldurcombe House and Carisbrooke Castle

Amazon World

A simulated rainforest with a large Jurassic-themed adventure park, exotic animals, falconry displays and talks by the keepers. **Watery Lane, Newchurch, near Arreton** www.amazonworld.co.uk ☎ 01983 867122 **34 C5**

Brickfields Horse Country

An equestrian attraction with shire horses, miniature Shetland ponies, a farm corner, a museum, a blacksmith's forge, a riding school, a play area and special events. **Newnham Road, Binstead, Ryde** ☎ 01983 566801 • www.brickfields.net **11 E3**

Butterfly and Fountain World

Indoor landscaped gardens (a Japanese garden with koi carp, a tropical garden and an Italian garden) with freeflying butterflies, fountain displays and more. **Staplers Road, Wootton** • www.butterfly-world-iow.co.uk ☎ 01983 883430 **10 B2**

Coastal Visitors Centre

The point of contact for those interested in or concerned about the island's coastline, the longest stretch in the UK, with themed rooms on different aspects of the coast and its management, from plant and animal life to marine archaeology, aquarium tanks and a children's touch pool. Guided walks, children's activities and talks. **Isle of Wight Centre for the Coastal Environment, Dudley Road, Ventnor** ☎ 01983 857220 • www.coastalwight. gov.uk/coastalcentre.htm **47 A5**

Colemans Animal Farm

A family farm with feeding and petting sessions, milking, pony rides, a tractor fun park, sand pits, an adventure play and picnic areas and daily activities. **Colemans Lane, Porchfield** • www.colemansfarmpark.co.uk ☎ 01983 522831 **7 E1**

Dinosaur Farm Museum

A conservation facility for and museum of locally discovered dinosaur remains, with a fossil identification service, children's activities and a tearoom. **Military Road (A3055), nr Brighstone** • www. isleofwight.com/dinosaurfarmmuseum ☎ 01983 740844 **38 G6**

Dinosaur Isle

A purpose-built attraction with the Isle's dinosaur types in a recreated landscape, interactive exhibits, and the opportunity to see volunteers working on new fossil finds. **Culver Parade, Sandown** ☎ 01983 404344 • www.dinosaurisle.com **36 B4**

Donkey Sanctuary

A donkey-rescue charity housing more than 200 donkeys and other animals over 50 acres, and offering an 'Adopt a Donkey' scheme. **Lower Winstone Farm, Whiteley Bank, Wroxall** www.iwdonkeysanctuary.co.uk ☎ 01983 852693 **42 B7**

Flamingo Park Wildlife Encounter

Animal park with flamingos, pelicans, penguins, owls, wallabies, meerkats, Asian otters, beavers, red squirrels, an aviary, a Discovery Zone, feeding sessions and landscaped gardens overlooking the Solent. **Springvale, Seaview** ☎ 01983 612153 • www.flamingopark.com **13 B4**

The Needles Rocks and Lighthouse

Fort Victoria Marine Aquarium and Sunken History Exhibition

An aquarium largely devoted to local sea fish and invertebrates, set in the remains of a Victorian fort with a tropical reef section and an exhibition on marine archaeology around the world. **Fort Victoria Country Park, near Yarmouth •www.fortvictoria.co.uk/aquarium/marine–aquarium.htm ✆ 01983 760283 14 F6**

Isle of Wight Zoo

Incorporating the Tiger and Big Cat Sanctuary – a collection of rare and endangered big cats. The zoo also features lemurs and monkeys, spiders, reptiles and amphibians, plus a children's play area and pets' corner. **Seafront, Yaverland, Sandown • www.isleofwightzoo.com ✆ 01983 403883 36 B4**

Natural History Centre

A 17th-century squire's cottage housing collections of shells, minerals, insects and birds, plus aquaria, a pond with koi carp and ornamental fountains, and a replica set of the Crown Jewels used during a rehearsal for the Queen's coronation. **High St, Godshill • www.shellmuseum.co.uk ✆ 01983 840333 41 D8**

Shanklin Chine

An historic gorge, once the haunt of smugglers, with waterfalls, nature trails (with the chance of red squirrels), nature hide, rare plants, a Heritage Centre with exhibitions, and a Victorian tea garden. It is part of The Chines, a special coastal feature (see also Blackgang Chine xv). **Old Village, Shanklin ✆ 01983 866432 www.shanklinchine.co.uk 43 C7**

Activities

Adgestone Vineyard

A vineyard and winery offering tastings and cellar tours. **Adgestone ✆ 01983 402503 • www.adgestonevineyard.co.uk 23 F2**

Bembridge Trail

A 10-mile walking trail from the middle of the island to its eastern tip, over downland and past marshes, historic houses and the village of Brading. **From Newport to Bembridge 22 E2**

Blackgang Chine

Dramatic 40-acre landscaped clifftop gardens with a range of family attractions, including Wild West Town, a roller coaster, Dinosaurland, a shipwreck collection and a maze. **Chale, near Ventnor ✆ 01983 730330 •www.blackgangchine.com 44 C4**

Cowes Week

The world's most famous sailing regatta, held annually in early August since 1826. There are 8 or 9 days of racing involving about 900 craft, and a host of social events, including balls and a fireworks finale. **Cowes ✆ 01983 296621 •www.cowesweek.co.uk**

Fort Victoria Country Park

A country park with seashore and woodland walks, a nature trail, ranger tours, and fine views over the Solent, and containing an aquarium (see xiv), a planetarium (see xiii) and a model railway (see xiii). **Fort Victoria, near Yarmouth ✆ 01983 823893 • www.fortvictoria.co.uk 14 F6**

Freshwater Golf Club

One of two 18-hole courses on the island, with panoramic views of the Solent and English Channel, and Neolithic and Bronze Age burial mounds forming natural 'hazards', set on a Site of Special Scientific Interest with many rare and endangered plant and animal species. **Afton Down, Freshwater • www.freshwaterbaygolfclub.co.uk ✆ 01983 752966 27 E6**

Hamstead Trail

A 7-mile walking trail crossing the island from north to south, passing saltwater marshes and ancient burial grounds, including the Long Stone (see xii). At the south coast the remains of a fossil forest can be seen at low tide. **From Hamstead to Brook 16 F3**

Island Brass Rubbing Centre,

A craft centre with reproduction medieval brasses depicting chivalrous scenes; tuition is provided. **Arreton Barns Craft Village, Arreton ✆ 01983 528353 21 E2**

Island Sailing Club

A friendly family yachting club with excellent facilities. **70 High Street, Cowes www.islandsc.org.uk ✆ 01983 296911 3 B5**

Island Speedway

Motorcycle speedway races. **Smallbrook Stadium, Ashey Road, Ryde • www.islandspeedway.co.uk ✆ 01983 811180 12 C1**

Isle of Wight Steam Railway

5-mile country trips in restored Victorian and Edwardian steam trains, plus a museum, woodland walk and play area. **Railway Station, Havenstreet • www.iwsteamrailway.co.uk ✆ 01983 882204 22 E8**

The Needles Park

A park offering views of the spectacular Needles Rocks and lighthouse. Features a chairlift to the beach with its coloured sand, children's attractions, a pier with shopping arcade, glass manufactory, sand shop, Jurassic golf, junior driver and boat trips, as well as summer fireworks displays. **Alum Bay ✆ 01983 752401 • www.theneedles.co.uk 26 D5**

Robin Hill Countryside Adventure Park

A country park with activities for all ages, including a Countryside Centre with a sensory zone, a play village, a wooden maze, a toboggan run, woodland walks and a treetop trail. **Downend, Arreton ✆ 01983 730052 • www.robin-hill.com 21 F4**

Rosemary Vineyard

One of Britain's biggest vineyards, with both guided walks and self-guided trails, and free tastings. **Smallbrook Lane, Ryde ✆ 01983 811084 •www.rosemaryvineyard.co.uk 12 C3**

Round the Island Cycling Route

A route taking in dedicated cycle-ways, disused

▲ Isle of Wight Steam Railway

railway lines, bridleways and quiet country lanes. Maps are available from tourist centres. **✆ 01983 813818**

St Helens Beach

One of the island's 13 award-winning beaches, adjoining some National Trust land that is home to a variety of interesting wildlife. A calm spot with wonderful views over Bembridge Harbour, it is excellent for swimming. **St Helens 25 B7**

Solent and Wight Line cruises

Half-hour Cowes Harbour sightseeing trips, cruises taking in Cowes, Yarmouth and the Needles, full-day trips to Portsmouth and more. **66 Newnham Road, Binstead, Ryde ✆ 01983 564602**

Tennyson Trail

A 12½-mile walk across the downs and through forests, passing ancient burial sites and the Tennyson Monument, and affording excellent views. **From Carisbrooke Castle to the Needles 20 A3**

Walking Festival

The UK's biggest walking festival, held each May, with more than 130 volunteer-led walks, including castles, the Red Squirrel Safari, storytime walks, lanternlit strolls, ghost walks, a pram walk and a 70-mile 24-hour walk around the island. **✆ 01983 813818**

Waltzing Waters

An indoor synchronised water, light and music show. **Westridge, Ryde ✆ 01983 811333 •www.waltzingwaters.co.uk 12 F1**

Worsley Trail

A 12½-mile walk past pine forests and farm buildings, over chalk downlands, fields and a disused railway line. **From Mottistone Down to Old Shanklin 30 C5**

Coastal Path

Major administrative and Postcode boundaries

County and unitary
authority boundaries
Postcode boundaries
Area covered by this atlas

30　40　50　60　70

20

S017
S018
S015
Southampton
S014 S019
S040

**City of
Southampton**

Hampshire

10

**City of
Portsmouth**

SU
SZ

Hampshire

P02
P012　P01
Gosport　Portsmouth
P05　P04

SU
SZ

100

P041
Lymington

Cowes
East Cowes
P031　P032
Northwood
Fishbourne
Ryde
Little
Whitehouse
Wootton
Bridge
Binstead
Havenstreet
P034
Nettlestone
Hamstead
P033
Yarmouth
St Helens
90
Shalfleet
Newport
Bembridge
Norton Green
Wellow
Carisbrooke
P035
P040
P041
Calbourne
Brading
Totland
Isle of Wight
P036
P039
Newchurch
Freshwater
Bay
Brook
P030
Sandown
Brighstone
Shorwell
Godshill
Shanklin
P037
Luccombe
Village
80
Chale
Green
P038
Wroxall
Blackgang
Ventnor
Niton

30　40

Scale
0　5　10　15 km
0　5　10 miles

50　60　70

Key to map symbols

Motorway with junction number	
Primary route – dual/single carriageway	
A road – dual/single carriageway	
B road – dual/single carriageway	
Minor road – dual/single carriageway	
Other minor road – dual/single carriageway	
Road under construction	
Tunnel, covered road	
Speed cameras – single, multiple	
Rural track, private road or narrow road in urban area	
Gate or obstruction to traffic – restrictions may not apply at all times or to all vehicles	
Path, bridleway, byway open to all traffic, restricted byway	
Pedestrianised area	
Postcode boundaries	
County or unitary authority boundaries	
Railway with station	
Tunnel	
Railway under construction	
Metro station	
Private railway station	
Miniature railway	
Tramway, tramway under construction	
Tram stop, tram stop under construction	
Bus, coach station	

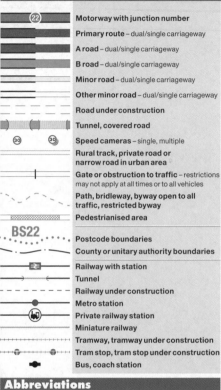

Ambulance station	
Coastguard station	
Fire station	
Police station	
Accident and Emergency entrance to hospital	
Hospital	
Place of worship	
Information centre – open all year	
Shopping centre, parking	
Park and Ride, Post Office	
Camping site, caravan site	
Golf course, picnic site	
Non-Roman antiquity, Roman antiquity	
Important buildings, schools, colleges, universities and hospitals	
Woods, built-up area	
Water name	
River, weir	
Stream	
Canal, lock, tunnel	
Water	
Tidal water	
Adjoining page indicators and overlap bands – the colour of the arrow and band indicates the scale of the adjoining or overlapping page (see scales below)	

The dark grey border on the inside edge of some pages indicates that the mapping does not continue onto the adjacent page

The small numbers around the edges of the maps identify the 1-kilometre National Grid lines

Abbreviations

Acad	Academy	Meml	Memorial
Allot Gdns	Allotments	Mon	Monument
Cemy	Cemetery	Mus	Museum
C Ctr	Civic centre	Obsy	Observatory
CH	Club house	Pal	Royal palace
Coll	College	PH	Public house
Crem	Crematorium	Recn Gd	Recreation ground
Ent	Enterprise	Resr	Reservoir
Ex H	Exhibition hall	Ret Pk	Retail park
Ind Est	Industrial Estate	Sch	School
IRB Sta	Inshore rescue boat station	Sh Ctr	Shopping centre
Inst	Institute	TH	Town hall / house
Ct	Law court	Trad Est	Trading estate
L Ctr	Leisure centre	Univ	University
LC	Level crossing	W Twr	Water tower
Liby	Library	Wks	Works
Mkt	Market	YH	Youth hostel

Enlarged maps only

Railway or bus station building	
Place of interest	
Parkland	

The map scale on the pages numbered in blue is 2⅔ inches to 1 mile
4.2 cm to 1 km • 1:23810

0	¼ mile	½ mile	¾ mile	1 mile
0	250m	500m	750m	1km

The map scale on the pages numbered in red is 5⅓ inches to 1 mile
8.4 cm to 1 km • 1:11900

0	220yds	440yds	660yds	½ mile
0	125m	250m	375m	500m

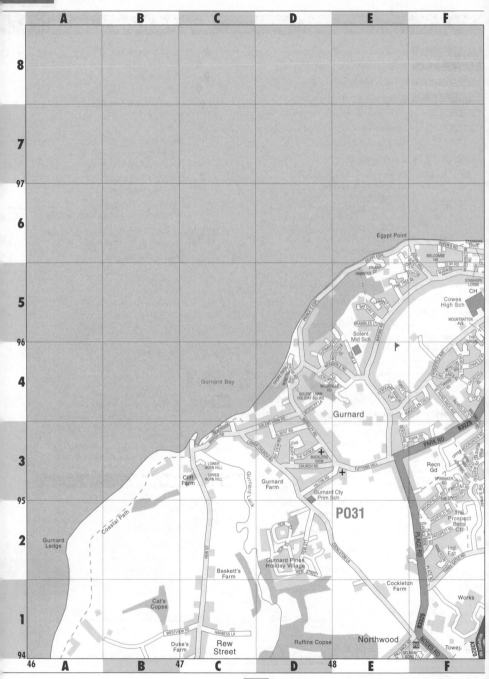

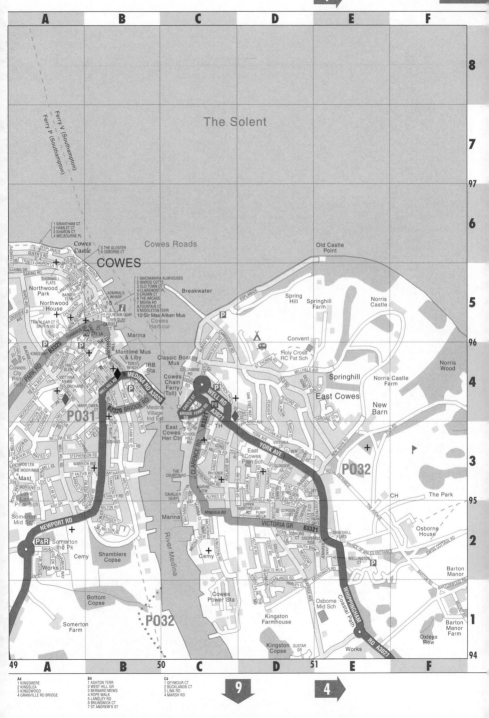

The Solent

Cowes Roads

Old Castle Point

Cowes Castle
COWES

Ferry V (Southampton)
Ferry P (Southampton)

1 GRANTHAM CT
2 HAMLET CT
3 SHARON CT
4 MELBOURNE PL

5 THE GLOSTER
6 OSBORNE CT

1 MACNAMARA ALMHOUSES
2 WARDS COTTS
3 OLD TOWN CT
4 CLAREMONT PL
5 CROWN CT
6 THE ARCADE
7 MOIRA HO
8 FOUNTAIN ST
9 MIDDLETON TERR
10 Sir Max Aitken Mus

Breakwater

Esplanade
Spring Hill
Springhill Farm
Norris Castle

Convent
Holy Cross RC Fst Sch
Springhill
Norris Castle Farm
Norris Wood

ADMIRALS WHARF
FOUNTAIN QUAY
TOWN QUAY
Cowes Harbour
Marina

Maritime Mus & Liby
IRB Sta
Classic Boat Mus

MEDINA RD A3020
Cowes Chain Ferry (Toll) V

Medina Village Ind Est

East Cowes Her Ctr

East Cowes

New Barn

Northwood Park
Northwood House

THORNHILL FLATS

PO31

MEDINA RD A3020
B3320 BRIDGE RD

WELL RD PO

East Cowes Prim Sch
YORK AVE
PO32

Medina

School Hill
CLARENCE RD
B3321
FERRY RD A3021

NEWPORT RD

The Siding
PO31

PO32

Love Lane Prim Sch
Mast
Somerton Mid Sch

P&R
Somerton Ind Pk

Works

Cemy
Shamblers Copse

River Medina

Bottom Copse

Somerton Farm

PO32

Marina

Cemy

Phoenix Flats
Cavalier Quay
Minerva Rd

VICTORIA GR
B3321

Cowes Power Sta

Kingston Farmhouse

Kingston Copse
GUSTAR GR

Daneshill Flats
PRINCE OF WALES ENTRANCE
WELLINGTON CT

Osborne Mid Sch

Osborne House

PO32

The Park
CH

Barton Manor

Barton Manor Farm
Oxleys Rew

WHIPPINGHAM COASTAL PATH
RD A3021
Works

A4
1 KINGSMERE
2 KINGSLEA
3 KINGSWOOD
4 GRANVILLE RD BRIDGE

B4
1 ASHTON TERR
2 WEST HILL GR
3 BERNARD MEWS
4 ROPE WALK
5 LANGLEY RD
6 BRUNSWICK CT
7 ST ANDREWS ST

C4
1 SEYMOUR CT
2 BUCKLANDS CT
3 LINK RD
4 MARSH RD

	A	B	C	D	E	F

8

7

97

6

5

96

Norris
Wood

4

Pier
Wood

PIER RD

BOUNDARY DR

WHITE WLK

3

Osborne
Bay

95

SWISS COTTAGE RD

Swiss
Cottage
Mus

2

PO32

PRIORY WOODS DR

Barton
Wood

Barton
Hard

BARTONWOOD RD

Barton
Manor

Barton
Pond

1

MOUNT B

Combe
Copse

Cockcrow
Rew

King's
Quay

94

52 **A**   **B**   53   **C**   **D**   54   **E**   **F**

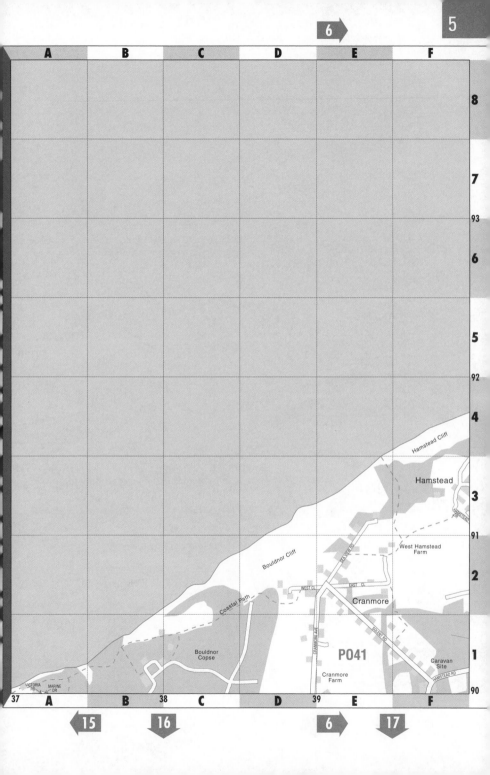

A   B   C   D   E   F

8

7

93

6

5

92

4

Hamstead Cliff

Hamstead

3

91

West Hamstead
Farm

Bouldnor Cliff

SEA VIEW RD

2

WEST CL.   EAST CL.

Cranmore

Coastal Path

CRANMORE AVE

SOLENT RD

Bouldnor
Copse

P041

Caravan
Site

1

Cranmore
Farm

HAMSTEAD RD

VICTORIA   MARINE
RD   DR

90

37   A   B   38   C   D   39   E   F

5

A
B
C
D
E
F
8
7
93
6
5
92
4
3
91
2
1
90
40
41
42
Newtown Bay
DANGER AREA
Brickfield Farm House
PO30
Hamstead Point
Hamstead Ledge
Hamstead Dover
Coastal Path
Clamerkin Lake
Newtown Marshes Nature Reserve
Hamstead Farm
Hamstead
PO41
Newtown River
Quay
Lower Hamstead Copse
Lower Hamstead Farm
Lower Hamstead
Newtown Harbour National Nature Reserve
Newtown
Hart's Farm
Hamstead Trail
Creek Farm
Causeway Lake
Piggery
HAMSTEAD DR
Town Hall
PO30
Western Haven
Quay
Pigeon Coo Farm
HAMSTEAD RD
Coastal Path
Shalfleet Lake
Corf Lake
PO30
Corf Camp
Fleetlands Farm
Fleetlands Copse
OLD VICARAGE LA

5
17
18

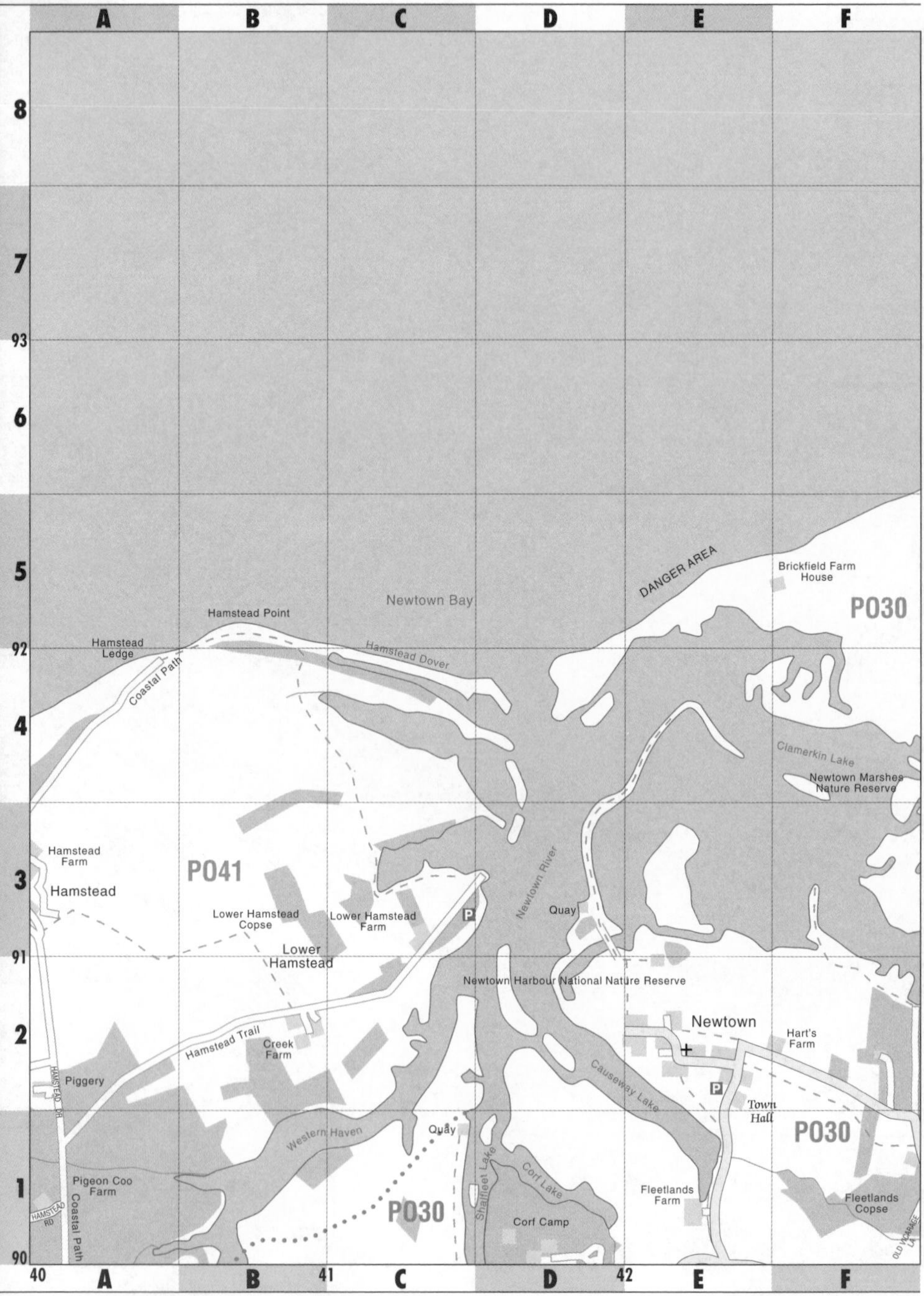

7
2

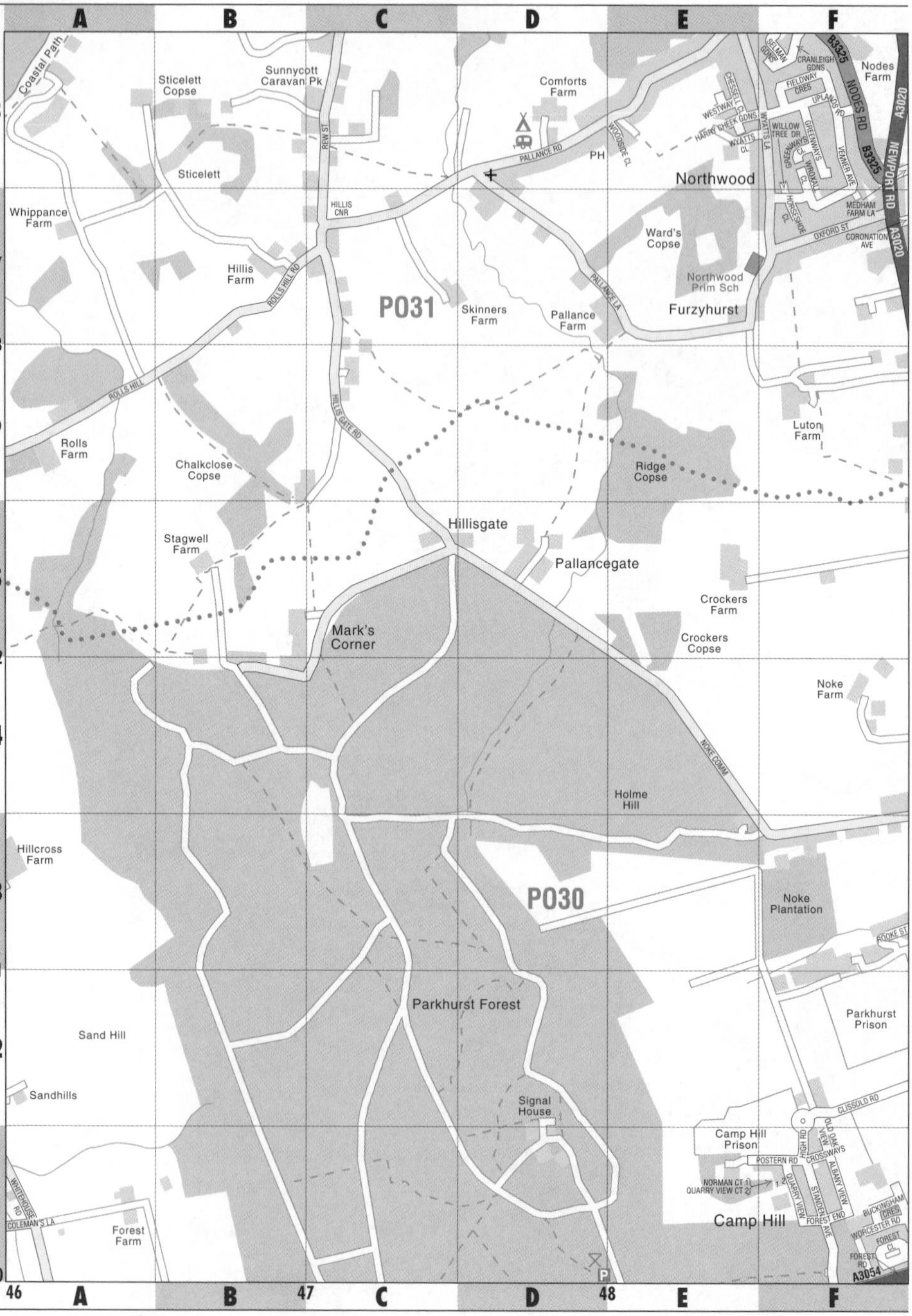
A
B
C
D
E
F
8
7
93
6
5
92
4
3
91
2
1
90
46
47
48
Coastal Path
Sticelett Copse
Sunnycott Caravan Pk
Comforts Farm
SELMAN GDNS
CRANLEIGH GDNS
B3325
Nodes Farm
FIELDWAY CRES
CHESSELL CL
WESTWAY
HARRY CHEEK GDNS
WYATTS LA
WYATTS CL
WILLOW TREE DR
GREENWAYS
GREENWAYS CL
WROXALL CL
UPLANDS RD
NODES RD
VEMNER AVE
A3020
NEWPORT RD
REW ST
PALLANCE RD
WOODSIDE CL
PH
Northwood
Sticelett
HILLIS CNR
Whippance Farm
HORSESHOE CL
MEDHAM FARM LA
OXFORD ST
CORONATION AVE
Ward's Copse
Hillis Farm
ROLLS HILL RD
Northwood Prim Sch
PALLANCE LA
PO31
Skinners Farm
Pallance Farm
Furzyhurst
ROLLS HILL
HILLS GATE RD
Luton Farm
Rolls Farm
Chalkclose Copse
Ridge Copse
Hillisgate
Stagwell Farm
Pallancegate
Crockers Farm
Mark's Corner
Crockers Copse
Noke Farm
NOKE COMM
Holme Hill
Hillcross Farm
PO30
Noke Plantation
ROOKE ST
Parkhurst Forest
Parkhurst Prison
Sand Hill
Sandhills
CLISSOLD RD
Signal House
Camp Hill Prison
HIGH RD
OLD OAK VIEW
CROSSWAYS
POSTERN RD
NORMAN CT 1
QUARRY VIEW CT 2
QUARRY VIEW
STANDEN AVE
ALBANY VIEW
BUCKINGHAM CRES
WHITEHOUSE RD
COLEMAN'S LA
Camp Hill
FOREST END
WORCESTER RD
Forest Farm
FOREST CL
FOREST RD
A3054
P

7
19
20

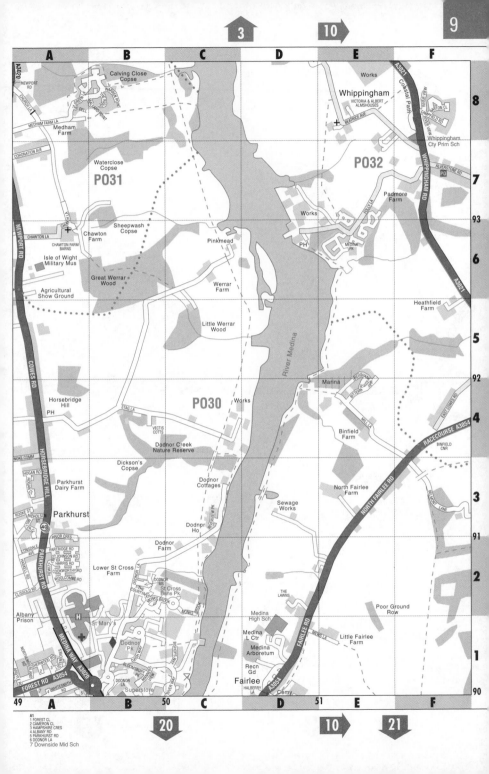

9
4

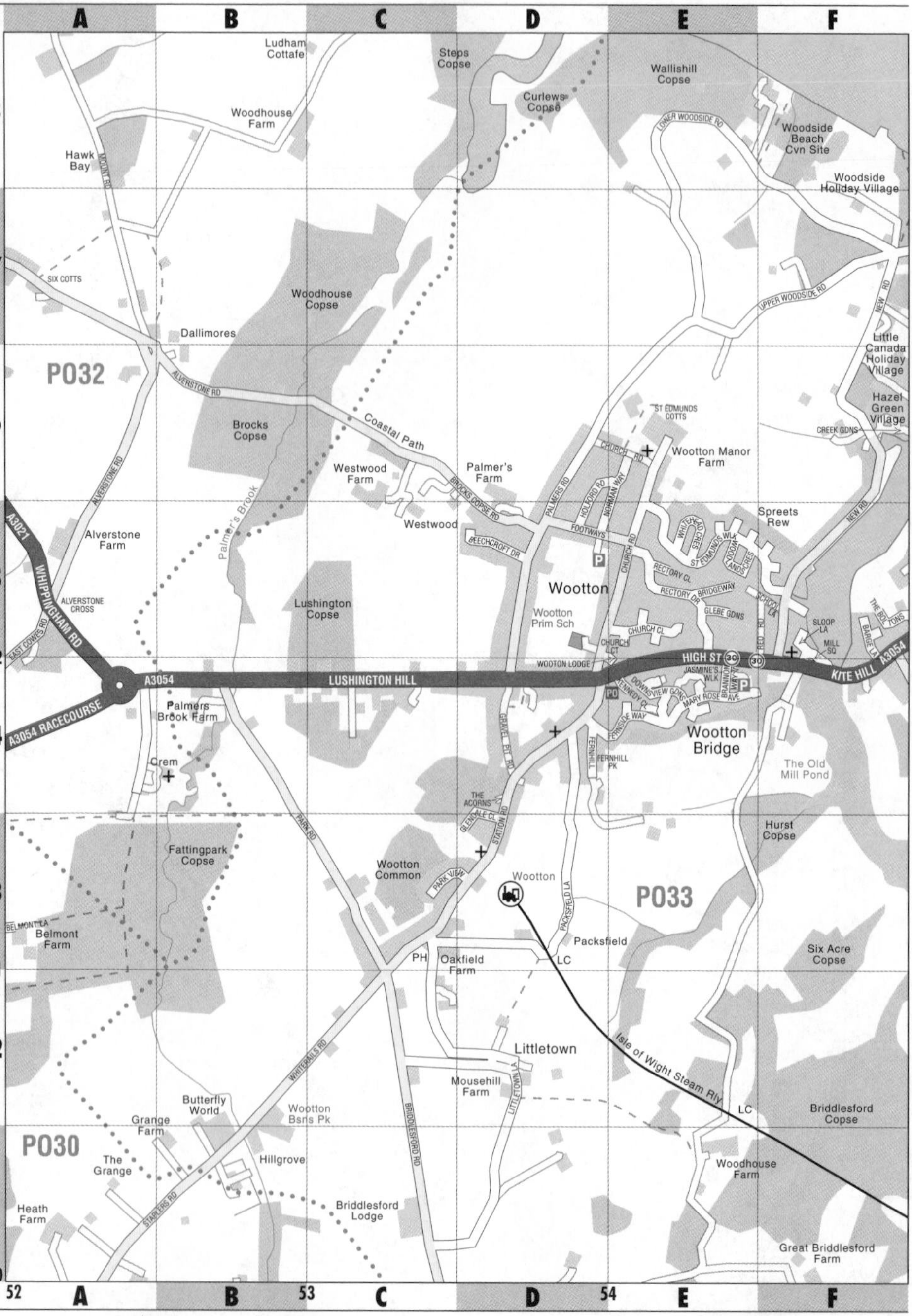

A B C D E F
8 7 93 6 5 92 4 3 91 2 1 90
52 53 54
Ludham Cottafe
Steps Copse
Wallishill Copse
Curlews Copse
Woodhouse Farm
Hawk Bay
MOUNT RD
LOWER WOODSIDE RD
Woodside Beach Cvn Site
Woodside Holiday Village
SIX COTTS
Woodhouse Copse
UPPER WOODSIDE RD
NEW RD
Little Canada Holiday Village
Dallimores
PO32
ALVERSTONE RD
Hazel Green Village
Brocks Copse
Coastal Path
ST EDMUNDS COTTS
CREEK GDNS
CHURCH RD
Wootton Manor Farm
Westwood Farm
Palmer's Farm
ALVERSTONE RD
BROCKS COPSE RD
PALMERS RD
HOLFORD RD
NORMAN WAY
Palmer's Brook
Westwood
Spreets Rew
A3021
Alverstone Farm
BEECHCROFT DR
FOOTWAYS
WHITEHEAD CRES
ST EDMUNDS WLK
WOODLANDS CRES
WHIPPINGHAM RD
Wootton
RECTORY CL
ALVERSTONE CROSS
Lushington Copse
RECTORY DR
BRIDGEWAY
SCHOOL LA
EAST COWES RD
Wootton Prim Sch
GLEBE GDNS
THE BOLTONS
BARGE LA
CHURCH CL
SLOOP LA
MILL SQ
CHURCH CT
RED RD
HIGH ST
WOOTON LODGE
A3054
LUSHINGTON HILL
JASMINE'S WLK
BRANNON WAY
KITE HILL A3054
Palmers Brook Farm
A3054 RACECOURSE
DOWNSVIEW GDNS
KENNEDY CL
MARY ROSE AVE
FERNSIDE WAY
Wootton Bridge
GRAVEL PIT RD
FERNHILL
FERNHILL PK
Crem
The Old Mill Pond
THE ACORNS
GLENDALE CL
STATION RD
PARK RD
Fattingpark Copse
Hurst Copse
Wootton Common
Wootton
PARK VIEW
PACKSFIELD LA
PO33
BELMONT LA
Belmont Farm
Packsfield
Six Acre Copse
PH
Oakfield Farm
LC
Littletown
WHITERAILS RD
Isle of Wight Steam Rly
Mousehill Farm
LITTLETOWN LA
Butterfly World
Wootton Bsns Pk
BRIDDLESFORD RD
LC
Briddlesford Copse
Grange Farm
PO30
The Grange
Hillgrove
Woodhouse Farm
STAPLERS RD
Briddlesford Lodge
Heath Farm
Great Briddlesford Farm

9
21
22

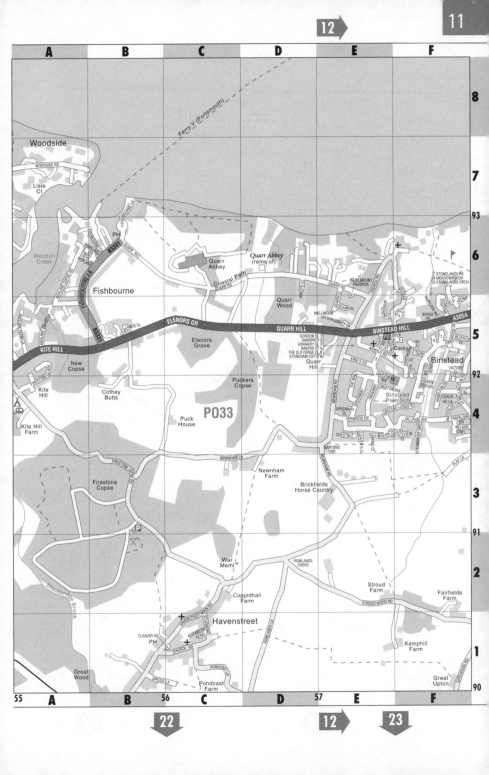

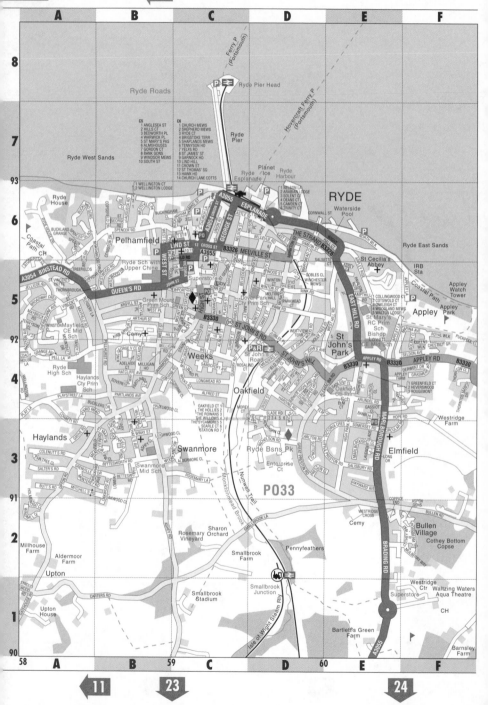

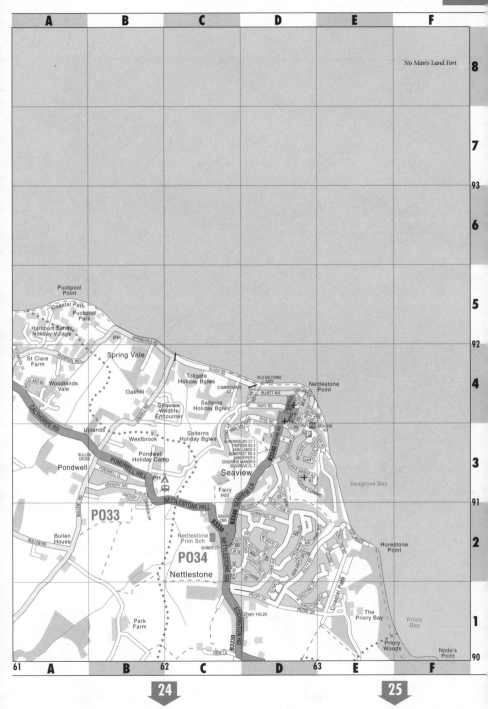

No Man's Land Fort

8

7

93

6

5

92

Puckpool
Point

Coastal Path

Puckpool
Park

Harcourt Sands
Holiday Village

PH

SPRINGVALE RD

Spring Vale

St Clare
Farm

PUCKPOOL HILL

Woodlands
Vale

Oakhill

PICKFORD CL

OAKLAND CL

CALTHORPE RD

DUVER RD

Tollgate
Holiday Bglws

OLD SALTERNS
GATE

COMMODORES
CT

Salterns
Holiday Bglws

BLUETT AVE

FAIRY RD

Nettlestone
Point

ESPLANADE

Seaview
Wildlife
Encounter

Uplands

Westbrook

ORDNEL RD

Salterns
Holiday Bglws

HIGH ST

SALTERNS RD

RYDE RD

4

PO

SEAVIEW
RD

PH

BULLEN
CROSS

POND WELL HILL

Pondwell

Pondwell
Holiday Camp

BULLEN RD

GREGORY AVE

HUTCHINGTON DR

GREGORY CL

POND WELL CL

SHREWSBURY CT 1
TIMPSON HO 2
SANDLANDS 3
SOMERSET RD 4
SANDPIPER 5
SEAGROVE MANOR 6
SEAGROVE CL 7

SEAVIEW LA

B3340

Seaview

SEAGROVE MANOR RD

SEAGROVE CL

SEAGROVE BAY RD

Seagrove Bay

3

91

Fairy
Hill

HOLGATE LA

GREEN
CNR

MATLOCK RD

SALT VIEW RD

ROWANTREE DR

Horestone
Point

2

PO33

Bullen
House

BULLEN RD

NETTLESTONE HILL

B3330

B3330

Nettlestone
Prim Sch

SHINER CT

PO34

Nettlestone

EDDINGTON RD

NETTLESTONE GN

EAST GN

ELM CL

THE GLADE

BIRCHWOOD

OLD WOOD CL

CHERRYTREE

CARS AVE

GULLY RD

SPRING VIEW

OAKFIELD RD

HORESTONE DR

HORESTONE RISE

Coastal Path

The
Priory Bay

Priory
Bay

1

Park
Farm

PRIORY DR

KERRY FIELDS

PARK LA

PRIORY DR

Priory
Woods

Node's
Point

90

61

A   **B**   62   **C**   **D**   63   **E**   **F**

24

25

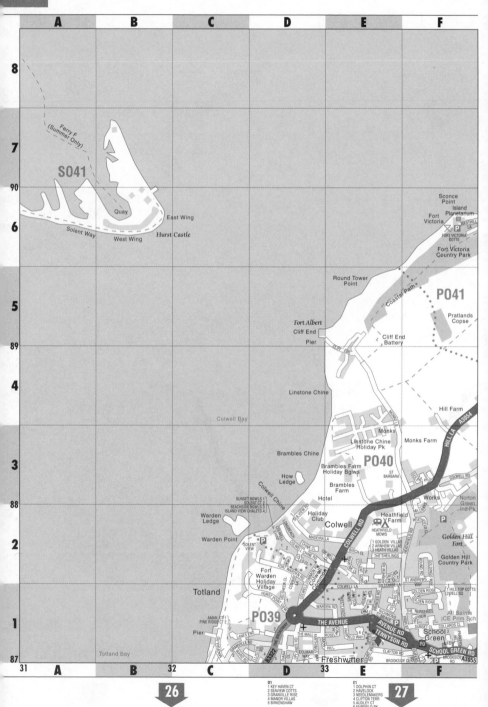

Ferry F
(Summer Only)

S041

Solent Way

Quay

East Wing

West Wing

Hurst Castle

Sconce
Point

Island
Planetarium

Fort
Victoria

FORT VICTORIA
COTTS

WESTHILL

Fort Victoria
Country Park

Round Tower
Point

Coastal Path

P041

Pratlands
Copse

Fort Albert

Cliff End

Pier

Cliff End
Battery

CLIFF END

Linstone Chine

Hill Farm

HILL LA

A3054

Colwell Bay

Monks

Linstone Chine
Holiday Pk

Monks Farm

MARSH RD

Brambles Chine

P040

COLWELL RD

How
Ledge

Brambles Farm
Holiday Bglws

ST
BARBARA

Brambles
Farm

Colwell Chine

SUNSET BGWLS 1
SOLENT CT 2
BEACHSIDE BGWLS 3
ISLAND VIEW CHALETS 4.

Hotel

Works

Norton
Green
Ind Pk

MILL RD

Warden
Ledge

Holiday
Club

Colwell

Heathfield
Farm

P

Golden Hill
Fort

Warden Point

SOLENT
VIEW

P

HEATHFIELD
MDWS

1 GOLDEN VILLAS
2 ARNHEM VILLAS
3 HEATH VILLAS

COLWELL RD

BIRCH CL

THE SHEILINGS

Golden Hill
Country Park

MADEIRA LA

COLWELL CHINE RD

ST ANDREWS
WAY

GOLDEN RIDGE

1 HILL TOP COTTS
2 DELL SQ

Fort
Warden
Holiday
Village

Totland

HURST POINT RD

COLWELL COMMON RD

COLWELL LA

WARDEN RD

SILCOMBE LA

All Saints
CE Prim Sch

GOLDEN RIDGE

THE NURSERIES

SEAVIEW

SUNSET CL

COLLARDS CT

P039

AMAN CT 1
PINE RIDGE CT 2

Pier

LANES RD

THE AVENUE

RICHMOND

SUNSET RD

AVENUE RD

P

School
Green

Library

SCHOOL GREEN RD

A3055

Totland Bay

THE MALL

GRANVILLE RD

B3322

DIANA

COLMAR WAY

HILL

ROSEL

FIELD WAY

TENNYSON RD

CLAYTON RD

BROOKSIDE CL

Freshwater

BROOKSIDE
RD

31 A B 32 C D 33 E F

8 7 90 6 5 89 4 3 88 2 87 1

26 **27**

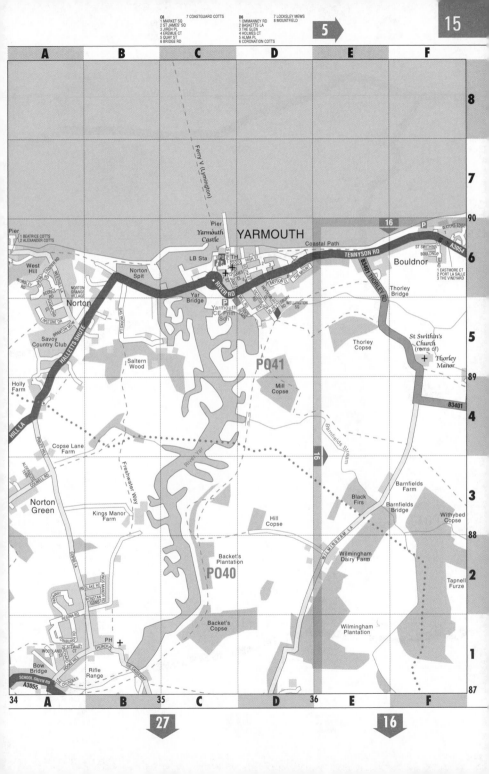

	A	B	C	D	E	F

8

Coastal Path

A3054 Tennyson Rd

B3401 THORLEY RD

St Swithins
BOULDNOR
Bouldnor

WATERS EDGE

MARINE DR

VICTORIA RD

ALEXANDRA RD

THE AVENUE

Byecross

Cranmore
Park

CRANMORE AV

1 EASTMORE CT
2 PORT LA SALLE
3 THE VINEYARD

Purbeck
House

NINGWOOD HILL A3054

Thorley
Bridge

HOLBROOKES
COTTS

Lucketts
Farm

7

Thorley
Copse

St Swithin's
Church
(rems of)

Thorley
Manor

MILL PIGHTLE

Lee
Copse

93

Thorley Brook

6

Barnfields Stream

Thorley

LATTISS LA

HOLMFIELD AVE

N X CRESHELD LA

+

Lee
Farm

NORTH VIEW

Thorley
Street

5

Black
Firs

WILMINGHAM LA

Barnfields
Farm

Barnfields
Bridge

Withybed
Copse

New Barn
Farm

Mattingley
Farm

Wellow

DODPITS LA

WELLOW TOP RD

B3401

88

Wilmingham
Dairy Farm

Dog Kennel
Cottage

PO41

4

Tapnell
Furze

3

Wilmingham
Plantation

BROAD LA

Hummet
Copse

Hamstead Trail

87

PO40

15

2

Tapnell Farm

Tapnell
Farm

1

B3399

NEWPORT RD

East Afton
Farm

TAPNELL
COTTAGES

The
Quarries

86

East Afton Down

B3399

Shalcombe
Holding

36	A	B	37	C	D	38	E	F

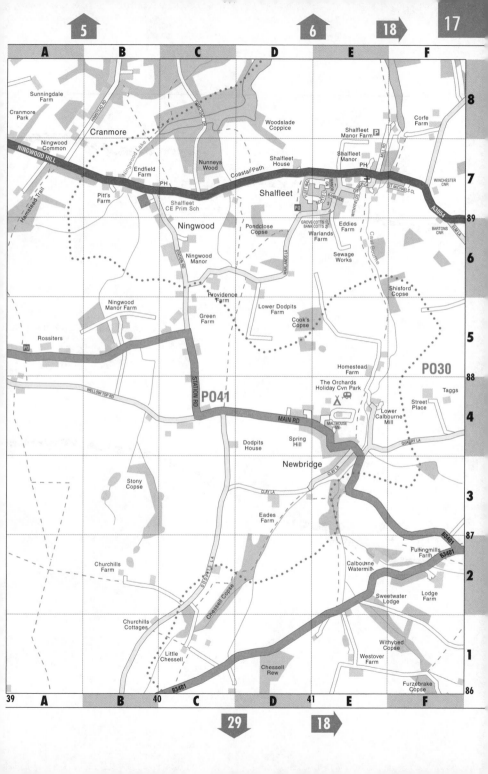

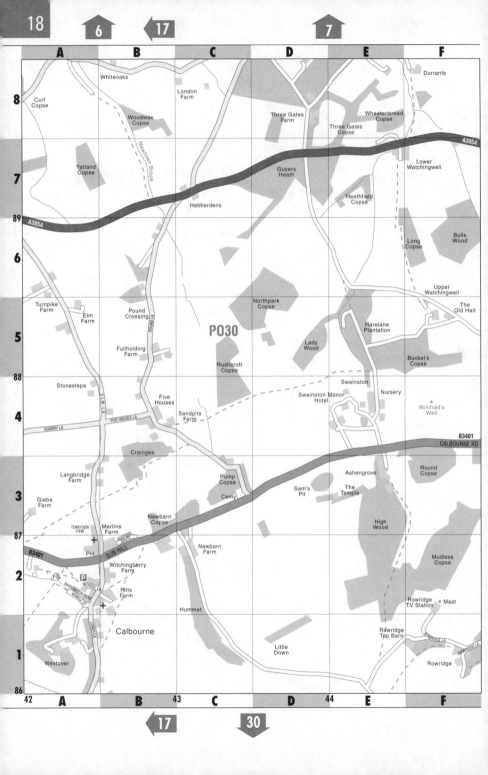

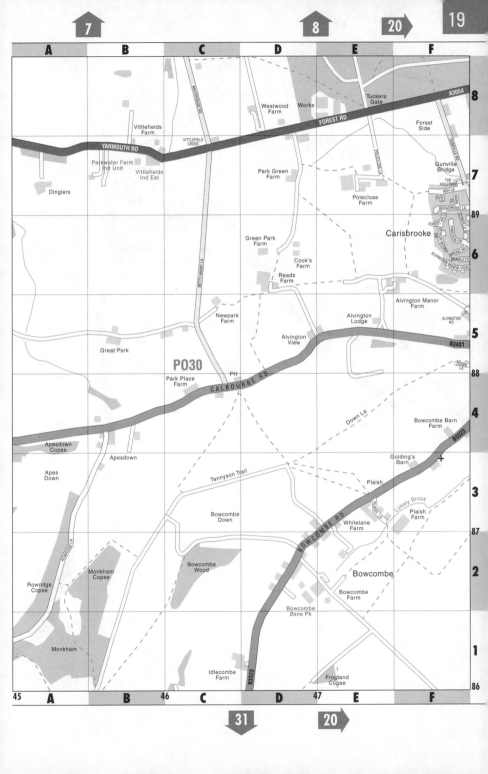

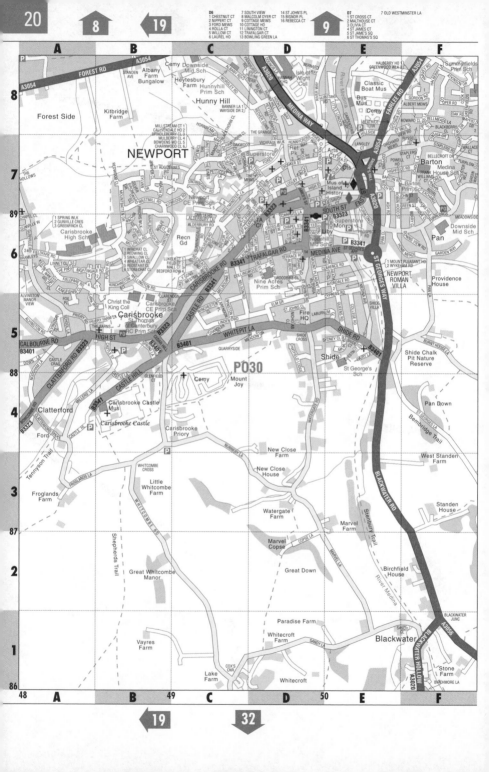

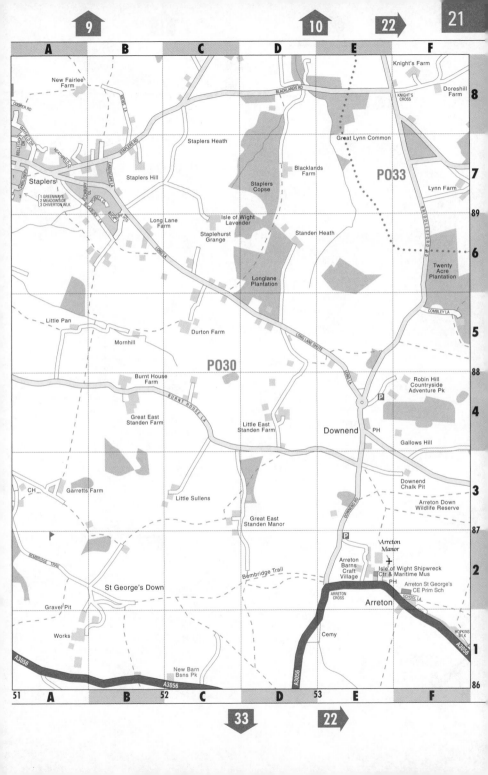

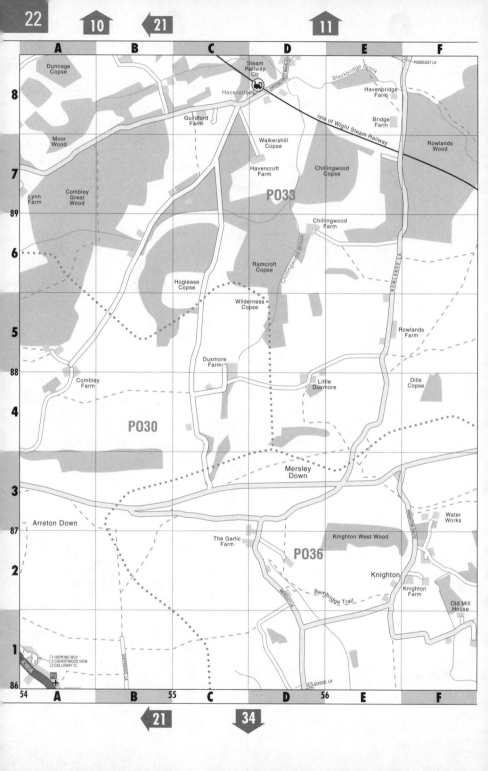

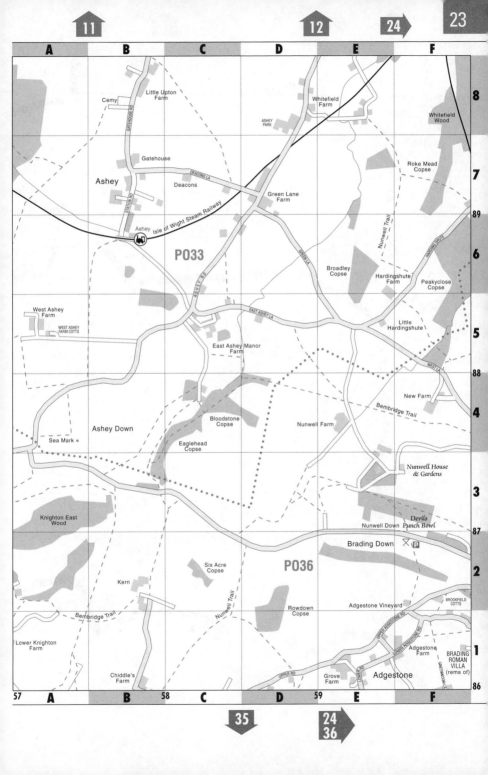

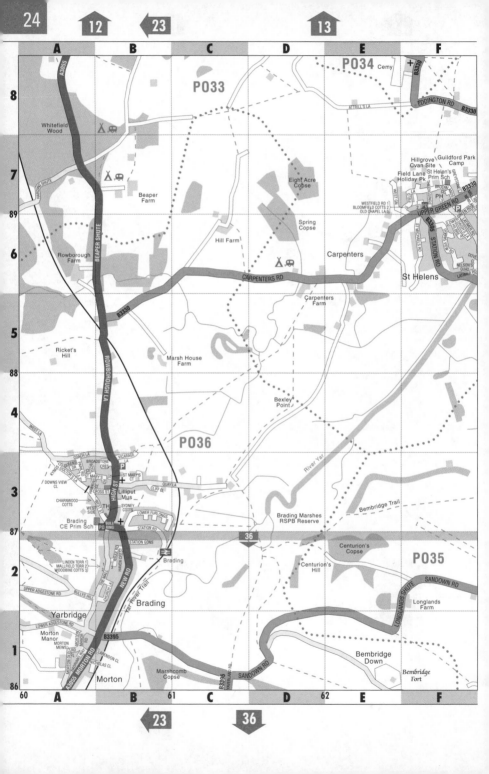

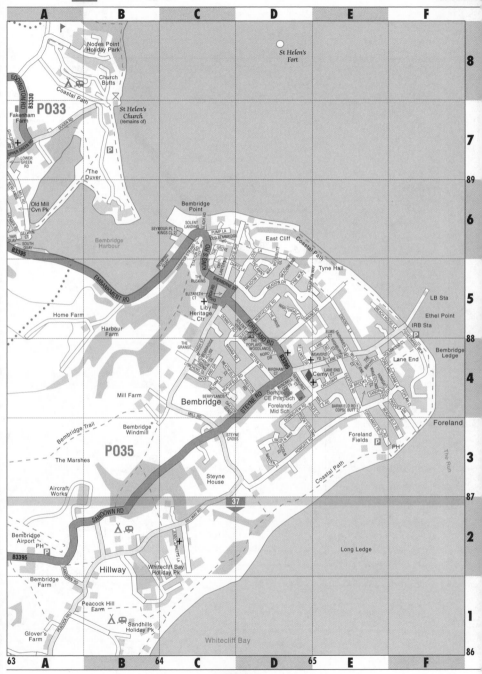

13

A · **B** · **C** · **D** · **E** · **F**

8

Nodes Point
Holiday Park

St Helen's
Fort

Church
Butts

Coastal Path

PO33

Fakenham
Farm

St Helen's
Church
(remains of)

7

LOWER
GREEN
RD

UPPER GREEN RD

DUVER RD

89

'The
Duver

Old Mill
Cvn Pk

YAR
QUAY

SOUTH
QUAY

B3395

EMBANKMENT RD

Bembridge
Harbour

Bembridge
Point

6

SOLENT
LANDING

SEYMOUR PL 1
KINGS CL 2

OLD BEMBRIDGE
PUMP LA

East Cliff

Coastal Path

GROVE

Tyne Hall

KING'S RD

PICKING
QUAY

STATION RD

FORELAND RD

SHERBONE RD

THE RUSKINS

LB Sta

5

Home Farm

Harbour
Farm

ELIZABETH
CT

Liby
Heritage
Ctr

NIGHTINGALE CL

THE DRIVE

Ethel Point
IRB Sta

88

THE
GRANGE

DUCKETT RD

MANN RD

WILLOW CL

THE
POPLARS
WOODLANDS

NORTH CLOSE RD

NORFCLT
DR

ELMS

WEAVERS
YD

LANE END RD

Lane End

Bembridge
Ledge

4

Mill Farm

BERRYLANDS

PRESTON

BIRDHAM
CT

Bembridge
CE Prim Sch

Cemy

CROSSWAY

BARNFIELD RD 1
COPSE BUTT 2

Bembridge

STEYNE RD

MILL RD

Forelands
Mid Sch

Foreland

3

PO35

Bembridge Trail

The Marshes

Bembridge
Windmill

STEYNE
CROSS

LINCOLN WAY

MARSDEN CL

Foreland
Fields

PH

The Run

Aircraft
Works

Steyne
House

Coastal Path

87

37

Bembridge
Airport

PH

SANDOWN RD

HILLWAY RD

Long Ledge

2

B3395

Hillway

Whitecliff Bay
Holiday Pk

Bembridge
Farm

Peacock Hill
Farm

PEACOCK HILL

Sandhills
Holiday Pk

1

Glover's
Farm

Whitecliff Bay

86

63 **A** · **B** 64 **C** · **D** 65 **E** · **F**

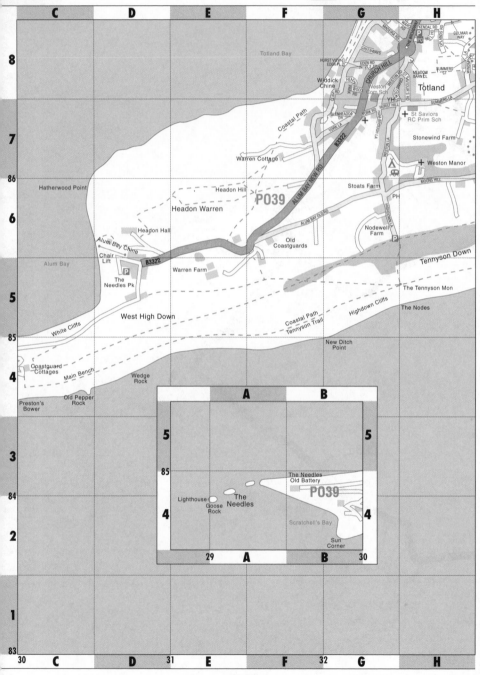

C **D** **E** **F** **G** **H**

8

Totland Bay

HURST VIEW
EDEN PL
GREENWAYS
HEADON
WOOD RD
YORK RD
Widdick
Chine
Weston Com Sch
YH
CHURCH HILL
EDEN RD
KENDAL RD
COLMAR WAY
THE BROADWAY
SUMMERS CT
MEADOW
BARN EL
SAVIOURS RD
Totland
St Saviors
RC Prim Sch
SUMMERS LA

7

Coastal Path
BLENHEADON BR
YORK LA
B3322
HURST HILL
WESTON RD
HORDLE RD
Stonewind Farm
Weston Manor
MOONS HILL

86

Hatherwood Point
Headon Hill
PO39
Stoats Farm
PH
ALUM BAY NEW RD

6

Headon Warren
Headon Hall
ALUM BAY OLD RD
Old
Coastguards
Nodewell
Farm
P

Alum Bay Chine
Chair
Lift
B3322
Alum Bay
P
Warren Farm
Warren Cottage
Tennyson Down

5

The
Needles Pk
Warren Farm
West High Down
Highdown Cliffs
The Tennyson Mon
The Nodes

85

White Cliffs
Coastal Path
Tennyson Trail
New Ditch
Point

4

Coastguard
Cottages
Main Bench
Wedge
Rock
Preston's
Bower
Old Pepper
Rock

A **B**

5   5

85

The Needles
Old Battery
PO39

84

Lighthouse
The Needles
Goose
Rock

4   4

Scratchell's Bay

2

Sun
Corner

29 **A**   **B** 30

3

1

83

30 **C**   **D** 31 **E**   **F** 32 **G**   **H**

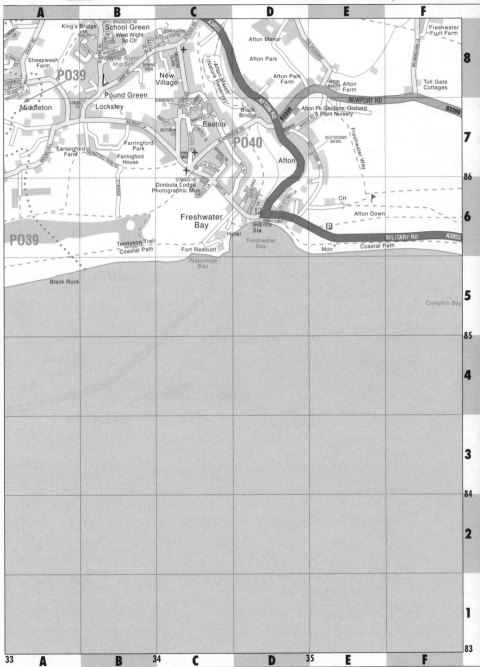

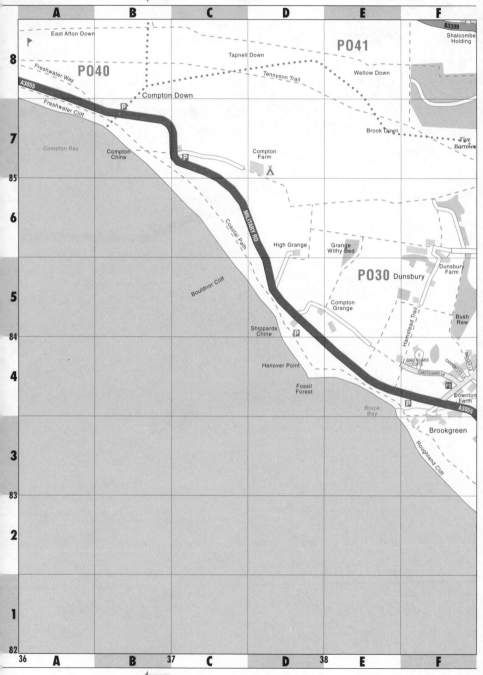

East Afton Down

P040

P041

Tapnell Down

Shalcombe
Holding

B3399

Freshwater Way

A3055

Freshwater Cliff

Tennyson Trail

Wellow Down

Compton Down

P

Compton Bay

Compton
Chine

P

Compton
Farm

Brook Down

Five
Barrows

Coastal Path

MILITARY RD

High Grange

Grange
Withy Bed

P030 Dunsbury

Dunsbury
Farm

Bouldnor Cliff

Compton
Grange

Hamstead Trail

Bush
Rew

Shippards
Chine

P

COASTGUARD
COTTS

COASTGUARD LA

CARPENTERS

BRAZIERS

Hanover Point

PO

Fossil
Forest

P

Downton
Farm

A3055

Brook
Bay

Brookgreen

Roughland Cliff

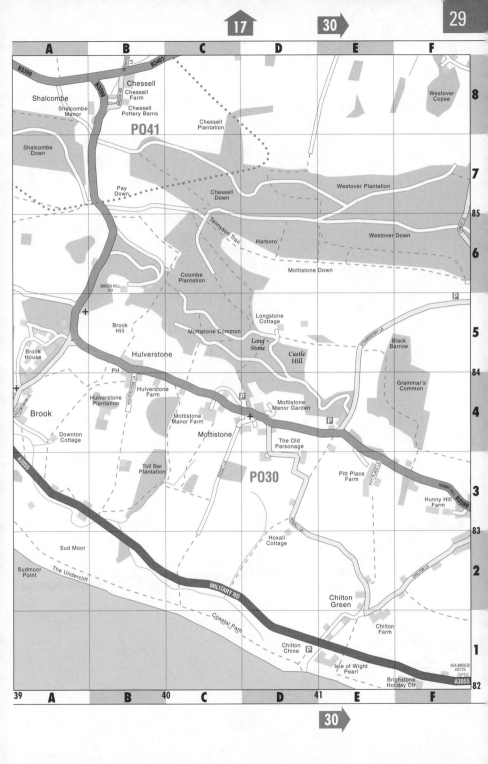

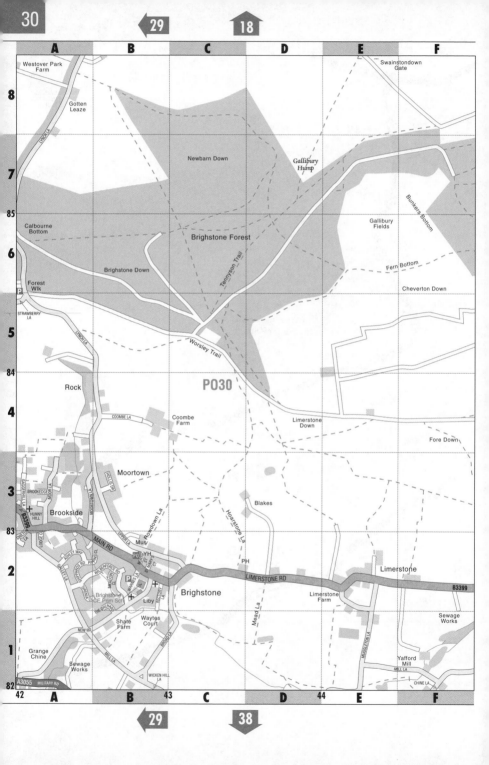

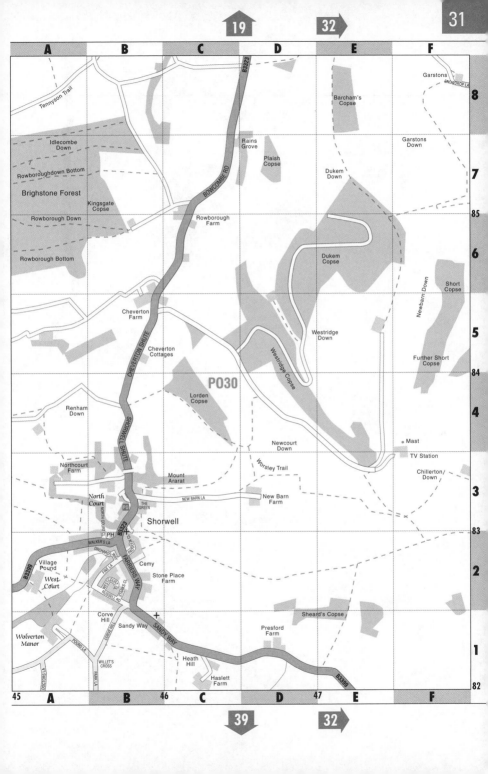

A B C D E F

8

Gatcombe
Withy Bed

SNOWDROP LA

Hill
Farm

VICTORY LA

SANDY LA

A3020

BIRCHMORE LA

Stenbury
Trail

7

Newbarn
Farm

Little
Gatcombe
Farm

Tuckers
Farm

Gatcombe

GATCOMBE RD

Gatcombe
Mill

Birchcombe
Farm House

BLACKWATER HOLLOW

85

Gatcombe House

Home Farm

Champion
Farm

6

Sheat Farm
Ind Est

HIGHWOOD LA

Pidford
Manor

Little Pidford
Farm

BROOK LA

Sheat
Manor

Chillerton &
Rookley
Prim Sch

Tolt
Copse

5

Chillerton

Sibdown
Farm

Rookley

BURNTERS LA

MAIN RD

PO

A3020

Long
Copse

Shepherds Trail

84

+

DOG CROFT RD

MANOR

CREST RD

HILL

4

HILLSIDE

GREENLANDS

MAIN LANE

FACTORY RD

GREENLAND CL
Kervil
Dairy

Loverstone
Farm

PO38

Rookley
Manor Farm

Rookley
Green

MITCH RD

PO30

Chillerton
Farm

River Medina

Harts
Farm

HARTS LA

Elliot's
Hill

3

Upper
Rill

Rookley
Farm

83

Lower
Rill

2

Berry
Hill

Ramsdown
Farm

Shepherds Trail

Berry
Copse

Roslin
Farm

Worsley Trail

Cridmore

Cridmore
Farm

BERRY SHUTE

1

Roslin

82

48 A B 49 C D 50 E F

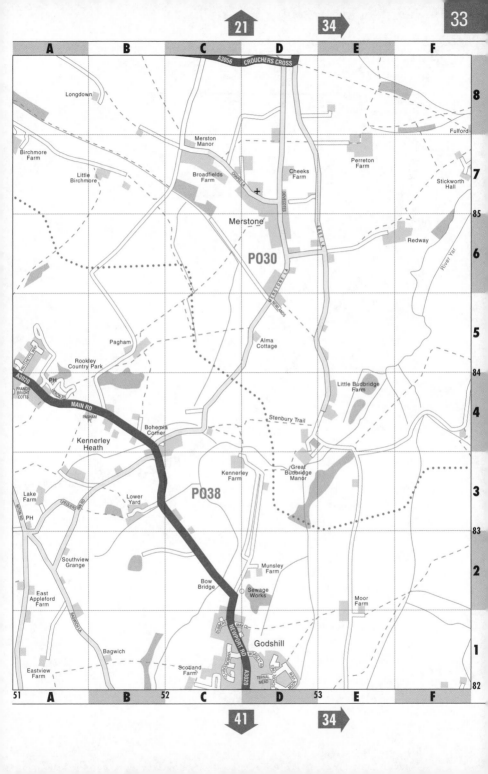

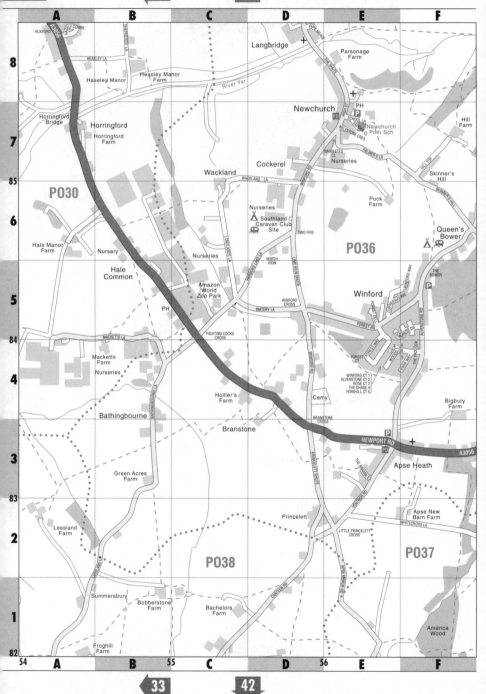

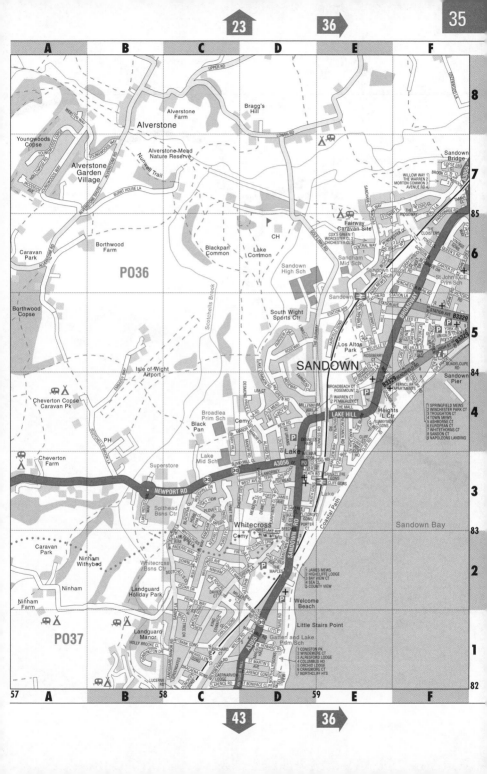

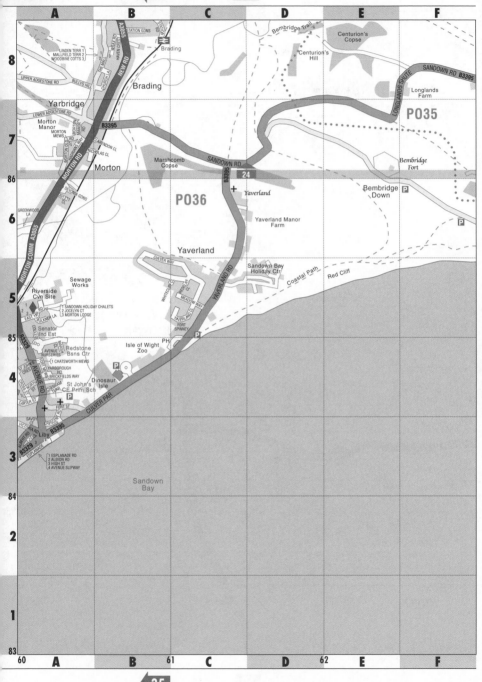

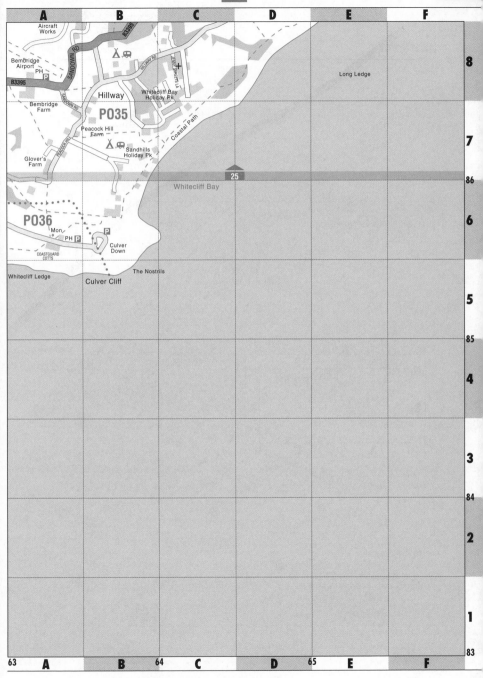

30

29

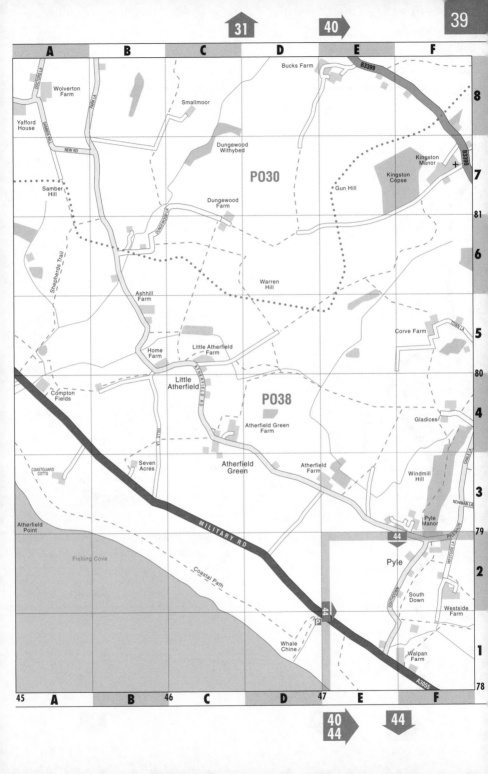

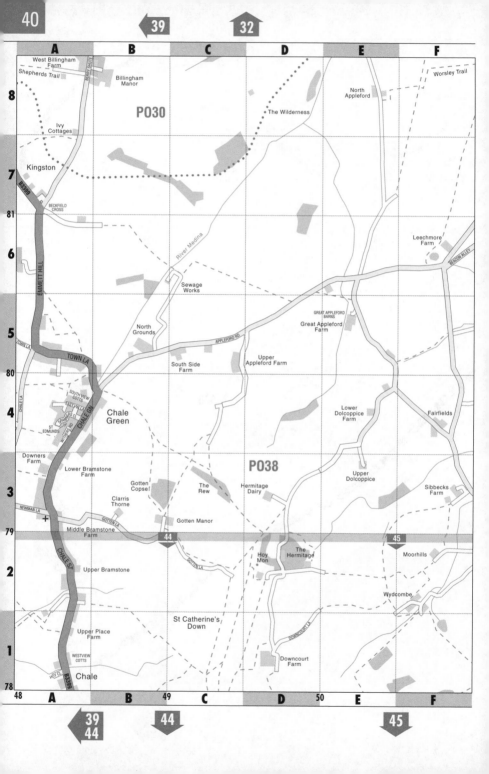

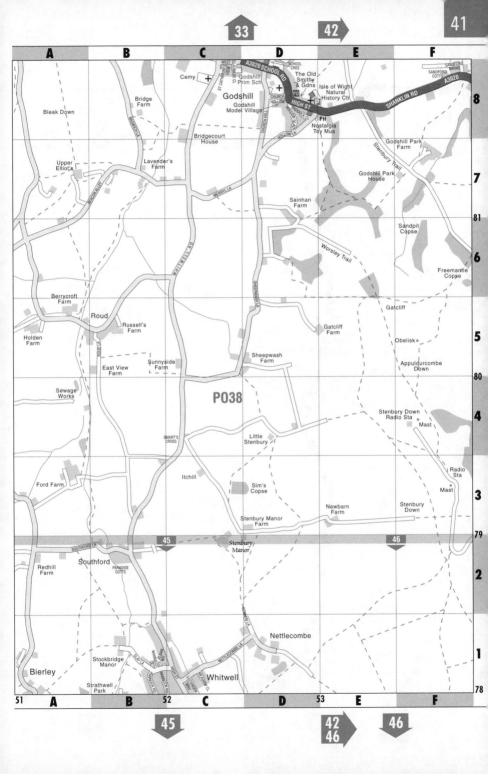

41
34

A B C D E F

8

7

81

6

5

80

4

3

79

2

1

78

54 A B 55 C D 56 E F

41
46
46
47

Froghall Farm
Sandford
SHANKLIN RD
A3020
Whiteley Bank
Pound Farm
French Hill
B3327
Apse Manor
Apsecastle Wood
SHANKLIN RD
VICTORIA AVE
UPPER HYDE LA
A3020
CLIFF ROAD (FOOT)
WINDSOR

Isle of Wight Donkey Sanctuary
Winstone Farm
Upper Hyde
Cliff Farm

Park Hill Farm
REDHILL LA
Sewage Works
PO37

Redhill Farm
Yard Farmhouse
ST JOHN'S RD
PO38

Appuldurcombe Farm
Appuldurcombe Cvn Pk
Clevelands Holiday Bglws
Worsley Trail
St Martin's Down
Shanklin Down

Appuldurcombe Park
RED SCHOOL LA
APPULDURCOMBE RD
ORCHARD LA
MIDDLE LA
AVENUE RD
YARBOROUGH CL
CASTLE RD
CAWTE RD

Cleveland Terr
Cemy
Wroxall Prim Sch

Appuldurcombe House
Isle of Wight Owl & Falconry Ctr
PH
P
Wroxall
MOTTLEY CRES
MOTTLEY RD
WEST ST
BRADFORD RD

Appuldurcombe Terr 1
Yarborough Terr 2
Wroxall Ho 3

Baycroft Farm
CLARENCE RD
ST JOHN'S RD

Span Lodge
PRIORY VIEW
MANOR RD
Wroxall Cross Farm
Middle Barn
MIDDLE BARN LANE

Little Span Farm
Wroxall Manor Farm

46
Span Farm
47

REW LA
Wroxall Copse
Wroxall Down

Homelands Pit Farm
P
P
Ventnor Radar Sta
Masts

Rew Farm
Lowtherville
NEWPORT RD
B3327
CHESTNUT CL
ST MARGARETS
MIDDLETON CL
LOWTHERVILLE RD
St Margarets CE Prim Sch
St Boniface Down

Rew Valley Sports Ctr
Ventnor Mid Sch
BANAS CL
A3055
WHITWELL RD

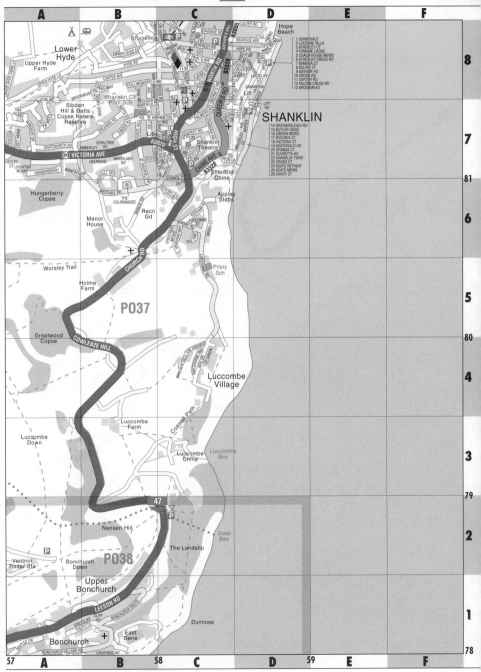

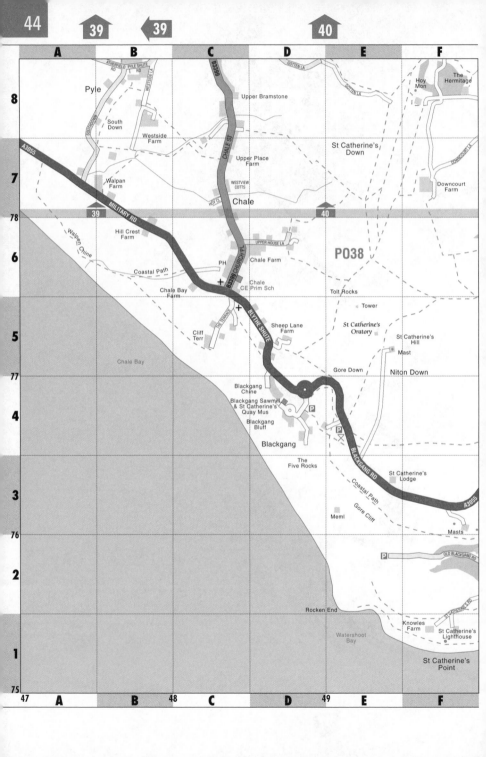

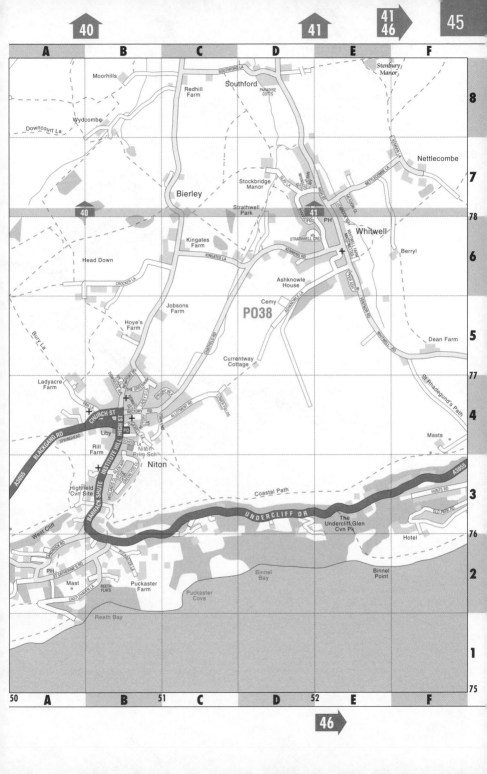

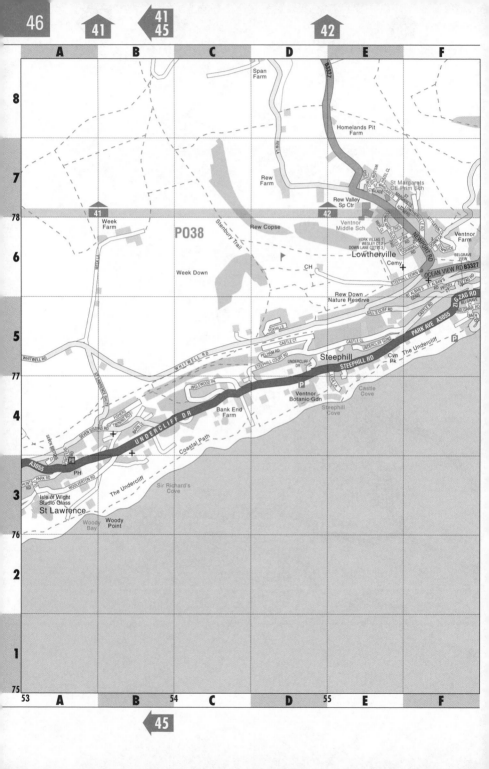

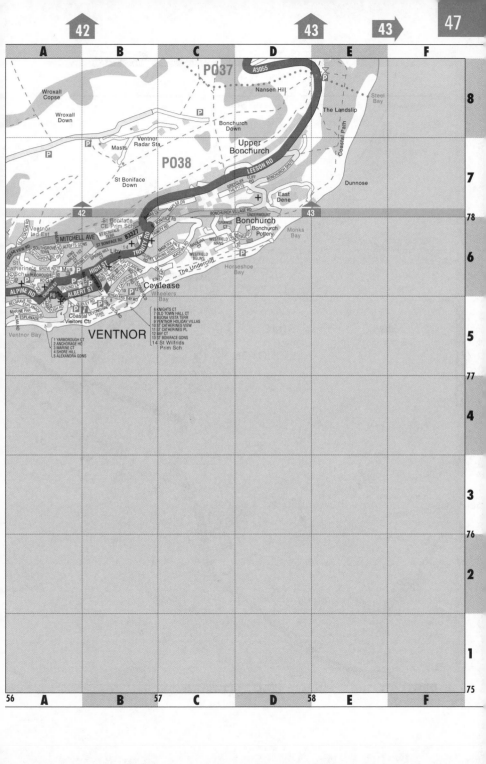

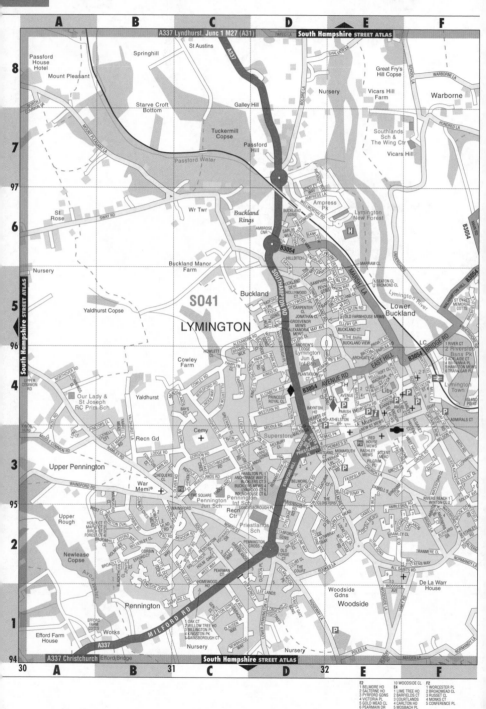

E2	10 WOODSIDE CL	F2
1 BELMORE HO	E4	1 WORCESTER PL
2 SALTERNE HO	1 LIME TREE HO	2 BROADMEAD CL
3 PYRFORD GDNS	2 BARFIELDS CT	3 RUSSET CL
4 VICTORIA PL	3 COURTLANDS	4 MONKS CT
5 GOLD MEAD CL	4 CARLTON HO	5 CONFERENCE PL
6 PEARMAIN DR	5 MOSBACH PL	
7 PEARTREE CT	6 KEEL GDNS	
8 PIPPIN CL	7 UNION PL	
9 CHURCH MEAD		

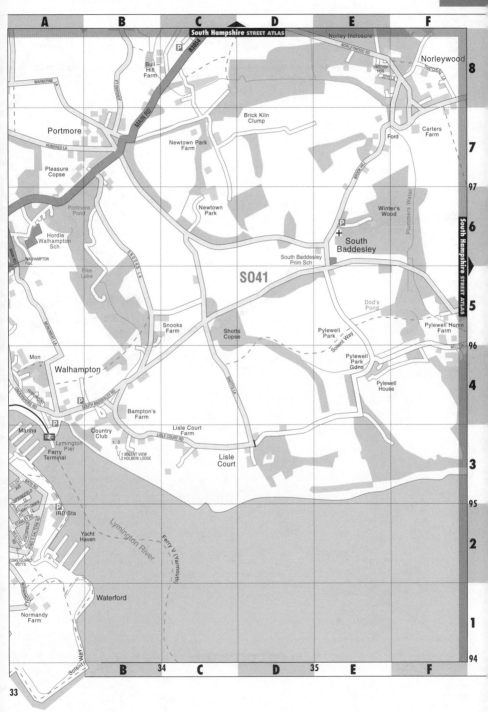

A B C D E F

Norley Inclosure

NORLEYWOOD RD

Norleywood

SWEDISH HOS

8

WARBORNE LA

Bull
Hill
Farm

P

B3054

MAIN RD

JORDANS LA

THATCHER'S RD

SYSLA

Brick Kiln
Clump

Ford

Carters
Farm

Portmore

Newtown Park
Farm

7

HUNDRED LA

97

Pleasure
Copse

Portmore
Pond

Newtown
Park

BRICK HILL

Winter's
Wood

Plummers Water

Hordle
Walhampton
Sch

South Baddesley
Prim Sch

+ **South
Baddesley**

6

WALHAMPTON
HILL

Pike
Lake

ST ODES LA

SO41

Dod's
Pond

5

MAIN RD

Snooks
Farm

Shotts
Copse

Pylewell
Park

Solent Way

Pylewell Home
Farm

MILL LA

96

Mon

Walhampton

MONTAGU LA

Pylewell
Park
Gdns

Pylewell
House

4

FERRY POINT

HAMPSHIRE LA

P

SOUTH BADDESLEY RD

Bampton's
Farm

SHOTTS LA

Lisle Court
Farm

Marina

Lymington
Pier

Ferry
Terminal

P

Country
Club

LISLE COURT RD

**Lisle
Court**

3

P

IRB Sta

1 2
1 SOLENT VIEW
2 HOLBEIN LODGE

95

COASTGUARD
COTTS

Yacht
Haven

Lymington River

Ferry V (Yarmouth)

2

NORMANDY LA

Normandy
Farm

Waterford

1

Solent

New

94

B 34 C D 35 E F

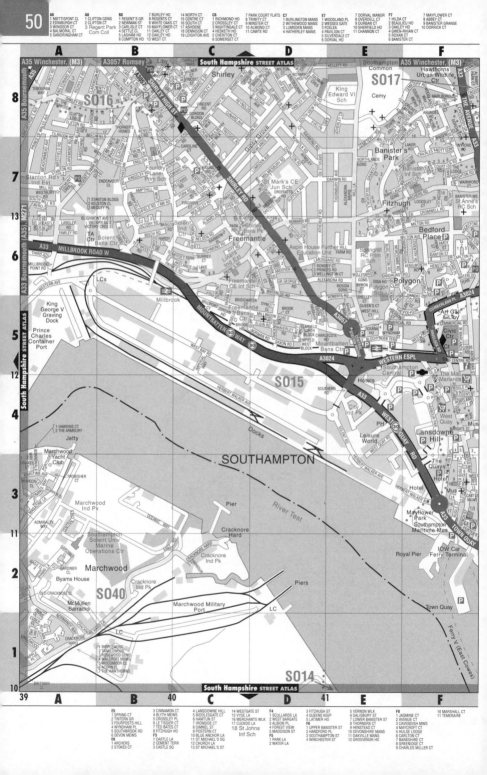

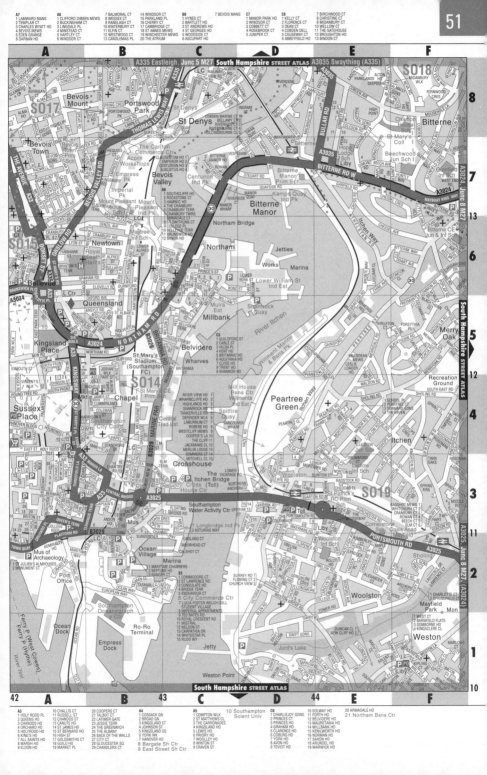

A7
1 LAMWARD MANS
2 TEMPLAR CT
3 CHARLES WYATT HO
4 BEVOIS MEWS
5 EDEN GRANGE
6 DARNAN HO

A8
1 CLIFFORD DIBBEN MEWS
2 BUCKINGHAM CT
3 LINGDALE PL
4 MINSTEAD CT
5 HARTLEY CT
6 WINDSOR CT

7 BALMORAL CT
8 WESSEX CT
9 RANELAGH CT
10 KINTERBURY CT
11 ELFIN CT
12 WESTWOOD CT
13 CANDLEMAS PL

14 WINDSOR CT
15 PARKLAND PL
16 CHERRY CT
17 CAMBRIDGE CT
18 ST ANNES MEWS
19 WINCHESTER MEWS
20 THE ATRIUM

B8
1 HYNES CT
2 BARTLETT HO
3 ST ANDREWS HO
4 ST GEORGES HO
5 WOODSIDE CT
6 ASCUAMPT HO

7 BEVOIS MANS

E7
1 MANOR PARK HO
2 WINDSOR CT
3 COBBETT CT
4 ROSEBROOK CT
5 JUNIPER CT

E8
1 KELLY CT
2 FLORENCE CT
3 DEAN CT
4 COBDEN DELL
5 CAUSEWAY CT
6 ABBEYFIELD HO

7 BIRCHWOOD CT
8 CHRISTINE CT
9 MIDANBURY CT
10 WELLOW CT
11 THE GATESHOUSE
12 BROUGHTON HO
13 BINDON CT

A   B   C   D   E   F

8
7
13
6
5
12
4
3
11
2
1
10

42   A   B   43   C   D   44   E   F

A3
1 HOLY ROOD PL
2 QUEENS HO
3 CHANDOS HO
4 ORCHARD HO
5 HOLYROOD HO
6 KING'S HO
7 ALL SAINTS HO
8 MARSH HO
9 ELDON HO

10 CHALLIS CT
21 RUSSELL CT
13 CHANDOS ST
18 CANUTE HO
14 ST JAMES HO
15 ST BERNARD HO
16 HIGH ST
17 GOLDSMITHS CT
18 GUILD HO
19 MARKET PL

20 COOPERS CT
21 TALBOT CT
22 LATIMER GATE
23 JESSIE TERR
24 THE GREENWICH
25 THE ALBANY
26 BACK OF THE WALLS
27 CITY CT
28 EXECUTIVE SQ
29 CHANDLERS CT

A4
1 COSSACK GN
2 BROAD GN
3 KINGSLAND CT
4 JOHNSON ST
5 KINGSLAND SQ
6 YORK WK
7 HANOVER ST
8 Bargate Sh Ctr
9 East Street Sh Ctr

A5
1 COMPTON WLK
2 ST MATTHEWS CL
3 THE CARRONADES
4 KINGSLAND HO
5 LEWIS HO
6 PRIORY HO
7 WOOLLEY HO
8 CRAVEN ST

10 Southampton
Solent Univ

C6
1 CHARLIEJOY GDNS
2 PRINCES CT
3 PRINCES HO
4 GRAHAM HO
5 CLARENCE HO
6 COBURG HO
7 YORK HO
8 AVON HO
9 TEVIOT HO

10 SOLWAY HO
11 FORTH HO
12 BELVIDERE HO
13 MAURETANIA HO
14 MILLBANK HO
15 KENILWORTH HO
16 NORMAN HO
17 SAXON HO
18 ARUNDEL HO
19 WARWICK HO

20 ARMADALE HO
21 Northam Bsns Ctr

B3
1 COMMODORE CT
2 ST LAWRENCE RD
3 CONSULATE CT
4 BRIDGE TERR
5 ENDEAVOUR CT
6 City Commerce Ctr
7 LUCIA FOSTER WELCH HALL
STUDENT VILLAGE
8 IMPERIAL APARTMENTS
9 TED BATES RD
10 ROYAL CRESCENT RD
11 MISTRAL
12 NELSON ST
13 CARPATHIA DR
14 WHITESTAR PL
15 RUDD WY

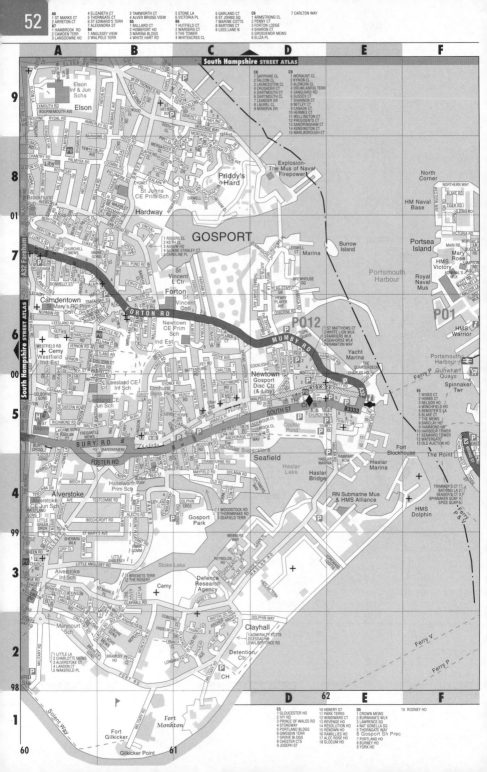

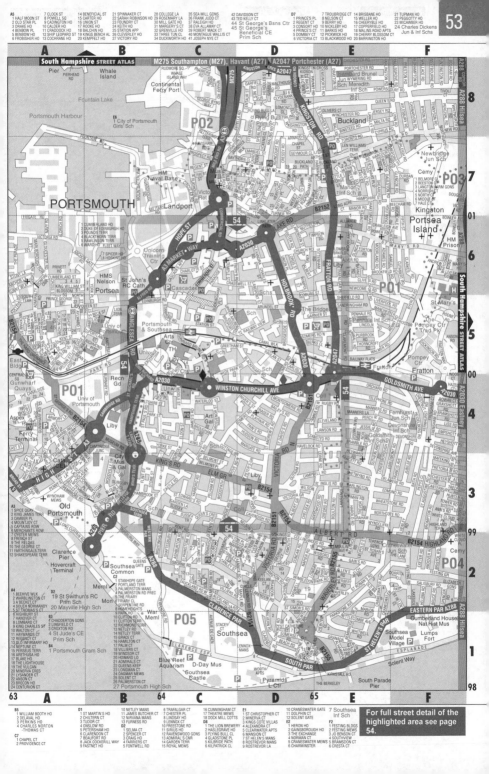

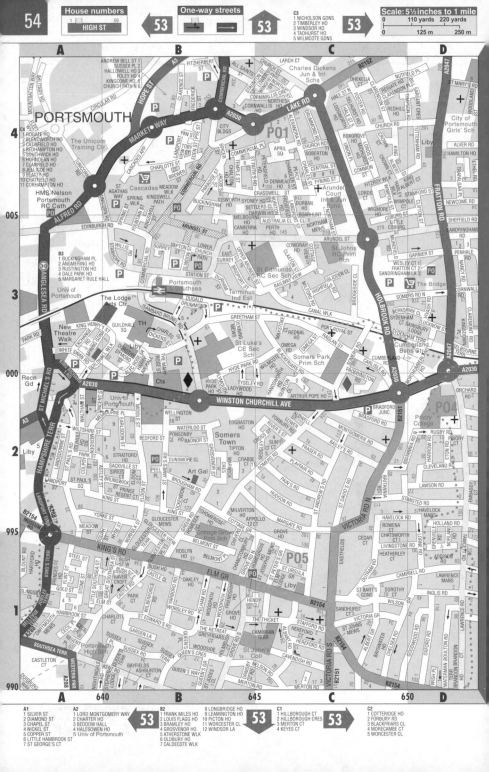

Index

Place name May be abbreviated on the map

Location number Present when a number indicates the place's position in a crowded area of mapping

Locality, town or village Shown when more than one place has the same name

Postcode district District for the indexed place

Page and grid square Page number and grid reference for the standard mapping

Church Rd 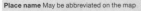 **6** Beckenham BR2..........**53** C6

Cities, towns and villages are listed in CAPITAL LETTERS Public and commercial buildings are highlighted in magenta
Places of interest are highlighted in blue with a star★

Abbreviations used in the index

Acad	Academy	Comm	Common	Gd	Ground	L	Leisure	Prom	Promenade
App	Approach	Cott	Cottage	Gdn	Garden	La	Lane	Rd	Road
Arc	Arcade	Cres	Crescent	Gn	Green	Liby	Library	Recn	Recreation
Ave	Avenue	Cswy	Causeway	Gr	Grove	Mdw	Meadow	Ret	Retail
Bglw	Bungalow	Ct	Court	H	Hall	Meml	Memorial	Sh	Shopping
Bldg	Building	Ctr	Centre	Ho	House	Mkt	Market	Sq	Square
Bsns, Bus	Business	Ctry	Country	Hospl	Hospital	Mus	Museum	St	Street
Bvd	Boulevard	Cty	County	HQ	Headquarters	Orch	Orchard	Sta	Station
Cath	Cathedral	Dr	Drive	Hts	Heights	Pal	Palace	Terr	Terrace
Cir	Circus	Dro	Drove	Ind	Industrial	Par	Parade	TH	Town Hall
Cl	Close	Ed	Education	Inst	Institute	Pas	Passage	Univ	University
Cnr	Corner	Emb	Embankment	Int	International	Pk	Park	Wk, Wlk	Walk
Coll	College	Est	Estate	Intc	Interchange	Pl	Place	Wr	Water
Com	Community	Ex	Exhibition	Junc	Junction	Prec	Precinct	Yd	Yard

Index of towns, villages, streets, hospitals, industrial estates, railway stations, schools, shopping centres, universities and places of interest

A

Abbey Ct **8** SO15.........50 F7
Abbeyfield Ho **6** SO18...51 E8
Abbey La PO33...........12 E5
Abbots Brook SO41.......48 F2
Abbots Cl PO33..........11 D6
A'Becket Ct **3** PO1.....53 A4
Abingdon Cl PO12........52 B5
Abingdon Rd PO33........12 C5
Above Bar St SO14.......50 F5
Acacia Cl PO30..........20 F7
Acacia Rd SO19..........51 F5
Acorn Cl SO40...........50 A1
Acorn Gdns PO32.........3 D2
Acorns The PO33.........10 D4
Acorn Workshops SO14...51 B7
Adames Rd PO1..........53 E6
Addison Rd PO4..........54 D1
Adelaide Ct
　Lymington SO41.........48 F4
　Ryde PO33..............12 B4
Adelaide Gr PO32........3 C3
Adelaide Pl PO33........12 B4
Adelaide Rd SO17........51 C8
ADGESTONE..............23 E1
Adgestone Vineyard★
　PO36..................23 F2
Admiral's Cnr **18** PO5...53 D2
Admirals Ct
　Lymington SO41.........48 F4
　2 Portsmouth PO5....53 C2
Admirals Wharf PO31.....3 B5
Admiral's Wlk PO1.......52 F7
Admiralty Cl PO12.......52 C8
Admiralty Cotts PO12...52 C2
Admiralty Ho SO14......51 A2
Admiralty Rd PO1.......53 A5
Admiral Way PO31.......2 F3
Afton Barns PO40........27 E8
Afton Marsh Nature
　Reserve★ PO40.........27 C8
Afton Park Gdns★ PO40..27 D7
Afton Rd PO40...........27 D7
Agincourt Rd PO2.......53 D7
Agnew Ho PO12..........52 B7
Aisla La SO19...........51 D4
Akban Way PO38.........49 F2
Albany Cl PO12..........52 B6
Albany Park Ct SO17.....50 F8
Albany Rd
　East Cowes PO32........3 C5

Albany Rd continued
　Newport PO30...........20 C8
　Portsmouth PO5.........54 C1
　Southampton SO15......50 C6
Albany The **28** SO14....51 A3
Albany View PO30........8 F1
Albemarle Ave PO12......52 B9
Albert Gr PO5...........54 C1
Albert Mews PO30........20 F8
Albert Rd
　Gurnard PO31...........2 D3
　Portsmouth PO4, PO5...53 E2
　Sandown PO36..........36 A3
　Shanklin PO37..........43 B7
Albert Road N SO14......51 B3
Albert Road S SO14......51 B3
Albert St
　Cowes PO31.............3 A4
　Gosport PO12...........52 C6
　Newport PO30...........20 D6
　Ryde PO33..............12 C5
　Ventnor PO38...........47 B6
Albion Pl **3** SO14.....50 F4
Albion Rd PO36..........36 A3
Albion Towers SO14......51 B4
Alcantara Cres SO14.....51 B3
Alderbury La PO30.......20 C6
Alderbury Rd PO30.......20 C6
Aldermore Cl PO33.......12 C3
Aldermore Terr PO40.....15 A3
Aldrich Rd PO1..........53 A6
Aldwell St PO5..........54 C2
Alec Rose Ho **17** PO12..52 C5
Alec Rose La PO1........54 B3
Alecto Rd PO12..........52 B4
Alec Wintle Ho PO2......53 D8
Alencon Cl **3** PO12....52 C9
Alexander Cotts PO41...15 A6
Alexander Ct
　Southampton SO15......50 D6
　Southampton, Woolston
　SO19..................51 E2
Alexandra Ct **4** PO4...53 E1
Alexandra Gdns PO38....47 A5
Alexandra La PO30.......20 D6
Alexandra Mews
　Lymington SO41.........48 D5
　Southampton SO15......50 E7
Alexandra Rd
　Cowes PO31.............3 A3
　Lymington SO41.........48 C5
　Portsmouth PO1.........54 C4
　Ryde PO33..............12 E4

Alexandra Rd continued
　Shanklin PO37..........43 C7
　Southampton SO15......50 E6
Alexandra Road E PO41...16 C8
Alexandra St **7** PO12..52 A7
Alfred Rd
　Portsmouth PO1.........54 A4
　Sandown PO36..........35 D4
Alfred St
　East Cowes PO32........3 C3
　Ryde PO33..............12 C4
　Southampton SO14......51 B6
Alhambra Rd PO4........53 E1
Allen's Rd PO4..........53 E2
Alliance Ho PO1.........53 E6
Allotment Rd PO38.......45 C4
All Saints CE Prim Sch
　PO40..................14 F1
All Saints Ho **7** SO14..51 A3
All Saints Rd SO41......48 F2
All Saints' Rd PO1......53 D7
All Saints' St PO1......54 B4
Alma Ho SO14...........51 A8
Alma Pl **5** PO41.......15 D6
Alma Rd
　Southampton SO14......51 A8
　Ventnor PO38...........47 A5
Alma St PO12............52 B7
Almond Ct **10** SO15....50 C6
Almond Rd SO15.........50 C6
Almshouses **8** PO33...12 C5
Alpine Rd PO38..........47 A6
Alresford Lodge PO37....35 D1
Alresford Rd PO37.......35 D1
Altofts Gdns PO38.......47 A6
Alton Rd SO18..........51 E8
Alum Bay New Rd PO39...26 F6
Alum Bay Old Rd PO39...26 F6
Alvara Rd PO12..........52 C5
Alver St PO12...........52 B7
Alver Bridge View **4**
　PO12..................52 B4
Alver Quay PO12.........52 B4
Alver Rd
　Gosport PO12...........52 B4
　Portsmouth PO1.........53 E6
ALVERSTOKE..........52 B4
Alverstoke CE Jun Sch
　PO12..................52 A4
Alverstoke Inf Sch PO12..52 A3
ALVERSTONE..........23 E4
Alverstone Cross PO32...10 A5
Alverstone Ct PO36......34 E4

**ALVERSTONE GARDEN
VILLAGE**..............35 B7
Alverstone Rd
　Alverstone Garden Village
　PO36..................35 B7
　Winford PO36...........34 F5
　Wootton PO32...........10 A6
Alverstone Shute PO36...35 B7
Alverston Mead Nature
　Reserve★ PO36.........35 B7
Alvington Cl PO30.......20 A5
Alvington Manor View
　PO30..................19 F6
Alvington Rd PO30.......20 A5
Alyne Ho SO15..........50 F8
Aman Ct PO39...........14 C1
Amazon World Zoo Park★
　PO36..................34 C5
Amberley Ho PO37.......43 B7
Amberley Rd PO12.......52 A9
Ambleside Rd SO41......48 F3
Ambrose Cnr SO41.......48 D6
Amherst Pl PO33........12 E4
Amos Hill PO39..........14 E1
Amoy St SO15...........50 F6
Ampress La SO41........48 D6
Ampress Pk SO41........48 D6
Ampthill Rd
　Ryde PO33..............12 E5
　Southampton SO15......50 B7
Ancasta Rd SO14........51 B7
Anchorage Ho PO38......47 A5
Anchorage The PO12.....52 C5
Anchorage Way
　East Cowes PO32........3 C2
　Lymington SO41.........48 D3
Anchor Gate Rd PO1.....53 A6
Anchor La PO1..........53 B4
Anchor Mews SO41......48 E4
Anderri Way PO37.......35 C2
Anderson's Rd SO14.....51 B3
Andes Cl SO14..........51 C3
Andover Rd
　Portsmouth PO4........53 F2
　Southampton SO15......50 D6
Andrew Bell St PO1......54 B4
Andrew Cl PO1..........54 B4
Andrew's Lodge SO41....48 D5
Angel Ct SO41..........48 E4
Anglesea PO1...........53 B5
Anglesea Rd PO1........54 A3
Anglesea St **1** PO33...12 C5
Anglesea Terr SO14......51 B3

Abb–Arm

Anglesey Arms Rd PO12..52 A3
Anglesey Rd PO12.......52 A3
Anglesey View **1** PO12..52 B4
Angmering Ho **2** PO1...54 B3
Ann's Hill Rd PO12......52 A6
Ansells PO34...........13 D2
Anson Ct **22** PO1......53 A4
Anson Ho SO14..........51 B3
Appleford Rd PO38......40 C5
APPLEY................12 F5
Appley Farm PO33.......12 E4
Appley La PO33.........12 E5
Appley Rd PO33.........12 F4
Appley Rise PO33.......12 F5
Appley Twr★ PO33......12 F5
Apollo Ct PO5..........54 B2
Appuldurcombe Ho★
　PO38..................42 A4
Appuldurcombe Rd PO38..42 B5
Appuldurcombe Terr
　PO38..................42 C4
April Sq PO1...........54 C4
APSE HEATH............42 A4
Apse Manor Rd PO36, PO37,
　PO38..................34 E1
Aquitania Ho **6** SO14..51 C5
Arabian Lodge PO33.....12 D6
Araluen Way PO36.......35 E3
Arcade The PO31........3 B5
Archer Ho PO12.........12 B5
Archers **1** SO15.......50 E6
Archers Rd SO15........50 F7
Archery Gdns SO19......51 F2
Archery Gr SO19........51 F2
Archery Rd SO19........51 E1
Archgate SO41..........48 E4
Arctic Rd PO31.........3 B4
Arethusa Ho **16** PO1...53 A4
Argyle Rd
　Newport PO30...........9 A1
　Southampton SO14......51 A5
Argyll Pl PO33..........12 B5
Argyll St PO33..........12 B5
Ariel Rd PO1...........53 E5
Arlott Ct SO15.........50 E7
Armadale Ho **20** SO14..51 C6
Arminers Cl PO33.......52 B2
Armory La PO1..........53 A3
Armoury The SO40.......50 A3
Armstrong Cl **1** PO12..52 B5

Arnaud Cl PO2 . . . . .53 D7
Arnhem Rd PO40 . . . . .14 E2
Arnhem Villas PO40 . . . . .14 E2
Arnold Rd
  Cowes PO31 . . . . .3 A3
  Ryde PO33 . . . . .11 E5
ARRETON 21 E2
Arreton Barns Craft Village*
  PO30 . . . . .21 E2
Arreton Cross PO30 . . . . .21 E2
Arreton Ct **2** PO12 . . . . .52 B4
Arreton St George's CE Prim
  Sch PO30 . . . . .21 F2
Arrow Cl SO19 . . . . .51 D1
Arthur Cott PO32 . . . . .3 E2
Arthur Moody Dr PO30 . . . . .19 F6
Arthur Pope Ho PO5 . . . . .54 C2
Arthur Rd SO15 . . . . .50 D6
Arthur's Hill PO37 . . . . .35 D1
Arthur St
  Portsmouth PO2 . . . . .53 E7
  Ryde PO33 . . . . .12 B5
Arundel Cl PO33 . . . . .12 E4
Arundel Ct Inf Sch PO1 . . . . .54 C4
Arundel Ct Jun Sch PO1 . . . . . . .54 C4
Arundel Ho
  Southampton, Banister's Pk
  SO15 . . . . .50 F8
  18 Southampton, Northam
  SO14 . . . . .51 C6
Arundel Rd PO33 . . . . .12 E4
Arundel St PO1 . . . . .54 C4
Ascupart Ho **16** SO17 . . . . .51 B8
Ascupart St SO14 . . . . .51 B4
Ashborne Ct PO36 . . . . .35 F5
Ashburnham Cl SO19 . . . . .51 D5
Ashburton Ct PO33 . . . . .54 B1
Ashburton Rd PO5 . . . . .53 C2
Ashby Cl
  Gosport PO12 . . . . .52 B5
  Newport PO30 . . . . .19 F7
Ashby Pl PO5 . . . . .53 C2
Ash Gr
  Cowes PO31 . . . . .3 A2
  Shanklin PO37 . . . . .43 C6
Ashdene **17** SO15 . . . . .50 B8
ASHEY 23 B7
Ashey Cl PO33 . . . . .12 B3
Ashey Pk PO33 . . . . .23 D8
Ashey Rd PO33 . . . . .23 C6
Ashey View PO36 . . . . .35 C3
Ash La
  Cowes PO31 . . . . .3 A2
  Shanklin PO37 . . . . .43 C6
Ashknowle La PO38 . . . . .45 D5
Ashlake Copse La PO33 . . . . .11 A5
Ashlake Copse Rd PO33 . . . . .11 A6
Ashlake Farm La PO33 . . . . .11 A5
Ashley Ct PO12 . . . . .52 A6
Ashley Way PO30 . . . . .30 A2
Ash Rd PO33 . . . . .12 A6
Ashridge Cl SO15 . . . . .50 F8
Ashton Ho SO19 . . . . .51 F1
Ashton Terr **1** PO31 . . . . .3 B4
Ashtree Way PO34 . . . . .13 D2
Aspen Cl PO30 . . . . .20 C7
Aspen Gdns PO33 . . . . .12 F2
Aspex (Gall)* PO1 . . . . .53 A4
Aspin House Further
  Education Unit SO15 . . . . .50 B6
Astley St PO5 . . . . .54 A2
Aston Rd PO4 . . . . .53 F3
Astra Wlk PO12 . . . . .52 B5
Asturias Way SO14 . . . . .51 C3
Asylum Rd SO15 . . . . .51 A6
Athelstan Rd SO19 . . . . .51 E6
Athelston Ct SO14 . . . . .51 A6
ATHERFIELD GREEN 39 C3
Atherfield Rd PO38 . . . . .39 C4
Atherley Cross PO37 . . . . .43 C8
Atherley Ct
  Shanklin PO37 . . . . .43 C8
  Southampton SO15 . . . . .50 B8
Atherley Rd
  Shanklin PO37 . . . . .43 C8
  Southampton SO15 . . . . .50 B8
Atherstone Wlk **6** PO5 . . . . .54 B2
Atkinson Cl PO12 . . . . .52 A3
Atkinson Dr PO30 . . . . .20 F8
Atlantic Cl SO14 . . . . .51 B2
Atrium The **20** SO17 . . . . .51 A8
Attrill's La PO33 . . . . .24 E8
Auckland Road E PO5 . . . . .54 C2
Auckland Road W PO5 . . . . .53 C2
Audley Ct **8** PO40 . . . . .14 E1
Augusta Rd PO33 . . . . .12 B6
Augustine Rd SO14 . . . . .51 B6
Augustus Ho SO14 . . . . .51 C7
Australia Cl PO1 . . . . .54 C3
Autumn Rd SO40 . . . . .50 A1
Avenue Ct
  Gosport PO12 . . . . .52 A3
  2 Southampton SO17 . . . . .50 F8
Avenue De Caen PO5 . . . . .53 C1
Avenue Nurseries PO36 . . . . .36 A4
Avenue Rd
  Freshwater PO40 . . . . .14 E1
  Gosport PO12 . . . . .52 C5
  Lymington SO41 . . . . .48 E4
  Sandown PO36 . . . . .36 A4
  Shanklin PO37 . . . . .43 C8
  Southampton SO14 . . . . .51 A8
  Wroxall PO38 . . . . .42 B4
Avenue Slipway PO36 . . . . .36 A3
Avenue The
  Bouldnor PO41 . . . . .16 C8
  East Cowes PO32 . . . . .3 E2

Avenue The continued
  Gosport PO12 . . . . .52 A4
  Gurnard PO31 . . . . .2 D3
  Totland PO39 . . . . .14 E1
Avery La PO12 . . . . .52 A8
Avon Cl SO41 . . . . .48 C3
Avondale Rd
  Newport PO30 . . . . .20 E6
  Portsmouth PO1 . . . . .53 F7
Avon Ho **80** SO14 . . . . .51 C5
Avro Cl SO15 . . . . .50 A7
Aylesbury Rd PO2 . . . . .53 F8
Aylett Cl PO36 . . . . .36 A6
Aylward St PO1 . . . . .53 A5
Aynsley Ct SO15 . . . . .50 D7

B

Back of the Walls **20**
  SO14 . . . . .51 A3
Bacon Cl SO19 . . . . .51 F1
Badger La PO30 . . . . .28 F4
Badgers Cl PO38 . . . . .42 C4
Badger Terr PO33 . . . . .3 A5
Bagshot Mews SO19 . . . . .51 F3
Bagwich La PO38 . . . . .33 A1
Bailey Cl PO33 . . . . .4 D3
Bailey's Rd PO5 . . . . .54 C2
Bakers Ct PO33 . . . . .11 F5
Baker St PO1 . . . . .53 D7
Balchin Ho **11** SO15 . . . . .53 A5
Ballard Cl **1** PO12 . . . . .52 B5
Balliol Rd PO2 . . . . .53 E8
Balmoral Ct
  4 Southampton, Millbrook
  SO15 . . . . .50 A6
  7 Southampton SO17 . . . . .51 A8
Banas Cl PO38 . . . . .47 B7
Banbury Cl PO33 . . . . .12 E4
Bangor Rd SO15 . . . . .50 B6
Banister Ct **6** SO15 . . . . .50 F7
Banister Gdns SO15 . . . . .50 F7
Banister Grange **9** SO15 . . . . . . .50 F7
Banister Inf Sch SO15 . . . . .50 F7
Banister Mews SO15 . . . . .50 F7
Banister Rd SO15 . . . . .50 F7
BANISTER'S PARK 50 E7
Bank Cotts PO30 . . . . .17 C7
Bank Gdns **8** PO33 . . . . .12 C5
Bankhill Dr SO41 . . . . .48 D5
Bank Rd PO33 . . . . .12 C5
Bankside
  Lymington SO41 . . . . .48 D6
  Shalfleet PO30 . . . . .17 E7
Bankview SO41 . . . . .48 D6
Banner La PO30 . . . . .20 C8
Bannock Rd PO38 . . . . .45 D6
Barclay Ho **8** PO12 . . . . .52 E5
Barfield PO33 . . . . .12 C5
Barfields Cl SO41 . . . . .48 E4
Barfields Ct **2** SO41 . . . . .48 E4
Barkis Ho **4** SO14 . . . . .51 D7
Barkshire Ct **7** SO15 . . . . .50 F8
Barn Cl PO38 . . . . .46 B4
Barnes Rd PO1 . . . . .53 E6
Barnfield Cl SO19 . . . . .51 E1
Barnfield Ct SO19 . . . . .51 F1
Barnfield Flats SO19 . . . . .51 F1
Barnfield Rd
  Bembridge PO35 . . . . .25 C4
  Southampton SO19 . . . . .51 F1
Barnfield Way SO19 . . . . .51 F1
Barns The PO30 . . . . .20 B5
Baronsmere PO12 . . . . .52 A5
Barrack Shute PO38 . . . . .45 B3
Barrington Rd **20** PO1 . . . . .53 D7
Barrington Row PO18 . . . . .18 A2
Bars Hill PO31 . . . . .3 A5
Bartlett Ho **2** SO17 . . . . .51 B8
Bartletts Cl PO36 . . . . .34 E7
BARTON .20 F7
Barton Prim Sch PO30 . . . . .20 F7
Barton Rd
  East Cowes PO32 . . . . .3 F2
  Newport PO30 . . . . .20 E7
Bartons Cnr
  Ryde PO33 . . . . .11 E4
  Shalfleet PO30 . . . . .17 F6
Bartons Ct **8** PO12 . . . . .52 B6
Bartonwood Rd PO32 . . . . .4 A1
Basepoint Ent Ctr SO14 . . . . .51 B3
Basing Rd SO15 . . . . .50 C7
Basin St PO2 . . . . .53 D8
Basketts La **2** PO41 . . . . .15 D6
Bathingbourne La PO36 . . . . .34 B4
Bathing La PO1 . . . . .52 F5
Bath Rd
  Cowes PO31 . . . . .3 B5
  Lymington SO41 . . . . .49 A3
  Portsmouth PO4 . . . . .53 F3
  Ventnor PO38 . . . . .46 F5
Bath Sq PO1 . . . . .52 F5
Batten St SO14 . . . . .51 A7
Battenburg Rd PO12 . . . . .52 C6
Battery Row PO1 . . . . .53 A3
Battery Row PO1 . . . . .53 A3
Batts Rd PO37 . . . . .43 B7
Bay Ct PO38 . . . . .47 B6

Bayfields PO5 . . . . .54 B1
Baynton Ho SO41 . . . . .48 D4
Bay Rd PO40 . . . . .27 D7
Bays Ct SO41 . . . . .48 C4
Bays Rd SO41 . . . . .48 C4
Bayswater Ho PO5 . . . . .54 C1
Baythorn Cl PO1 . . . . .54 C4
Bay View Cr PO36 . . . . .35 D2
Bay View Rd PO31 . . . . .2 D3
Beachfield Rd
  Bembridge PO35 . . . . .25 F3
  Sandown PO36 . . . . .35 F5
  Wroxall PO38 . . . . .42 B4
Beach House La PO35 . . . . .25 F5
Beach Rd
  Bembridge PO35 . . . . .25 C6
  Portsmouth PO5 . . . . .53 D1
Beachside PO33 . . . . .2 C3
Beachside Bgwls PO36 . . . . .14 D2
Beacon Alley PO38 . . . . .41 B7
Beaconsfield Rd PO38 . . . . .47 B6
Beaper Shute PO33, PO36 . .24 B6
Beatrice Ave
  Cowes PO32 . . . . .9 E8
  Shanklin PO37 . . . . .43 D8
Beatrice Cl PO33 . . . . .11 F5
Beatrice Cotts PO41 . . . . .15 A6
Beatrice Rd
  Portsmouth PO4 . . . . .53 E2
  Southampton SO15 . . . . .50 C7
Beatrice Terr PO30 . . . . .20 E8
Beatty Ho **9** PO1 . . . . .54 C4
Beaufort Rd **7** PO5 . . . . .53 D1
Beaulieu Ho **2** SO15 . . . . .50 F7
Beaumont Ct PO12 . . . . .52 A9
Beckfield Cross PO38 . . . . .40 A7
Beckford Rd PO1 . . . . .3 B4
Beck St PO1 . . . . .53 B5
Bedbury La PO40 . . . . .27 B7
Beddow Hall **3** PO38 . . . . .54 A2
Bedford Ave SO19 . . . . .51 E2
Bedford Pl SO15 . . . . .50 F6
BEDFORD PLACE 50 F6
Bedford Row PO30 . . . . .20 C6
Bedford St
  Gosport PO12 . . . . .52 A7
  Portsmouth PO5 . . . . .54 B2
Bedhampton Ho **4** PO1 . . . . .54 C4
Bedhampton Rd PO2 . . . . .53 F8
Bedworth Pl **3** PO33 . . . . .12 C5
Beecham Rd PO1 . . . . .53 F7
Beech Ave SO19 . . . . .51 F1
Beechcroft Dr PO33 . . . . .10 D5
Beechcroft Rd PO12 . . . . .52 B4
Beech Ct
  Shanklin PO37 . . . . .43 C6
  Southampton SO19 . . . . .51 F3
Beeches The PO36 . . . . .35 D3
Beechfield Ct SO15 . . . . .50 B8
Beech Gr
  Gosport PO12 . . . . .52 A4
  Ryde PO33 . . . . .12 A6
Beech Rd
  Newport PO30 . . . . .20 E7
  Southampton SO15 . . . . .50 B6
Beech Tree Dr PO37 . . . . .35 C1
Beechwood Gdns SO18 . . . . .51 F8
Beechwood Rd SO17 . . . . .51 C8
Beechwood Jun Sch SO18 . .51 F7
Beehive Vlle **1** PO1 . . . . .53 A4
Beeston Ct PO12 . . . . .53 E7
Behrendt Cl PO12 . . . . .52 A7
Belgrave St PO38 . . . . .46 F5
Belgrave Rd PO38 . . . . .47 A5
Belgrave View PO38 . . . . .46 F6
Bellamy St SO17 . . . . .51 D8
Bellcroft Dr PO30 . . . . .21 A6
BELLEVUE 51 C5
Bellevue Rd
  Cowes PO31 . . . . .3 A3
  Ryde PO31 . . . . .12 D6
  Southampton SO15 . . . . .51 A6
Bellevue Terr
  Portsmouth PO5 . . . . .54 A1
  10 Southampton SO14 . . . . . . .51 A6
Belmede La PO30 . . . . .20 F8
Bell St SO14 . . . . .51 A3
Belmont La PO32 . . . . .9 F3
Belmont Pl PO5 . . . . .54 B1
Belmont St PO5 . . . . .54 B1
Belmore Cl PO33 . . . . .11 F5
Belmore Ho **1** SO41 . . . . .48 E2
Belmore La SO41 . . . . .48 E3
Belmore Rd SO41 . . . . .48 E3
Belvedere St PO33 . . . . .12 C5
BELVIDERE 51 C5
Belvidere Ho **12** SO14 . . . . .51 C5
Belvidere Rd SO14 . . . . .51 C5
Belvidere Terr SO14 . . . . .51 C5
BEMBRIDGE 25 C4
Bembridge Airport PO35 . . . . .25 A2
Bembridge CE Prim Sch
  PO35 . . . . .25 D4
Bembridge Cres **4** PO5 . . . . .53 E1
Bembridge Her Str*
  PO35 . . . . .25 C5
Bembridge House Cl
  PO35 . . . . .25 D4
Bembridge Trail PO30 . . . . .21 A2
Bembridge Windmill*
  PO35 . . . . .25 B3
Bemister's La **5** PO12 . . . . .52 B5
Benbow Ho **5** PO1 . . . . .53 A5
Benbow Pl **4** PO1 . . . . .53 A5
Beneficial St **10** PO1 . . . . .53 A5
Benett St PO33 . . . . .12 D5
Benjamen Mews PO36 . . . . .35 F5

Benson Rd SO15 . . . . .50 B8
Bentham Rd PO12 . . . . .52 B4
Bentley Way SO41 . . . . .48 D6
Bently Way SO41 . . . . .48 D7
Benton Cl PO32 . . . . .3 D3
Beresford Rd SO41 . . . . .48 C4
Berkeley Cl SO15 . . . . .50 E7
Berkeley Rd SO15 . . . . .50 F6
Berkeley The PO5 . . . . .53 E1
Berkshire Cl PO1 . . . . .54 D3
Bernard Mews **3** PO31 . . . . .3 B4
Bernard Rd PO31 . . . . .3 B4
Bernard St SO14 . . . . .51 A3
Bernard Way PO30 . . . . .20 D8
Berry Cl PO30 . . . . .20 F6
Berry Hill PO36 . . . . .35 C4
Berry Ho **9** PO1 . . . . .53 D7
Berrymead PO38 . . . . .42 C4
Berry Shute PO30 . . . . .32 A1
Beryton Cl PO12 . . . . .52 A7
Beryton Rd PO12 . . . . .52 A7
Bettesworth Rd
  Portsmouth PO1 . . . . .53 E7
  Ryde PO33 . . . . .12 B3
Betty Haunt La PO30 . . . . .19 C6
Bevan Cl SO19 . . . . .51 E1
Bevis Rd PO12 . . . . .52 B6
Bevois Gdns SO14 . . . . .51 A7
Bevois Hill SO14 . . . . .51 B8
Bevois Mans **7** SO14 . . . . .51 B8
Bevois Mews **4** SO14 . . . . .51 A7
BEVOIS MOUNT 51 A8
BEVOIS TOWN 51 B8
Bevois Town Prim Sch
  SO14 . . . . .51 A7
BEVOIS VALLEY 51 B7
Bevois Valley Rd SO14 . . . . .51 B7
Biddlesgate Ct **5** SO14 . . . . .50 F3
BIERLEY .41 A1
Bignor Pl **15** PO30 . . . . .20 D6
Billington Pl SO41 . . . . .48 D2
Bill Sargent Cres PO1 . . . . .54 D4
Bindon Ct **3** SO18 . . . . .51 E8
Binfield Cnr PO30 . . . . .9 F4
Bingham Dr SO41 . . . . .48 E3
BINSTEAD 11 F5
Binstead Hill PO33 . . . . .11 E5
Binstead Lodge Rd PO33 . . . . . . .11 F5
Binstead Prim Sch PO33 . . . . .11 F4
Binstead Rd PO33 . . . . .12 A5
Birch Cl
  East Cowes PO32 . . . . .3 D3
  Freshwater PO40 . . . . .14 E2
Birch Cl SO41 . . . . .48 B2
Birch Gdns
  Newport PO30 . . . . .20 D7
  Ryde PO33 . . . . .11 F5
Birchmore La PO30 . . . . .32 F8
Birchwood Ct **7** SO18 . . . . .51 E8
Birdham Cl PO33 . . . . .12 A5
Birkenshaw **8** PO30 . . . . .19 D1
Birmingham Rd PO1 . . . . .3 B4
Bishop Lovett CE Mid Sch
  PO33 . . . . .12 E4
Bishops Cl PO36 . . . . .35 E6
Bishops Cres SO19 . . . . .51 F4
Bishops Rd SO19 . . . . .51 E8
Bishop St PO1 . . . . .53 A5
Bishops Way PO30 . . . . .9 C1
Bittern Cl PO12 . . . . .52 B8
BITTERNE 51 F6
Bitterne CE Inf Sch SO19 . . . . . . .51 F6
Bitterne CE Jun Sch SO19 .51 F6
BITTERNE MANOR 51 D7
Bitterne Manor Ho SO18 . . . . . . .51 C7
Bitterne Manor Prim Sch
  SO18 . . . . .51 D7
Bitterne Road W SO18 . . . . .51 E7
Bitterne Sta PO37 . . . . .51 D7
Bitterne Way
  Lymington SO41 . . . . .48 D2
  Southampton SO19 . . . . .51 F6
Bittern Pl **7** PO30 . . . . .9 E4
Blackberry Rd PO38 . . . . .20 F8
Blackberry La PO33 . . . . .3 A4
Blackberry Terr SO14 . . . . .51 B7
Blackbridge Rd PO40 . . . . .27 C7
Blackfriars Cl **3** PO5 . . . . .54 C2
Blackfriars Rd PO5 . . . . .54 C2
BLACKGANG 44 D4
Blackgang Chine* PO38 . . . . . .44 C4
Blackgang Rd PO38 . . . . .44 E4
Blackgang Sawmill & St
  Catherine's Quay Mus*
  PO38 . . . . .44 D4
Blacklands Rd PO30, PO33 . .21 D8
Blackpan Cl PO36 . . . . .35 C3
Blacksmiths La PO41 . . . . .16 D6
Blackthorn Cl
  Lymington SO41 . . . . .48 B2
  Newport PO30 . . . . .20 D7
Blackthorn Rd SO19 . . . . .51 F5
Blackthorn Terr PO1 . . . . .53 A6
BLACKWATER 20 E1
Blackwater Hollow PO30,
  PO38 . . . . .32 F7
Blackwater Junc PO30 . . . . .20 E1
Blackwater Rd PO30 . . . . .20 E3
Blake Ct **3** PO12 . . . . .52 E5
Blake Ho PO38 . . . . .47 B7
Blake Rd
  Gosport PO12 . . . . .52 C6
  Portsmouth PO1 . . . . .52 E5

Blechynden Terr SO15 . . . . .50 E5
Blendworth Ho **2** PO1 . . . . .54 C4
Blenheim Gdns PO12 . . . . .52 B9
Blighmont Ave SO15 . . . . .50 B6
Blighmont Cres SO15 . . . . .50 B6
Bloomfield Cotts PO33 . . . . .24 F7
Bloomsbury Pk PO30 . . . . .9 B1
Bloomsbury Wlk SO19 . . . . .51 E2
Blossom Sq PO1 . . . . .53 A5
Blount Rd PO1 . . . . .53 B3
Blue Anchor La **10** SO14 . . . . . . .50 F3
Blue Reef Aquarium*
  PO5 . . . . .53 C1
Bluett Ave PO34 . . . . .13 D4
Blythe Shute PO38 . . . . .44 D5
Blythe Way PO37 . . . . .43 A8
Blyth Mews **4** SO15 . . . . .50 E6
Boardwalk Way SO40 . . . . .50 A3
Boarhunt Cl PO15 . . . . .54 C3
Boldens Rd PO12 . . . . .52 B2
Boldre La SO41 . . . . .48 D8
Bolton Dr PO12 . . . . .52 C8
Boltons The PO33 . . . . .10 F5
BONCHURCH 47 D6
Bonchurch Pottery*
  PO38 . . . . .47 D7
Bonchurch Shute PO38 . . . . .47 D7
Bonchurch Village Rd
  PO38 . . . . .47 C7
Bond St SO14 . . . . .51 C6
Bonfire Cnr PO1 . . . . .53 A6
Bosham Rd PO2 . . . . .53 F8
BOULDNOR 15 F6
Bouldnor Mead PO41 . . . . .15 F6
Boulton Rd PO5 . . . . .54 D1
Boundary Dr PO32 . . . . .4 B3
Bound Rd PO40 . . . . .14 F2
Bourn Cl PO33 . . . . .11 E4
Bournemouth Ave PO12 . .52 A9
Bourne St PO33 . . . . .50 D5
BOWCOMBE 19 E2
Bowcombe Bsns Pk PO30 .19 D2
Bowcombe Rd PO30 . . . . .19 E3
Bowdens Mead Cl PO30 . . . . . . .20 C7
Bower Cl SO19 . . . . .51 F1
Bower Rd PO36 . . . . .34 F5
Bowler Ave PO1 . . . . .53 F6
Bowler Ct PO1 . . . . .53 F6
Bowling Green La **13**
  PO30 . . . . .20 D6
Boxgrove Ho PO1 . . . . .54 C4
Bracken Dell PO37 . . . . .43 C4
Brackens Way PO41 . . . . .48 F2
Brackleshamn Cl SO19 . . . . .51 F3
Bradford Junc PO5 . . . . .54 C2
Bradford Rd PO5 . . . . .54 C2
BRADING 24 A3
Brading CE Prim Sch
  PO36 . . . . .24 A3
Brading Marshes RSPB
  Reserve* PO35 . . . . .24 B3
Brading Rd PO33 . . . . .12 E2
Brading Roman Villa*
  PO36 . . . . .23 F1
Brading Sta PO36 . . . . .24 B2
Braeside Cl SO19 . . . . .51 E5
Braeside Cres SO19 . . . . .51 E5
Braeside Rd SO19 . . . . .51 E5
Bramber Rd PO12 . . . . .52 A8
Bramble Rd PO34 . . . . .53 E4
Brambles La PO31 . . . . .2 E5
Brambles The
  Apse Heath PO36 . . . . .34 E3
  Bembridge PO35 . . . . .25 E4
Bramble Wlk SO41 . . . . .48 C4
Bramdean Mews SO19 . . . . .51 E5
Bramley Cl SO41 . . . . .48 E2
Bramley Gdns PO12 . . . . .52 B2
Bramley Ho
  Gosport PO12 . . . . .52 B2
  3 Portsmouth PO5 . . . . .54 B2
Bramleys PO30 . . . . .20 A6
Bramsdon Ct **5** PO4 . . . . .53 F2
Bramshott Rd PO4 . . . . .53 F4
Branazor Rd SO15 . . . . .50 C8
Brandon Ct PO5 . . . . .54 D1
Brandon Ho PO5 . . . . .54 D1
Brandon Rd PO5 . . . . .53 D2
Brannon Way PO33 . . . . .10 E4
BRANSTONE 34 D3
Branstone Cross PO36 . . . . .34 D3
Braxton Mdw PO41 . . . . .15 A5
Brecon Ho **22** PO1 . . . . .53 A4
Brewer St PO1 . . . . .54 B4
Brewhouse Sq PO12 . . . . .52 D7
Briary Ct PO12 . . . . .2 E5
Brickets Terr PO12 . . . . .52 B3
Brickfield La
  Freshwater PO39 . . . . .27 A8
  Lymington SO41 . . . . .48 D7
Brickfields Horse Country*
  PO33 . . . . .11 E3
Brickfields Way PO36 . . . . .36 A4
Briddlesford Rd PO30,
  PO33 . . . . .21 F6
Bridge Ho SO15 . . . . .50 C5
Bridge Rd
  Cowes PO31 . . . . .3 B4
  East Cowes PO32 . . . . .3 C4
  Lymington SO41 . . . . .48 F5
  Southampton SO19 . . . . .51 D3
  6 Yarmouth PO41 . . . . .15 C6
Bridge Sh Ctr The PO1 . . . . .54 D3
Bridgeside Cl PO1 . . . . .54 D3
Bridge Sq PO32 . . . . .3 C4
Bridge Terr **4** SO14 . . . . .51 B3
Bridge Way PO33 . . . . .10 F5
Bridgeway The SO19 . . . . .51 E3

Clarendon Rd continued
Southampton SO16 . . . .**50** A8
Clarendon St
Newport PO30 . . . .**20** C6
Portsmouth PO1 . . . .**54** C4
Clarkes Rd PO1 . . . .**53** F6
Classic Boat Mus★
Cowes PO32 . . . .**3** C4
Newport PO30 . . . .**20** E8
CLATTERFORD **20** A4
Clatterford Rd PO30 . . . . . .**20** A4
Clatterford Shute PO30 . . .**20** A4
Clausentum Ho SO18 . . . . . .**51** C7
Clausentum Rd SO14 . . . . . .**51** B7
Clausen Way SO41 . . . .**48** C1
Claxton St PO1 . . . .**54** C3
CLAYHALL **52** D2
Clayhall Rd PO12 . . . .**52** B3
Clay La PO41 . . . .**17** E3
Clayton Rd PO41 . . . .**14** E1
Clearwater Apartments 5
PO4 . . . .**53** E1
Cleaver Ho PO33 . . . .**11** C1
Cleaver's Cl PO33 . . . .**11** E4
Cleveland Rd
Gosport PO12 . . . .**52** B4
Portsmouth PO5 . . . .**54** D2
Clevelands Rd PO38 . . . .**42** C5
Cleveland Terr PO33 . . . .**12** C6
Cleverley Ho 26 PO1 . . . .**53** A5
Cliff Cl PO36 . . . .**24** B3
Cliff Cl PO36 . . . .**35** E4
Cliff End PO40 . . . .**14** E4
Cliff Farm App PO37 . . . . . .**42** F7
Cliff Gdns PO35 . . . .**35** E3
Cliff Ho
Sandown PO36 . . . .**35** E4
Ventnor PO38 . . . .**47** D7
Cliff La PO30 . . . .**38** C8
Clifford Dibben Mews 1
SO14 . . . .**51** A8
Clifford St
Newport PO30 . . . .**20** C6
Southampton SO14 . . . .**51** B5
Cliff Rd
Cowes PO31 . . . .**2** F5
Shanklin PO36 . . . .**35** E4
Southampton SO15 . . . .**50** D5
Totland PO39 . . . .**26** G8
Cliff The SO39 . . . .**51** D3
Cliff Way PO36 . . . .**35** E3
Clifton Cl 2 SO15 . . . .**50** A8
Clifton Gdns 1 SO15 . . . . . .**50** A8
Clifton Lodge SO15 . . . .**50** A8
Clifton Rd
10 Portsmouth PO5 . . . . . .**53** C2
Southampton SO15 . . . .**50** A8
Clifton Terr
11 Portsmouth PO5 . . . . . .**53** C2
4 Totland PO40 . . . .**14** E1
Clinton Rd SO41 . . . .**48** E5
Clissold Rd PO30 . . . .**9** A2
Clive Rd PO1 . . . .**53** E6
Clock St 7 PO1 . . . .**53** A5
Cloisters The
Lymington SO41 . . . .**48** E3
Shanklin PO36 . . . .**35** F6
Close The PO34 . . . .**13** E2
Clovelly Rd SO14 . . . .**51** B6
Clydebank Rd PO2 . . . .**53** D8
Clyde Ho
7 Southampton SO14 . . . . .**51** C5
Ventnor PO38 . . . .**47** B6
Coach House La PO33 . . . . . .**12** A4
Coach La PO36 . . . .**24** A3
Coastal Visitors Ctr★
PO38 . . . .**47** A5
Coastguard Cotts
Bembridge PO35 . . . .**37** A6
Brighstone PO30 . . . .**38** C8
Brook PO30 . . . .**28** F4
Little Atherfield PO38 . . . . .**39** A3
Lymington SO41 . . . .**49** A2
7 Yarmouth PO41 . . . .**15** C6
Coastguard La
Brook PO30 . . . .**28** F4
Freshwater Bay PO40 . . . . .**27** D6
Cobbett Ct 3 SO18 . . . .**51** E7
Cobbett Rd SO18 . . . .**51** E8
Cobden Ave SO18 . . . .**51** F8
Cobden Cres SO18 . . . .**51** F8
Cobden Ct SO18 . . . .**51** E8
Cobden Dell 4 SO18 . . . .**51** F8
Cobden Marine SO17 . . . . . .**51** D8
Cobden St PO12 . . . .**52** B6
Coburg Ct PO32 . . . .**3** D7
Coburg Ho 6 SO14 . . . .**51** C6
Coburg St
Portsmouth PO1 . . . .**54** C3
Southampton SO14 . . . .**51** C6
Cochrane Ho 13 PO1 . . . .**53** A5
COCKEREL **34** D7
Cockerell Rise PO32 . . . .**3** D2
Cockleshell Sq PO12 . . . .**52** D6
Cockleton La PO32 . . . .**2** E2
Colborne Cl SO41 . . . .**48** E4
Coleman's Animal Farm★
PO30 . . . .**7** E1
Coleman's La PO30 . . . .**7** E1
Coleman St SO14 . . . .**51** B4
Colenutt's Rd PO33 . . . .**12** A3
Coles Cl PO40 . . . .**14** D2
Coleson Rd SO18 . . . .**51** E8

Collards Cl PO40 . . . .**14** F1
College Cl PO36 . . . .**36** A4
College Keep SO14 . . . .**51** B3
College La 22 PO1 . . . .**53** A5
College Pl 9 SO15 . . . .**51** A6
College Rd
Newport PO30 . . . .**20** E5
Portsmouth PO1 . . . .**53** A5
Southampton SO19 . . . .**51** E2
College St
Portsmouth PO1 . . . .**53** A5
Southampton SO14 . . . .**51** A3
College Way PO32 . . . .**3** D2
Collier Cl SO17 . . . .**51** C8
Collingwood Ct PO33 . . . . . .**12** E5
Collingwood Rd
Newport PO30 . . . .**20** D6
Portsmouth PO5 . . . .**53** D2
Shanklin PO37 . . . .**43** B8
Colmar Rd PO39 . . . .**14** D1
Colonnades The PO37 . . . . . .**43** B6
Colonnade Rd SO19 . . . .**51** D3
Colpoy St PO5 . . . .**54** A2
Columbine Rd PO32 . . . .**3** C4
Columbus Ho PO37 . . . .**35** D1
COLWELL **14** E2
Colwell Chine PO40 . . . .**14** D2
Colwell Chine Rd PO40 . . . .**14** D2
Colwell Cl PO40 . . . .**14** E2
Colwell Common Rd
PO39 . . . .**14** D1
Colwell La PO40 . . . .**14** E1
Colwell Rd
Freshwater PO39 . . . .**14** E2
Norton Green PO40 . . . .**15** A3
Combley La PO30 . . . .**21** F5
Comforts Farm PO31 . . . .**8** D7
Commercial Pl PO1 . . . .**54** B4
Commercial Rd
Portsmouth PO1 . . . .**54** B4
Southampton SO15 . . . .**50** E5
Commodore Ct 1 SO14 . . . .**51** B3
Commodore Pl PO12 . . . .**52** D7
Commodores Ct PO34 . . . . . .**13** C4
Common St PO1 . . . .**54** C4
Compton Ho 6 SO16 . . . .**50** B8
Compton Wlk 1 SO14 . . . . . .**51** A5
Condor Cl SO19 . . . .**51** E3
Conference Pl 6 SO41 . . . . . .**48** F2
Conifer Cres SO41 . . . .**48** B3
Coniston Ave PO33 . . . .**11** E4
Coniston Dr PO33 . . . .**12** B6
Coniston Pk PO37 . . . .**35** C2
Connaught Rd PO32 . . . .**3** D3
Consort Ho 3 PO1 . . . .**53** D7
Consort Rd PO31 . . . .**3** B4
Constable Cl 2 PO12 . . . .**52** C2
Consulate Ho 8 SO14 . . . . . .**51** B3
Conway La PO39 . . . .**14** D2
Cook Ave PO30 . . . .**20** F8
Cook St SO14 . . . .**51** A4
Cookworthy Rd PO30 . . . .**9** A2
Coombe La PO30 . . . .**30** B4
Coombe Pk PO38 . . . .**42** B4
Coombe Rd PO12 . . . .**52** B8
Cooper Rd PO30 . . . .**20** F8
Coopers Cl PO40 . . . .**14** E1
Coopers Ct 20 SO14 . . . .**51** A3
Coopers La PO41 . . . .**16** F5
Coopers La SO19 . . . .**51** E3
Copperfield Ho 8 PO1 . . . . . .**53** D7
Copper St 8 PO5 . . . .**54** A1
Coppice End PO33 . . . .**12** E2
Coppins Cl PO30 . . . .**20** E7
Copse Butt PO35 . . . .**25** E4
Copse End PO36 . . . .**35** F7
Copse La
Blackwater PO30 . . . .**20** D2
Freshwater PO40 . . . .**15** A2
Copse Rd PO37 . . . .**43** B8
Corbett Rd PO33 . . . .**12** A3
Corbin Ct SO41 . . . .**48** B2
Corbin Rd SO41 . . . .**48** B2
Corhampton Ho 11 PO1 . . . .**54** C4
Cornel Rd SO19 . . . .**51** F5
Cornwallis Cres SO14 . . . . . .**54** C4
Cornwallis Rd PO1 . . . .**54** C4
Cornwall Ho
Portsmouth PO1 . . . .**53** E5
Ventnor PO38 . . . .**46** F6
Cornwall St PO33 . . . .**12** D6
Coronado Rd PO12 . . . .**52** B8
Coronation Ave PO31 . . . .**9** A2
Coronation Cotts
Freshwater PO40 . . . .**27** C8
6 Yarmouth PO41 . . . .**15** D6
Coronation Gdns PO37 . . . . .**35** C1
Coronation Rd PO31 . . . .**3** A4
Corve Hill PO30 . . . .**31** B1
Cossack Gn 1 SO14 . . . .**51** A4
Cothey Way PO33 . . . .**12** F2
Cotswold Cl PO33 . . . .**12** E5
Cottage Gr
Gosport PO12 . . . .**52** B6
Portsmouth PO5 . . . .**54** A2
Cottage Grove Prim Sch
PO5 . . . .**54** A1
Cottage Ho 10 PO30 . . . .**20** D6
Cottage Mews 9 PO30 . . . . .**20** D6
Cottage View PO31 . . . .**54** C3
Cotteridge Ho 6 PO5 . . . .**54** C2
Cotton Cl PO31 . . . .**3** A4
Coulmere Rd PO12 . . . .**52** A7
County View PO37 . . . .**35** D2
Court Cl SO41 . . . .**48** D2
Courtenay Pl SO41 . . . .**48** E3
Courtlands 3 SO41 . . . .**48** E4

Court Rd
Freshwater PO40 . . . .**27** A8
Southampton SO15 . . . .**50** F7
Court Royal Mews SO15 . . .**50** F8
Court The SO41 . . . .**48** D2
Courtyard The
East Cowes PO32 . . . .**3** C3
Newport PO30 . . . .**9** B2
Cousins Gr PO4 . . . .**53** F2
Coventry Rd SO15 . . . .**50** B8
Cowdray Ho PO5 . . . .**54** C3
COWES **3** B4
Cowes Cty Prim Sch PO31 . . .**3** A4
Cowes High Sch PO31 . . . .**2** F5
Cowes Maritime Mus★
PO31 . . . .**3** B4
Cowes Rd PO30 . . . .**9** A5
Cow La PO31 . . . .**2** E4
COWLEASE **47** B6
Cowleaze Hill PO37 . . . .**43** B4
Cowley Rd SO41 . . . .**48** C4
Cowper Rd PO1 . . . .**53** E7
Cox's Cnr PO30 . . . .**20** C1
Cox's Green PO36 . . . .**35** E6
Cox's La SO19 . . . .**51** D3
Cozens Cl SO19 . . . .**51** F4
Crabbe Ct PO5 . . . .**54** B2
Cracknore Hard SO40 . . . . . .**50** A1
Cracknore Hard La SO40 . . .**50** A1
Cracknore Ind Pk SO40 . . . .**50** C2
Cracknore Rd SO15 . . . .**50** D5
Craddock Ho 11 PO1 . . . .**53** A5
Craig Ho 3 PO5 . . . .**53** D2
Craigmore Ct PO37 . . . .**35** D1
Cranbourne Rd PO12 . . . .**52** C4
Cranbury Ave PO1 . . . .**54** B6
Cranbury Ct SO19 . . . .**51** F3
Cranbury Pl SO14 . . . .**51** A6
Cranbury Rd SO19 . . . .**51** F3
Cranbury Terr 5 SO14 . . . . . .**51** A6
Cranbury The 4 SO14 . . . . . .**51** A6
Cranbury Twrs 6 SO14 . . . . .**51** A6
Craneswater Ave PO4 . . . . . .**53** E1
Craneswater Gate PO4 . . . . .**53** E1
Craneswater Jun Sch PO4 . .**53** F2
Craneswater Mews 5
PO4 . . . .**53** E2
Craneswater Pk PO4 . . . .**53** E2
Cranleigh Ave PO1 . . . .**53** E6
Cranleigh Gdns PO31 . . . .**8** F8
Cranleigh Ho SO17 . . . .**51** A8
Cranleigh Rd PO1 . . . .**53** E6
CRANMORE **16** F8
Cranmore Ave PO41 . . . .**5** D1
CRANMORE PARK **16** F8
Cranston Cl PO39 . . . .**26** G8
Craswell St PO1 . . . .**54** C4
Craven St 9 SO14 . . . .**51** A5
Cray Ho PO12 . . . .**52** D5
Creek Gdns PO33 . . . .**10** F6
Creek Rd PO12 . . . .**52** D5
Crescent Ct PO37 . . . .**43** D8
Crescent Rd
Gosport PO12 . . . .**52** A2
Sandown PO36 . . . .**36** A3
Shanklin PO37 . . . .**43** D8
Cressy Rd PO2 . . . .**53** D7
Cresta Ct 6 PO4 . . . .**53** F2
CRIDMORE **32** D2
Crocker La PO38 . . . .**45** B6
Crocker St PO30 . . . .**20** D7
Cromwell Rd SO15 . . . .**50** F7
Crossfield Ave PO31 . . . .**2** F4
CROSSHOUSE **51** C3
Cross House Ctr SO14 . . . . . .**51** C3
Crosshouse Rd SO14 . . . .**51** C3
Cross La PO30 . . . .**20** F8
Crossland Cl PO12 . . . .**52** C4
Crossley Ct 2 SO15 . . . .**50** C6
Crossley Pl 5 SO15 . . . .**50** E6
Cross Rd
Sandown PO36 . . . .**35** D3
Shanklin PO37 . . . .**43** C8
Cross St
Brading PO36 . . . .**24** B3
Cowes PO31 . . . .**3** B4
Newport PO30 . . . .**20** D6
Portsmouth PO5 . . . .**54** C2
Portsmouth, Portsea PO1 . . .**53** A6
Ryde, Oakfield PO33 . . . . . .**12** C4
Ryde PO33 . . . .**12** C6
Sandown PO36 . . . .**36** A4
Shanklin PO37 . . . .**43** C7
Crossway SO15 . . . .**25** E4
Crossways Rd
Camp Hill PO30 . . . .**8** F1
East Cowes PO32 . . . .**3** E2
Crossways The PO12 . . . .**52** B7
Crouchers Cross PO30 . . . . .**33** D8
Crown Ct
Cowes PO31 . . . .**3** B4
Portsmouth PO1 . . . .**54** C4
Crown Mews 1 PO12 . . . .**52** D5
Crown St
Portsmouth PO1 . . . .**54** C4
11 Ryde PO33 . . . .**12** C6
Southampton SO15 . . . .**50** B8
Croxton Rd PO1 . . . .**53** B3
Crozier Rd PO41 . . . .**15** A6
Crundles The PO40 . . . .**15** A1
Crusader Ct 4 PO12 . . . .**52** C8
Cuckoo La 8 SO14 . . . .**50** F3
Culver Par PO36 . . . .**36** B4
Culver Rd PO36 . . . .**43** D8
Culver Way PO36 . . . .**36** B5
Cumberland Bsns Ctr
PO1 . . . .**54** C3

Cumberland Ho PO1 . . . .**53** A6
Cumberland House Natural
History Mus**★** PO4 . . . .**53** F1
Cumberland Pl SO15 . . . .**50** F8
Cumberland Rd PO5 . . . .**54** D3
Cumberland St
Portsmouth PO1 . . . .**53** A6
Southampton SO14 . . . .**51** B4
Cunard Ave SO15 . . . .**50** C6
Cunard Rd SO14 . . . .**51** A2
Cunningham Ct 10 PO5 . . . . .**53** D2
Cupressus Ave PO36 . . . .**34** E5
Currie Rd PO36 . . . .**35** E4
Curzon Howe Rd PO1 . . . . . .**53** A5
Curzon Pl SO41 . . . .**48** D2
Cuthbert Rd PO1 . . . .**53** F6
Cut The PO31 . . . .**3** B5
Cygnet Ho PO12 . . . .**52** B8
Cynthia Gr PO30 . . . .**20** E8
Cypress Ave SO19 . . . .**51** F5
Cypress Rd SO19 . . . .**20** E5
Cyprus Rd PO2 . . . .**53** E8

D

Dagmar Mews 24 PO5 . . . . . .**53** C2
Dairy La PO30 . . . .**20** E5
Daish's La PO33 . . . .**24** F6
Daish Way PO30 . . . .**9** B1
Daisy La PO12 . . . .**52** B5
Dale Park Rd 4 PO5 . . . .**54** B3
Dame Anthonys Cl PO33 . . .**11** F4
Dandelion Flats PO32 . . . .**3** E2
Daniell's Cl SO41 . . . .**48** E3
Daniell's Wlk SO41 . . . .**48** E3
Daniel St PO33 . . . .**12** D5
Dapple Pl SO40 . . . .**50** A3
Darlington Rd PO4 . . . .**53** E3
Darnan Ho 6 SO14 . . . .**51** A7
Dart Ho SO18 . . . .**51** F8
Dartmouth Cl 6 PO12 . . . . . .**52** C8
Dartmouth Ct 3 PO12 . . . . . .**52** C8
Dartmouth Mews PO5 . . . . . .**54** A1
Darts La PO35 . . . .**25** C5
Darwin Ho PO1 . . . .**54** C4
Darwin Rd SO15 . . . .**50** E7
Daulston Rd PO1 . . . .**53** F7
Davidson Ct 42 PO1 . . . .**53** A5
Davies Ct SO19 . . . .**35** C2
Dawlish Ave SO15 . . . .**50** D8
D–Day Mus★ PO5 . . . .**53** C1
Deacons La PO12 . . . .**23** C7
Dean Ct 3 SO14 . . . .**51** A7
Dean Rd 8 PO1 . . . .**53** A5
Deans Cl PO36 . . . .**35** D3
Deans Ct PO33 . . . .**12** D6
Dean St PO1 . . . .**53** A5
Debourne Cl PO31 . . . .**2** E4
Debourne Manor Dr PO31 . . .**2** E4
Deeping . . . .
Shanklin PO37 . . . .**43** B7
Southampton SO18 . . . .**51** F1
Deeping Cl SO19 . . . .**51** F1
Defender Rd SO19 . . . .**51** D3
Defender Wlk SO19 . . . .**51** D3
Delamere Rd PO4 . . . .**53** D3
Delaval Ho 2 PO1 . . . .**53** B5
Dell Sq PO40 . . . .**14** F1
Dell The
Cowes PO31 . . . .**3** A8
Southampton SO15 . . . .**50** A8
Delphi Cl PO37 . . . .**43** D8
Delphi Rd PO37 . . . .**43** D8
De Mowbray Way SO41 . . . .**48** D2
Deneside Copse SO41 . . . . . .**48** B1
Denmark Rd PO1 . . . .**3** A4
Denmead Ho PO1 . . . .**54** C4
Denness Path SO41 . . . .**35** D4
Denness Rd PO36 . . . .**35** E4
Dennett Rd PO35 . . . .**25** C5
Denning Mews PO1 . . . .**54** B3
Dennison Ct 18 SO15 . . . . . .**50** B8
Denny Gdns PO37 . . . .**43** B8
Denton Gdns PO32 . . . .**3** D4
Denzil Ave SO14 . . . .**51** B6
Derby Rd SO14 . . . .**51** B6
Derwent Dr PO33 . . . .**12** F4
Desmond Price Cl PO36 . . . .**35** D4
Devonia Gdns PO37 . . . .**36** A6
Devon Mews 6 SO15 . . . .**50** E4
Devonshire Inf Sch PO4 . . . .**53** F4
Devonshire Mans 10 SO15 . .**50** F6
Devonshire Rd PO4 . . . .**53** F4
Devonshire Sq PO4 . . . .**53** F4
Devonshire Terr PO38 . . . . . .**47** B5
Dhekelia Cl PO12 . . . .**54** C4
Diamond St 3 PO5 . . . .**54** A1
Diana Cl PO37 . . . .**14** D1
Dickens Cl PO2 . . . .**53** D7
Dickinson Rd PO4 . . . .**53** F5
Diggings The PO33 . . . .**24** F7
Dight Rd PO12 . . . .**52** C2
Dimbola Lodge Photographic
Mus**★** PO40 . . . .**27** C6
Dimond Rd SO18 . . . .**51** E8
Dinosaur Farm Mus★
PO30 . . . .**38** G6
Dinosaur Isle★ PO36 . . . .**36** B4
Disa Ho SO15 . . . .**51** A6
Ditchbury SO41 . . . .**48** D6
Dock Mill Cotts 18 PO5 . . . . .**53** E2
Dock Rd PO12 . . . .**52** D5
Doctors La PO38 . . . .**39** A8
Doctor's La PO36 . . . .**24** A3
Dodnor Creek Nature
Reserve**★** PO30 . . . .**9** B4
Dodnor La PO30 . . . .**9** A1

Dodnor Mews PO30 . . . .**9** B2
Dodnor Pk PO30 . . . .**9** B1
Dodpits La PO30, PO41 . . . . .**17** C2
Dolcroft Rd PO38 . . . .**32** F5
Dolman Rd PO12 . . . .**52** C4
Dolphin Cres PO12 . . . .**52** C4
Dolphin Ct
11 Portsmouth PO5 . . . .**53** E1
1 Totland PO40 . . . .**14** E1
Dolphin Way PO12 . . . .**52** D2
Dombey Ct 5 PO12 . . . .**53** D7
Donnelly St PO12 . . . .**52** A7
Donnington Dr PO37 . . . .**35** B1
Dorchester Ct SO15 . . . .**50** F8
Dorothy Ct PO5 . . . .**54** C1
Dorothy Dymond St PO1 . . .**54** B3
Dorrick Ct 10 SO15 . . . .**50** F7
Dorrien Rd PO12 . . . .**52** B8
Dorrita Cl PO4 . . . .**53** F2
Dorset St SO14 . . . .**51** A6
Dorval Ho 6 SO15 . . . .**50** E7
Dorval Manor 7 SO15 . . . . . .**50** E7
Douglas Rd PO3 . . . .**53** F7
Dove Cl PO33 . . . .**24** F6
Dovecotes PO32 . . . .**3** D3
Dover Park Cty Prim Sch
PO33 . . . .**12** D5
Dover Rd PO32 . . . .**3** C4
Dover St
Ryde PO33 . . . .**12** D6
Southampton SO14 . . . .**51** A7
DOWNCOURT . . . .
Downcourt La PO38 . . . .**44** F7
DOWNEND **21** E4
Downend Rd PO30 . . . .**21** E3
Down La
Carisbrooke PO30 . . . .**20** A5
Ventnor PO38 . . . .**46** E6
Downlands Cres PO38 . . . . . .**46** E6
Downland View PO37 . . . .**35** C2
Downside PO38 . . . .**46** E6
Downside Ave PO38 . . . .**45** B4
Downside Mid Sch 7
PO30 . . . .**9** A1
Downs View PO40 . . . .**27** B8
Downs View Cl PO36 . . . .**24** A3
Downsview Gdns PO33 . . . . .**10** B3
Downsview Rd PO35 . . . .**25** D4
Downs View Rd
Newport PO30 . . . .**20** A5
St Helens PO33 . . . .**24** F6
Doyle Cl SO19 . . . .**51** F1
Drabbles La PO36 . . . .**35** E5
Dracaena Gdns PO37 . . . .**35** C1
Drake Cl SO40 . . . .**50** A2
Drake Ho 3 PO1 . . . .**53** A5
Drake Rd PO30 . . . .**20** D6
Drakes Cl SO40 . . . .**50** A3
Drill Hall Rd PO30 . . . .**20** D7
Drive The PO35 . . . .**25** D5
Droffatts Ho SO15 . . . .**50** D7
Drumlanrig Terr 4 PO12 . . . .**52** C9
Drummond Ct SO19 . . . .**51** E3
Drummond Dr SO14 . . . .**51** C8
Drummond Rd PO1 . . . .**54** C4
Dubbers SO18 . . . .**33** C1
Ducie Ave PO35 . . . .**25** C6
Duckworth Ho 34 PO1 . . . . . .**53** A5
Dudley Rd PO38 . . . .**47** B5
Dugald Drummond St
PO1 . . . .**54** B3
Duisburg Way PO5 . . . .**53** B2
Duke Cres PO1 . . . .**53** D7
Duke of Edinburgh Ho
PO1 . . . .**53** A6
Dukes Rd
Gosport PO12 . . . .**52** A7
Southampton SO14 . . . .**51** B7
Duke St SO14 . . . .**51** B3
Dumbarton Cl PO2 . . . .**53** D8
Duncan Cl SO19 . . . .**51** E1
Duncan Rd PO5 . . . .**53** D2
Duncroft Gdns PO37 . . . .**35** C1
Dundonald Cl SO19 . . . .**51** D1
Dungewood La PO30,
PO38 . . . .**39** B6
Dunkeld Rd PO12 . . . .**52** A8
DUNSBURY **28** F5
Dunsmore Cl PO5 . . . .**54** B2
Durban Cl 9 SO15 . . . .**50** E7
Durban Ho PO1 . . . .**54** C4
Durban Rd PO1 . . . .**53** F7
Durham St
Gosport PO12 . . . .**52** A7
Portsmouth PO1 . . . .**54** B3
Durley Rd PO12 . . . .**52** A7
Durnford Rd SO14 . . . .**51** B6
Duver Rd
Seaview PO34 . . . .**13** C4
St Helens PO33 . . . .**25** A7
Dyer Rd SO15 . . . .**50** C7
Dymott Cl SO15 . . . .**50** D5

E

Earley St SO41 . . . .**48** F4
Earlsdon St PO5 . . . .**54** B2
Earls Rd SO14 . . . .**51** A7
East Ashey La PO33 . . . .**23** D5
East Bldg PO1 . . . .**53** A5
Eastbourne Ave SO15 . . . . . .**50** D8
East Cl PO41 . . . .**5** E2
Eastcliff Ct PO33 . . . .**43** D8
Eastcliff Prom PO37 . . . .**43** D7
Eastcliff Rd PO37 . . . .**43** C7
EAST COWES **3** E4

East Cowes Heritage Ctr* PO32 — 3 C3
East Cowes Prim Sch PO32 — 3 D3
East Cowes Rd PO32 — 10 A5
East Ct PO1 — 53 E7
Eastern Par PO4 — 53 E2
Eastern Rd SO41 — 48 D4
Eastern Villas Rd PO4 — 53 D1
Eastfield Rd SO17 — 51 C8
Eastfields PO5 — 54 C1
Eastgate St SO14 — 51 A3
East Gn PO34 — 13 C2
East Hill SO41 — 48 E4
East Hill Rd PO33 — 12 E5
East La PO30 — 33 E6
East Mead PO37 — 43 A7
Eastmore Ct PO41 — 15 F6
East Mount Rd PO37 — 43 D8
Easton La PO40 — 27 C7
East Park Terr SO14 — 51 A5
East Rd SO40 — 50 B2
East St
  Newport PO30 — 20 E7
  Portsmouth PO1 — 53 A4
  Ryde PO33 — 12 D6
  Southampton SO14 — 51 A4
  Ventnor PO38 — 47 B6
East Street Sh Ctr SO14 — 51 A4
East Surrey St PO1 — 54 B3
East View PO30 — 20 D6
East Yar Rd PO36 — 36 A5
Easy View La PO38 — 40 A4
Eddington Rd PO4 — 53 E2
Eden Grange [6] SO14 — 51 A7
Eden Pl PO39 — 26 G8
Eden Rd PO39 — 26 G8
Eden St PO1 — 54 B4
Edgbaston Ho PO5 — 54 C2
Edinburgh Cl PO31 — 3 A4
Edinburgh Ct [2] SO15 — 50 A6
Edinburgh Rd
  Freshwater PO40 — 15 A1
  Portsmouth PO1 — 54 A3
Edith Haisman Cl SO15 — 50 D5
Edmund Rd PO4 — 53 F3
Edward Rd SO15 — 50 C7
Edwards Cl SO41 — 48 B3
Edward St PO33 — 12 C5
Edwin Jones Gn SO15 — 50 E8
Efford Cl SO41 — 48 B2
Efford Farm Cotts SO41 — 48 A1
Efford Way SO41 — 48 B2
Egerton Rd PO35 — 25 C4
Egypt Copse PO31 — 2 F5
Egypt Espl PO31 — 2 E6
Egypt Hill PO31 — 2 F5
Elder Cl SO40 — 50 A1
Eldon Cl PO5 — 54 B2
Eldon Ho [1] SO14 — 51 A3
Eldon St PO5 — 54 B2
Elenors Gr PO33 — 11 C5
Elfin Ct PO12 — 52 A3
Elgar Cl PO12 — 52 A3
Elgar Ct SO41 — 48 F4
Elgin Rd SO15 — 50 D5
Elizabeth Ct
  Bembridge PO35 — 25 C5
  [4] Gosport PO12 — 52 A7
Elizabeth Gdns
  Havenstreet PO33 — 11 C1
  Portsmouth PO4 — 53 F2
Eliza Pl [6] PO12 — 52 C6
Ellachie Gdns PO12 — 52 B2
Ellachie Mews PO12 — 52 B2
Ellachie Rd PO12 — 52 B2
Ellery Gr SO41 — 48 E5
Elliston Rd PO39 — 14 D1
Elm Ave SO41 — 48 C1
Elmbank Gdns PO36 — 35 E5
Elm Cl
  Freshwater PO40 — 14 E1
  Nettlestone PO34 — 13 C2
  Ryde PO33 — 12 D4
Elm Cr
  Ryde PO33 — 12 E4
  Southampton, Sholing SO19 — 51 F7
ELMFIELD — 12 E3
Elmfield North Block SO15 — 50 D5
Elmfield West Block SO15 — 50 D5
Elm Gr
  Cowes PO31 — 3 A3
  Gosport PO12 — 52 B6
  Newport PO30 — 20 D5
  Portsmouth PO5 — 54 B1
Elmhurst Bsns Pk PO12 — 52 B5
Elmhurst Rd PO12 — 52 C5
Elm La PO30 — 18 B4
Elm Lodge PO5 — 54 C1
Elms Ct PO35 — 25 E5
Elm St
  Portsmouth PO5 — 54 A1
  Southampton SO14 — 51 B4
Elmsworth La PO30 — 7 D3
Elm Terr SO14 — 51 B3
Elphinstone Rd PO5 — 53 C2
ELSON — 52 A9
Elson Inf Sch PO12 — 52 A9
Elson Jun Sch PO12 — 52 A9
Elson La PO12 — 52 A9
Elson Rd PO12 — 52 A9
Elstree Rd SO19 — 51 E5
Emanuel St PO2 — 53 D7
Embankment Rd PO35, PO35 — 25 B5
Embassy Ct PO4 — 54 D2

Embassy Way PO36 — 35 B4
Emmadale Ct [7] SO14 — 51 A6
Emmett Hill PO38 — 40 A6
Emperor Ho SO18 — 51 C7
Empress Pk SO14 — 51 B7
Empress Rd SO14 — 51 B7
Empshott Rd PO4 — 53 F4
Emsworth Rd
  Lymington SO41 — 48 E4
  Southampton SO15 — 50 B8
Endeavour Cl
  Gosport PO12 — 52 D5
  Southampton SO15 — 50 B7
Endeavour Ct [5] SO14 — 51 B3
Endle St SO14 — 51 C3
Enfield Gr SO19 — 51 E3
Englefield Rd SO18 — 51 D7
English Rd SO15 — 50 B7
Ensign Cl PO31 — 3 A3
Enterprise Cl PO33 — 12 D3
Enterprise Rd PO31 — 3 A2
Eremue Ct [4] PO41 — 15 C6
Ernest Rd PO1 — 53 E7
Esplanade
  Cowes PO31 — 3 A6
  East Cowes PO32 — 3 D5
  Nettlestone PO34 — 13 E2
  Ryde PO33 — 12 D6
  Sandown PO36 — 36 A3
  Seaview PO34 — 13 D4
  Shanklin PO37 — 43 D7
  Ventnor PO38 — 47 A5
Esplanade Rd
  Sandown PO36 — 36 A3
  Ventnor PO38 — 47 A5
Esplanade The PO12 — 52 C5
Esslemont Rd PO4 — 53 F3
Estella Rd PO2 — 53 D8
Ethel Rd PO1 — 53 E6
Eton Rd PO5 — 54 D2
European Ct PO4 — 35 F5
European Way SO14 — 51 B2
Eva Allaway Ct [38] PO1 — 53 A5
Evans St SO14 — 51 A4
Evelyn Cres SO15 — 50 D8
Everard Cl PO40 — 27 C7
Everton La PO37 — 43 C7
Ewart Rd PO1 — 53 E7
Ewer Comm PO12 — 52 B3
Exchange Rd PO1 — 54 A3
Exchange The [3] PO4 — 53 E2
Exeter Rd PO4 — 53 F2
Exmoor Rd SO14 — 51 B6
Exmouth Rd
  Gosport PO12 — 52 A9
  Portsmouth PO5 — 53 D2
Exmouth St SO14 — 51 A5
Explosion-The Mus of Naval Firepower* PO12 — 52 D8

F

Fairfield Cl SO41 — 48 E3
Fairfield Gdns PO36 — 35 E5
Fairfield Pk [1] PO19 — 14 E1
Fairfield Way PO39 — 14 E1
Fairhaven Cl PO35 — 25 E4
Fairholme Cl PO12 — 52 B8
Fairlead Rd PO31 — 3 A2
Fairlea Rd SO41 — 48 E5
FAIRLEE — 9 D1
Fairlee Rd PO30 — 9 D1
Fairmead Rd PO36 — 35 D4
Fairmount Dr PO20 — 20 F8
Fairthorne Gdns PO12 — 52 A5
Fairview Cres PO16 — 35 D5
Fairway Cvn Site PO36 — 35 E6
Fairway The PO36 — 35 E5
Fairy Rd PO34 — 13 D4
Fakenham Farm* PO33 — 25 A7
Falcon Cl [2] PO12 — 52 C8
Falcon Cross Rd PO37 — 43 C8
Falcon Rd PO32 — 3 C3
Falkland Rd SO15 — 50 A8
Fanshawe St SO14 — 51 A6
Farlington Rd PO4 — 53 E8
Farm La PO32 — 3 D2
Farnleys Mead SO41 — 48 E2
Farriers Ct [4] — 53 D2
Farriers Way PO30 — 31 B2
Farriers Wlk PO12 — 52 D6
Farringford Farm Rd PO40 — 27 B7
Farthingale Terr [11] PO1 — 53 A2
Farthing Ct PO12 — 52 A6
Farthing La PO1 — 53 A3
Farthings Way PO39 — 14 D1
Fastnet Ho [9] PO5 — 53 D1
Faulkner La PO1 — 53 A3
Fawcett Rd PO4 — 54 D2
Fawley Rd SO15 — 50 A6
Felix Rd PO12 — 52 B8
Fellows Rd PO31 — 3 A4
Fennel Gdns SO41 — 48 E5
Ferncliff Apartments PO36 — 35 F4
Ferncliff Rd PO36 — 35 F4
Fern Ct SO18 — 51 E7
Ferndene Way SO18 — 51 F8
Fernhill PO33 — 10 D4
Fernhill Ct PO36 — 10 D4
Fernhill Pk PO36 — 10 D4
Fernhurst Jun Sch PO4 — 53 F4
Fernhurst Rd PO4 — 53 F4
Ferniclose Rd PO34 — 13 C2
Fernside Way PO33 — 110 E4

Fernwood Cres SO18 — 51 F8
Ferrol Rd PO12 — 52 C7
Ferrypoint SO41 — 49 A4
Ferry Rd PO32 — 3 C4
Festing Bldgs [1] PO4 — 53 F2
Festing Mews [2] PO4 — 53 F2
Festing Rd PO4 — 53 F2
Fey Rd PO12 — 52 C6
Field Cl PO30 — 20 C6
Fieldfare Rd PO30 — 20 A6
Field La PO33 — 24 F7
Field Pl PO30 — 20 C6
Field View PO33 — 12 B3
Fieldway Cres PO31 — 8 F8
Field Wlk PO37 — 48 D5
Fifth St PO1 — 53 F6
Fighting Cocks Cross PO36 — 34 C5
Filton Rd PO12 — 48 D4
Finches The PO30 — 20 A6
Findon Rd PO12 — 52 B9
Fine La PO30 — 31 B2
Firbank Lodge PO37 — 43 C8
Firestone Copse Rd PO33 — 11 B3
Firestone Glade PO33 — 11 A4
Firgrove Ct SO15 — 50 C7
Firgrove Rd SO15 — 50 C7
Firs Cl PO31 — 2 F4
Fir Tree Cl PO37 — 35 D2
Fisgard Rd PO12 — 52 B8
FISHBOURNE — 11 B6
Fishbourne La PO33 — 11 A6
Fishermans Wlk PO35 — 25 F5
Fishers PO33 — 11 A4
Fitzherbert St PO1 — 54 B4
FITZHUGH — 50 E7
Fitzhugh Ho [6] SO15 — 50 E6
Fitzhugh Pl SO15 — 50 F7
Fitzhugh St [3] SO15 — 50 F5
Fitzroy St PO5 — 35 F5
Fitzroy Wlk PO1 — 54 C4
Five Houses La PO30 — 18 B4
Five Post La PO12 — 52 B7
Flagstaff Gn PO12 — 52 D7
Flathouse Rd PO1 — 53 C7
Fleet Cl PO33 — 11 F4
Fleet Way
  Portsmouth PO1 — 53 B6
  Portsmouth PO1 — 53 B6
  Shalfleet PO30 — 17 D7
Fleming Cl PO33 — 11 E4
Fleming Ct SO19 — 51 D2
Flint St PO5 — 54 A1
Flitcroft Gdns PO36 — 35 D5
Floating Bridge Rd SO14 — 51 C3
Florence Ct [2] SO18 — 51 E8
Florence Rd
  Portsmouth PO5 — 53 D1
  Shanklin PO37 — 43 D7
  Southampton SO19 — 51 D2
Flushards SO41 — 48 F3
Flying Bull Cl [1] PO2 — 53 D8
Flying Bull La PO2 — 53 D8
Flying Bull Prim Sch PO2 — 53 D8
Foley Ho PO1 — 54 B4
Folly La PO32 — 9 E7
Fontwell Rd [1] PO5 — 53 D2
Footways PO31 — 3 B1
Forbury Rd [8] PO5 — 54 C2
Ford Mews [1] PO30 — 20 D6
Foreland Farm La PO35 — 25 F4
Foreland Rd PO35 — 25 E5
Forelands Field Rd PO35 — 25 E5
Forelands Middle Sch PO35 — 25 D4
Foremans Cotts PO12 — 52 E3
Forest Cl PO30 — 8 F1
Forest
  Lymington SO41 — 48 B2
  Winford PO36 — 34 E4
Forest Dell PO36 — 34 E5
Forest Gate Gdns SO41 — 48 D1
Forest Hills PO30 — 19 F6
Forest Rd
  Newport PO30 — 19 E8
  Winford PO36 — 34 E5
FOREST SIDE — 20 A8
Forest Side PO30 — 19 E8
Forest View [3] SO14 — 50 F4
Forest Way PO36 — 34 E4
Forster Rd SO14 — 51 B7
Forsythia Pl SO19 — 51 F5
Forth Ho [11] SO14 — 51 B5
Fort Mews PO36 — 36 A4
FORTON — 52 C7
Forton Lodge [3] PO12 — 52 C6
Forton Rd
  Gosport PO12 — 52 B6
  Portsmouth PO1 — 53 C6
Fort Rd
  Gosport PO12 — 52 B2
  Southampton SO19 — 51 E3
Fort Spinney PO36 — 36 C5
Fort St PO36 — 36 A4
Fortune Ho PO12 — 52 A6
Fort Victoria Cotts PO41 — 14 F6
Fort Victoria Country Pk* PO41 — 14 F6
Fort Warden Rd PO39 — 14 D2
Forward Dr SO41 — 48 C2
Foster Rd
  Gosport PO12 — 52 B2
  Portsmouth PO1 — 54 C4
Foundry Ct [23] PO1 — 53 A5
Foundry La SO15 — 50 B7
Foundry Lane Prim Sch SO15 — 50 B7

Fountain Ct PO31 — 3 B5
Fountain Quay PO31 — 3 B5
Fountain Rd PO1 — 53 B7
Fountain St PO1 — 54 B3
Fourposts Hill [3] SO15 — 50 E5
Fourth St PO1 — 53 F6
Foxes Cl PO36 — 20 D7
Foxhills PO38 — 46 D5
Foxlea [1] SO15 — 50 E7
Foxlea Gdns PO12 — 52 B8
Fox Pd PO30 — 20 A5
Fox Pond La SO41 — 48 D1
Foyes Ct SO15 — 50 D5
Frampton Way PO35 — 25 D5
Francis Ave PO4 — 53 F3
Francis Bright Cotts PO38 — 33 A4
Frank Judd Ct [1] PO1 — 53 A5
Frank Miles Ho [1] PO5 — 54 B2
Frankton Way PO12 — 52 D6
Frank Williams Ct PO30 — 20 F7
Fraser Cl PO31 — 3 B2
Fraser Rd PO5 — 54 C2
FRATTON — 53 F5
Fratton Ct PO1 — 54 B4
Fratton Rd PO1 — 54 D4
Fratton Sta PO1 — 53 E5
Fratton Way PO4 — 53 F5
Frederick St
  Portsmouth PO1 — 53 A6
  Southampton SO14 — 51 B6
FREEMANTLE — 50 C5
Freemantle Bsns Ctr SO15 — 50 C5
Freemantle CE Controlled Inf Sch SO15 — 50 C5
Freemantle Cl SO19 — 51 F5
Freemantle Common Rd SO19 — 51 F6
Freemantle Rd PO12 — 52 B8
Freestone Rd [10] PO5 — 53 D2
French St
  [8] Portsmouth PO1 — 53 A3
  Southampton SO14 — 51 B3
Frensham Ct PO4 — 53 F4
Frensham Rd PO4 — 53 F4
Freshfield Rd SO15 — 50 B7
Freshfield Sq SO15 — 50 B7
FRESHWATER — 14 E1
FRESHWATER BAY — 27 C6
Friary Cl
  Gosport PO12 — 52 C2
  [1] Portsmouth PO5 — 53 C2
Friary The [5] PO5 — 53 C2
Friendship Ho PO5 — 54 B1
Frigate Rd PO1 — 53 A6
Frobisher Cl SO40 — 33 A3
Frobisher Ho [6] PO1 — 53 A5
Froddington Rd PO5 — 54 C4
Froglands La PO30 — 20 A3
Frome Cl SO40 — 50 A1
Fromond Cl SO41 — 48 E5
Froude Ave PO12 — 52 C3
Froude Rd PO12 — 52 D3
Froxfield Ho PO1 — 54 C4
Fullerton Rd SO41 — 48 C4
Funtington Rd PO2 — 53 F8
Furness Rd [13] PO5 — 53 D1
Furrlongs PO30 — 20 E6
Furze Hill Rd PO37 — 43 B7
FURZYHURST — 8 F7
Fyning St PO1 — 54 C4

G

Gage Cl SO40 — 50 A2
Gaggerhill La PO30 — 30 A3
Gainsborough Ct SO41 — 48 D2
Gainsborough Ho [2] PO4 — 53 E2
Gainsford Rd SO19 — 51 E5
Gain's Rd PO4 — 53 F3
Galley La PO30 — 30 A2
Gamble Cl SO19 — 51 F4
Gamble Rd PO2 — 53 D8
Garden La PO5 — 54 B1
Garden Terr [1] PO5 — 53 D2
Garden Way PO30 — 20 E6
Gardiner Cl SO40 — 50 A2
Garfield Rd
  Portsmouth PO2 — 53 D8
  Ryde PO33 — 12 C6
  Shanklin PO37 — 43 D7
  Southampton SO19 — 51 E7
Garland Ct [1] PO12 — 52 B6
Garlic Farm The* PO36 — 22 C2
Garnier St PO1 — 54 D3
Garnock Ho [9] PO33 — 12 C6
Garnock Rd SO19 — 51 D2
Garrow Dr SO41 — 48 E5
Garton Rd SO19 — 51 E7
Gassiot Cl PO33 — 12 E4
Gas Works La PO1 — 11 B5
GATCOMBE — 22 C7
Gatcombe Rd PO30 — 23 D8
Gatehouse Rd PO33 — 23 B8
Gatehouse The [1] SO18 — 51 E8
Gate La PO40 — 27 C7
Gawn Pl PO12 — 52 C2
Gaynor Ho PO37 — 43 C8
Genoa Cl SO41 — 48 C1
George Byng Way PO12 — 53 C8
George Ct PO5 — 53 D2
George Ct The [10] PO1 — 53 A3
George St
  Gosport PO12 — 52 C5
  Portsmouth PO1, PO2 — 53 F7
  Ryde PO33 — 12 C6

George St continued
  Sandown PO36 — 35 F5
Gibbs Rd SO14 — 50 F5
Gilbert Cl SO41 — 48 D2
Giles Cl PO12 — 52 A7
Gilkicker Rd PO12 — 52 C2
Gill's Cliff Rd PO38 — 46 F5
Glade The
  Nettlestone PO34 — 13 C2
  Sandown PO36 — 35 E4
  Wroxall PO38 — 42 C5
Gladstone Pl [4] PO2 — 53 D8
Gladstone Rd PO12 — 52 A8
Glamis Gdns PO32 — 3 D3
Glebe Gdns PO33 — 10 E5
Glebe Rd SO14 — 51 B3
Glen App PO38 — 45 B3
Glencoe Rd PO1 — 53 F7
Glendale Cl PO33 — 10 D4
Glenfield Ave SO18 — 51 F7
Glenfield Cres SO18 — 51 F7
Glenfield Ct PO30 — 20 B5
Glenfield Inf Sch SO18 — 51 F7
Glenfield Way SO18 — 51 F7
Glenheadon Dr PO39 — 26 G7
Glenmore Ct SO17 — 51 A8
Glen Rd SO19 — 51 D2
Glen The
  Cowes PO31 — 3 A4
  Niton PO38 — 45 B3
  [1] Yarmouth PO41 — 15 D6
Glidden Cl PO2 — 54 C3
Glossop Cl PO32 — 3 D3
Gloster The PO31 — 3 A3
Gloucester Ho [1] PO12 — 52 C5
Gloucester Mews PO5 — 54 B2
Gloucester Pl PO5 — 54 B1
Gloucester Rd
  Portsmouth PO1 — 53 A6
  Ventnor PO38 — 46 E6
Gloucester Sq [20] SO14 — 51 A3
Gloucester Terr PO5 — 54 B1
Gloucester View PO5 — 54 B2
Glynn Cl PO34 — 13 D1
Gobles Cl PO33 — 12 D5
GODSHILL — 41 D8
Godshill Model Village* PO38 — 41 D8
Godshill Prim Sch PO38 — 41 D8
Godwit Cl PO12 — 52 B9
Goldcrest Cl PO40 — 20 A6
Golden Gr SO14 — 51 B5
Golden Groves PO33 — 11 F4
Golden Hill Country Pk* PO40 — 14 F2
Golden Ridge PO40 — 14 F1
Golden Villas PO40 — 14 E2
Goldings Way PO41 — 14 E2
Gold Mead Cl [1] SO41 — 48 E2
Goldsmith Ave PO4 — 53 F4
Goldsmith Inf Sch PO4 — 53 E4
Goldsmiths Ct [17] SO14 — 51 A3
Gold St PO5 — 54 A1
Golf Links Rd PO36 — 35 E6
Goodwood Cl PO12 — 52 B9
Goodwood Rd
  Gosport PO12 — 52 B9
  Portsmouth PO5 — 54 D1
Gordon Ave SO14 — 51 A8
Gordon Bldgs SO15 — 50 C8
Gordon Cl
  Ryde PO33 — 11 E5
  Sandown PO36 — 35 F6
Gordon Ct [1] PO33 — 12 C5
Gordon Lodge PO32 — 3 D2
Gordon Rd
  Cowes PO31 — 3 B4
  Gosport PO12 — 52 A5
  Lymington SO41 — 48 C3
  Newport PO30 — 20 E8
  Portsmouth PO1 — 53 B3
Gort Rd PO32 — 3 D2
GOSPORT — 52 C5
Gosport Discovery Ctr* PO12 — 52 D5
Gosport St Pk Sch [1] PO12 — 52 D5
Gosport St SO41 — 48 F4
Gosport War Meml Hospl PO12 — 52 A5
Gotten La PO38 — 40 B3
Grace Cl PO12 — 53 C2
Graeme Rd PO41 — 15 A6
Grafton Cl PO12 — 52 C8
Grafton Gdns SO41 — 48 C1
Grafton La PO36 — 35 F5
Grafton St
  Portsmouth PO2 — 53 D7
  Sandown PO36 — 35 F5
Graham Ho [1] SO14 — 51 C6
Graham Rd
  Gosport PO12 — 52 A8
  Portsmouth PO4 — 53 E3
  Southampton SO14 — 51 B6
Graham St SO14 — 51 C6
Granada Rd PO4 — 53 E1
Granary Cl PO33 — 11 F5
Grand Par PO1 — 53 A3
Grange Ave PO33 — 12 A4
Grange Ct
  Shanklin PO37 — 43 C7
  Ventnor PO38 — 47 C6
Grange Dr PO30 — 20 D8
Grange Gdns PO35 — 25 C4
Grange Rd
  East Cowes PO32 — 3 D3

Grange Rd continued
Sandown PO36 . . . . .35 E4
Shanklin PO37 . . . . .43 C7
Grangeside PO38 . . . . .47 D6
Grange The
Bembridge PO35 . . . . .25 C4
Newport PO30 . . . . .20 D8
Grantham Ct PO31 . . . . .3 A6
Grantham Rd SO19 . . . . . . .51 F6
Granville Ct SO15 . . . . .50 E7
Granville Rd
Cowes PO31 . . . . .3 A4
Totland PO39 . . . . .14 C1
Granville Rise **3** PO39 . . .14 D1
Granville Road Bridge **4**
PO31 .3 A4
Granville St SO14 . . . . .51 B4
Grasmere Ave PO33 . . . . . .12 F4
Gravel Pit Rd PO33 . . . . . . .10 D4
Grays Cl PO31 . . . . .53 A4
Grayshott Rd PO4 . . . . .53 F4
Grayswood Cl PO38 . . . . . . .35 F6
Great Appleford Barns
PO38 . . . . .40 E5
Great Preston Rd PO33 . . . .12 D3
Great Southsea St PO5 . . . .54 B1
GREAT THORNESS 7 E6
Green Cnr PO34 . . . . .13 C2
Greenfield Cl PO33 . . . . . . .12 E4
Greenfields Rd PO30 . . . . . .20 F8
Greenfinch Cl PO30 . . . . . . .20 A6
Greengate Ind Est PO31 . . . .3 B4
Greengates PO37 . . . . .35 C1
Greenham Dr PO34 . . . . . . .13 D2
Greenidge Cl **6** SO15 . . . . .50 F8
Green La
Cowes PO31 . . . . .9 A8
Freshwater PO40 . . . . .27 B6
Gosport, Alverstoke PO12 . .52 A5
Gosport, Elson PO12 . . . . . .52 C7
Ryde PO33 . . . . .23 D6
Shanklin PO37 . . . . .43 C4
Green Land Cl PO30 . . . . . .32 B4
Greenlands PO30 . . . . .32 B4
Greenlands Rd PO32 . . . . . . .3 D2
Greenlydd Cl PO38 . . . . . . .45 B3
Green Mount Prim Sch
PO33 . . . . .12 C5
Green Rd
Gosport PO12 . . . . .52 A5
Portsmouth PO5 . . . . .54 B2
Green St
Newport PO30 . . . . .20 F7
Ryde PO33 . . . . .12 C5
Green The
Cowes PO31 . . . . .3 B5
Shanklin PO37 . . . . .43 C4
Shorwell PO30 . . . . .31 B3
Greenway PO33 . . . . .11 E4
Greenway Cl
Lymington SO41 . . . . .48 C3
Ryde PO33 . . . . .11 E4
Greenway Rd PO12 . . . . . .52 B7
Greenways
Cowes PO31 . . . . .8 F8
Newport PO30 . . . . .21 A7
Totland PO39 . . . . .26 G8
Greenway The PO38 . . . . .45 B4
Greenwich The **24** SO14 . . .51 A3
Greenwood La PO36 . . . . . .35 F8
Greenwood Wlk PO30 . . . . .20 F8
Greetham St PO5 . . . . .54 B3
Gregory Ave PO33 . . . . .13 B3
Gregory Cl PO33 . . . . .13 B3
Grenville Cl PO32 . . . . .3 D2
Grenville Dr PO33 . . . . .12 A3
Grenville Ho **45** PO1 . . . . . .53 A5
Grenville Rd SO14 . . . . .54 D1
Greville Rd SO15 . . . . .50 D7
Greycliff PO38 . . . . .47 D7
Greyfriars Ct PO5 . . . . .54 B1
Greystone La PO33 . . . . . . .24 F7
Greystones La PO40 . . . . . .27 D6
Griffin Cl SO17 . . . . .51 C8
Griffin Ho PO1 . . . . .3 A5
Grosvenor Ho
4 Portsmouth PO5 . . . . . . .54 B2
12 Southampton SO15 . . . .50 F6
Grosvenor Mews
5 Gosport PO12 . . . . .52 C6
Lymington SO41 . . . . .48 D5
Grosvenor Sq SO15 . . . . . . .50 F6
Grosvenor St PO5 . . . . .54 B2
Grove Ave PO12 . . . . .52 C6
Grove Bldgs **7** PO12 . . . . . .52 C5
Grove Cl PO30 . . . . .20 F6
Grove Cotts PO30 . . . . .17 E7
Grove Ho PO5 . . . . .54 B1
Grove Pastures SO41 . . . . . .48 E3
Grove Pl SO41 . . . . .48 E3
Grove Rd
Cowes PO31 . . . . .3 A3
Gosport PO12 . . . . .52 B8
Lymington SO41 . . . . .48 F3
Ryde PO33 . . . . .12 D5
Sandown PO36 . . . . .35 F6
Southampton SO15 . . . . . . .50 F6
Ventnor PO38 . . . . .47 A6
Wroxall PO38 . . . . .42 C4
Grove Road N PO5 . . . . . . .54 B1
Grove Road S PO5 . . . . . . .54 B1
Groves Cl PO40 . . . . .14 E2
Grove St SO14 . . . . .51 B4
Grove The
Bembridge PO35 . . . . .25 C6
Cowes PO31 . . . . .3 A5
Ventnor PO38 . . . . .47 A6
Guadeloupe Rd PO36 . . . . . .35 F5
Guardhouse Rd PO1 . . . . . . .53 B7
Guildford Park Camp
PO33 . . . . .24 F7
Guildford Rd
Portsmouth PO1 . . . . .53 E6
St Helens PO33 . . . . .25 A7
Guildford St **8** SO14 . . . . . .51 C5
Guildhall Sq PO1 . . . . .54 B3
Guildhall Wlk PO1 . . . . .54 A3
Guild Ho **18** SO14 . . . . .51 A3
Gully Rd PO34 . . . . .13 D2
Gunville Cres PO30 . . . . . . .20 A6
Gunville Rd PO30 . . . . .20 A6
Gunville W PO30 . . . . .19 F6
Gunwharf Quays PO1 . . . . . .53 E4
Gunwharf Quays (Sh Ctr)
PO1 . . . . .53 A4
Gunwharf Rd PO1 . . . . .53 A4
Guppy Cl PO31 . . . . .2 E4
GURNARD 2 F4
Gurnard Hts PO31 . . . . .2 D4
Gurnard Cty Prim Sch
PO31 . . . . .2 D3
Gurney Rd SO15 . . . . .50 C8
Gustar Gr PO32 . . . . .3 D1
Gusters Shute PO30 . . . . . . .18 B2
Guyers Rd PO40 . . . . .27 C7
Gwen-Rhian Ct **4** SO15 . . . .50 F7
Gwessin Terr **6** PO12 . . . . .52 C5
Gwydir Cl PO33 . . . . .12 A5

H

Hadrians Way PO36 . . . . . . .24 A1
Haglane Copse SO41 . . . . . .48 C2
Haig Cl PO33 . . . . .35 D3
Halberry Ho PO30 . . . . .20 F8
Halberry La PO30 . . . . .20 F8
HALE COMMON 34 B5
Hale Ct PO1 . . . . .53 E4
Halesowen Ho **4** PO5 . . . . .54 A2
Hale Street N PO1 . . . . .54 C4
Hale Street S PO1 . . . . .54 C4
Half Moon St **1** PO1 . . . . . .53 A5
Halford Cl PO33 . . . . .35 F7
Halfpenny La PO1 . . . . .53 A3
Halletts Shute PO41 . . . . . . .15 A5
Halliday Cl PO12 . . . . .52 B6
Hall of Aviation (Mus)* . . . . .
SO14 . . . . .51 B3
Hallowell Ho PO1 . . . . .54 A1
Hambrook Rd **1** PO12 . . . . .52 A7
Hambrook St PO5 . . . . .54 A1
Hambrough La PO39 . . . . . . .26 G7
Hambrough Rd PO38 . . . . . .47 A5
Hamilton Ct **3** PO5 . . . . . . .53 C2
Hamilton Ho PO1 . . . . .54 A1
Hamilton Mews SO41 . . . . . .48 F3
Hamilton Pl SO41 . . . . .48 D3
Hamilton Rd
Portsmouth PO5 . . . . .53 D2
Ryde PO33 . . . . .11 F4
Hamlet Ct PO31 . . . . .3 A6
Hammond Cl PO41 . . . . .15 A5
Hammond Ho **3** PO30 . . . . .52 E5
Hampshire Cres **3** PO30 . . . .9 A1
Hampshire St PO1 . . . . .53 E7
Hampshire Terr PO1 . . . . . . .54 A2
HAMSTEAD 5 F3
Hamstead Dr PO41 . . . . .6 A2
Hamstead Rd PO41 . . . . . . .17 B8
Hamtun St **6** SO14 . . . . . . .50 F3
Hamwic Ho **3** SO14 . . . . . . .51 A6
Handel Rd SO15 . . . . .50 E6
Handel Terr SO15 . . . . .50 E6
Handford Pl **2** SO15 . . . . . .50 F6
Handsworth Ho PO5 . . . . . . .54 C2
Hanley Rd SO15 . . . . .50 D8
Hannah Ho PO30 . . . . .20 D8
Hanover Bldgs SO14 . . . . . .51 A4
Hanover Ct **7** PO1 . . . . .53 C2
Hanover Ho SO14 . . . . .51 A4
Hanover St PO1 . . . . .53 A5
Hanway Rd PO1 . . . . .53 E7
Harborough Rd SO15 . . . . . .50 F6
Harbors Lake La PO36 . . . . .34 D6
Harbour Par SO40 . . . . .50 C2
Harbour Par PO5 . . . . .54 F4
Harbour Rd PO1 . . . . .52 E6
Harbour Strand SO15 . . . . . .50 C2
Harbour Twr **10** PO12 . . . . .52 C5
Harbour Way PO31 . . . . .2 F3
Harcourt Rd
Gosport PO12 . . . . .52 A6
Portsmouth PO1 . . . . .53 E7
Southampton SO18 . . . . . . .51 E8
Harding Rd SO41 . . . . .12 D4
Harding Shute PO33 . . . . . . .23 F6
Hard The PO1 . . . . .53 A5
HARDWAY 52 B8
Hardy Cl SO15 . . . . .50 B6
Harford Cl SO41 . . . . .48 C1
Harley Wlk PO1 . . . . .54 C4
Harness La PO31 . . . . .2 C1
Harold Rd
Portsmouth PO4 . . . . .53 E3
Southampton SO15 . . . . . . .50 C7
Harrison's Cut SO14 . . . . . . .51 A4
Harris Rd PO30 . . . . .9 A2
Harrow Rd PO5 . . . . .54 C2
Harry Cheek Gdns PO31 . . . . .8 E3
Harry Law Hall PO1 . . . . . . .54 B3
Hart Ct SO19 . . . . .51 F3
Hartford Ho PO1 . . . . .54 A1
Hartington Rd SO14 . . . . . . .51 B6
Hartley Ct **5** SO17 . . . . .51 A8
Harts La PO38 . . . . .32 F3
Harvester Way SO41 . . . . . .48 D6
Harvey Cl PO32 . . . . .3 D1
Harvey Rd PO30 . . . . .20 F8
Haselworth Dr PO12 . . . . . . .52 B2
Haselworth Prim Sch
PO12 . . . . .52 B4
Haskell Rd PO1 . . . . .9 A2
Haslar Marina PO12 . . . . . . .52 E4
Haslar Rd
Gosport, Clayhall PO12 . . . .52 D3
Gosport, Newtown PO12 . . .52 E5
Haslar Terr PO12 . . . . .52 D3
Haslegrave Ho **2** PO2 . . . . .53 D8
Haslemere Rd PO4 . . . . .53 E2
Hatherley Mans **3** SO15 . . .50 C7
Hatherton Rd PO37 . . . . . . .43 C7
Havant St PO1 . . . . .53 A5
Havelock Cl PO30 . . . . .20 B6
Havelock Mans PO5 . . . . . . .54 C2
Havelock Rd
Portsmouth PO5 . . . . .54 C2
Southampton SO14 . . . . . . .50 F5
Crawley Cres PO36 . . . . . . .24 B2
HAVENSTREET 11 C1
Havenstreet Main Rd
PO33 . . . . .11 C1
Havenstreet Sta* PO33 . . . .22 D8
Haven The
Gosport PO12 . . . . .52 B3
Southampton SO19 . . . . . . .51 E4
Havisham Rd PO2 . . . . .53 C7
Hawke St SO14 . . . . .51 B4
Hawkeswood Rd SO18 . . . . .51 C7
Hawk Ho **13** PO33 . . . . .12 C6
Hawkins Ho **3** 2 E5
Hawkins Cl PO36 . . . . .24 A3
Hawthorn Cl
Newport PO30 . . . . .20 C7
Ryde PO33 . . . . .11 F5
Hawthorns The SO40 . . . . . .50 A1
Hawthorns Urban Wildlife
Ctr* SO14 . . . . .50 F8
Haydens Ct SO41 . . . . .48 F4
HAYLANDS 12 A3
Haylands Cty Prim Sch
PO33 . . . . .12 A4
Hayling Cl PO12 . . . . .52 C9
Hayward Ave PO33 . . . . .12 E3
Haywards Cl **11** PO4 . . . . . .53 A4
Hazel Cl PO38 . . . . .46 E7
Hazel Ct PO4 . . . . .53 F4
Hazeleigh Ave SO19 . . . . . . .51 E2
Hazel Green Village PO33 . .10 F6
Hazelmount Paddock
PO33 . . . . .11 E6
Hazemere Ave PO33 . . . . . . .11 E4
Hearn St SO14 . . . . .20 D7
Hearts of Oak Mews
SO41 . . . . .48 D4
Heasley La PO30 . . . . .34 B8
Heath Cl PO33 . . . . .20 E6
Heatherley Ct PO5 . . . . .54 A1
Heatherwood Park Rd
PO39 . . . . .26 G8
Heathfield Cl
Bembridge PO35 . . . . .25 C4
Freshwater PO40 . . . . .14 F2
Newport PO30 . . . . .21 A7
Heathfield Ho PO37 . . . . . . .43 C7
Heathfield Mdws PO30 . . . .14 E2
Heathfield Rd
Bembridge PO35 . . . . .25 C4
Freshwater PO40 . . . . .14 F2
Heath Gdns PO36 . . . . .35 D3
Heath Rd PO36 . . . . .35 D3
Heath Villas PO40 . . . . .14 E2
Heaton Rd PO12 . . . . .52 A8
Hedley Cl PO37 . . . . .43 A7
Hefford Rd PO12 . . . . .3 D4
Heidelberg Rd PO4 . . . . .53 F4
Heights Leisure Ctr PO36 . .35 E4
Helena Rd PO4 . . . . .53 F2
Hendy Cl PO5 . . . . .54 B1
Hendy Rd PO32 . . . . .3 D4
Henery St **10** PO12 . . . . . . .52 C5
Henry Player Ave PO12 . . .52 D7
Henry St SO15 . . . . .50 F6
Henstead Ct **9** SO15 . . . . . .50 F6
Henstead Rd SO15 . . . . .50 F6
Henty Rd SO16 . . . . .50 B8
Herbert Rd PO4 . . . . .53 E2
Herbert St PO1 . . . . .53 C7
Herbert Walker Ave SO15 .50 C4
Hercules St PO2 . . . . .53 D8
Hereford Ct PO5 . . . . .54 C1
Hereford Rd PO5 . . . . .54 C1
Heritage Way, Priddy's Hard
PO12 . . . . .52 C9
Hermes Ct PO12 . . . . .52 C9
Heron Ho **1** PO5 . . . . .53 E2
Hersey Rise PO34 . . . . .13 D2
Hertford Pl PO1 . . . . .53 C7
Hesketh Ho **4** SO15 . . . . . . .50 C6
Heversword PO33 . . . . .12 E4
Hewitt Cl PO12 . . . . .52 A8
Hewitt Cres PO30 . . . . .9 A2
Hewitt's Rd SO15 . . . . .50 D5
Heysham Rd SO15 . . . . .50 B7
Heyshott Rd PO4 . . . . .53 F4
Heytesbury Cl PO41 . . . . . . .15 D5
Heytesbury Rd
Newport PO30 . . . . .20 D8
Yarmouth PO41 . . . . .15 D5
Heyward Rd PO4 . . . . .53 E4
Highbury Cl PO35 . . . . .25 B4
Highbury St **8** PO1 . . . . . . .53 A4
Highcliff Ave SO14 . . . . .51 A8
Highcliffe Lodge PO36 . . . . .35 D2
Highdown La PO39 . . . . .26 G6
Highfield SO41 . . . . .48 D3
Highfield Ave SO41 . . . . . . .48 C3
Highfield Cl PO33 . . . . .12 E4
Highfield Rd
Cowes PO31 . . . . .2 F2
Lymington SO41 . . . . .48 C3
Newport PO30 . . . . .20 E7
Portsmouth PO5 . . . . .54 C3
Shanklin PO37 . . . . .43 B7
Highlands Ho SO19 . . . . .51 D3
Highland Terr PO4 . . . . .53 F3
High Park Rd PO33 . . . . .12 E3
High Point SO18 . . . . .51 E8
High Rd PO30 . . . . .8 F1
High Salterns PO34 . . . . . . .13 D3
High St
Bembridge PO35 . . . . .25 C4
Brading PO36 . . . . .24 B3
Carisbrooke PO30 . . . . .20 B5
Cowes PO31 . . . . .3 B5
Freshwater PO40 . . . . .14 F1
Godshill PO38 . . . . .41 D8
Gosport PO12 . . . . .52 D5
Lymington SO41 . . . . .48 E4
Newchurch PO36 . . . . .34 E7
Newport PO30 . . . . .20 D7
Niton PO38 . . . . .45 B4
Portsmouth PO1 . . . . .53 A3
Rhyde, Oakfield PO33 . . . . .12 D4
Ryde PO33 . . . . .12 C5
Sandown PO36 . . . . .35 F5
Seaview PO34 . . . . .13 D4
Shanklin PO37 . . . . .43 C7
18 Southampton SO14 . . . .51 A3
Ventnor PO38 . . . . .47 B6
Whitwell PO38 . . . . .45 A5
Wootton PO33 . . . . .10 E5
Wroxall PO38 . . . . .42 C4
Yarmouth PO41 . . . . .15 D5
Hightrees SO41 . . . . .48 D1
Highview PO40 . . . . .14 F1
High View Way SO18 . . . . . .51 F8
Highway The PO37 . . . . .43 C4
Highwood La PO30, PO38 . .32 E6
Hilbre Rd PO33 . . . . .24 F6
Hilda Ct **1** SO15 . . . . .50 F7
Hilda Pl **5** SO14 . . . . .51 C5
Hildgards Cres PO37 . . . . . .35 D2
Hillborough Cres **2** PO5 . . .54 C1
Hillborough Ct **1** PO5 . . . . .54 C1
Hillcrest Rd PO38 . . . . .32 F4
Hillcroft PO33 . . . . .48 E4
Hillditch SO41 . . . . .48 D6
Hill Farm Rd SO15 . . . . .50 E6
Hillgrove Cvan Site PO33 . .24 F7
Hill Ho PO39 . . . . .26 H8
Hillis Cnr PO31 . . . . .8 C7
HILLISGATE 8 D5
Hillis Gate Rd PO30, PO31 . .8 C6
Hill La PO30 . . . . .14 F3
Hill Place La PO41 . . . . .16 C7
Hillrise Ave PO33 . . . . .11 F4
Hills Cl **2** PO33 . . . . .12 C5
Hillside
Chillerton PO30 . . . . .32 A4
Newport PO30 . . . . .20 E8
Hillside Rd SO41 . . . . .48 C3
Hills La PO38 . . . . .39 B4
Hill St
Ryde PO33 . . . . .12 B5
Sandown PO36 . . . . .35 E5
Southampton SO19 . . . . . . .51 D3
Hill Top Cotts PO40 . . . . . . .14 F1
Hill Top Cotts PO40 . . . . . . .14 F1
HILLWAY 25 B2
Hillway Rd PO35 . . . . .25 C2
Hilton Rd
Gosport PO12 . . . . .52 C4
Gurnard PO31 . . . . .2 D3
Hinton Rd PO30 . . . . .20 B6
Hives Way SO41 . . . . .48 F4
HMS Victory* PO1 . . . . .52 F7
HMS Warrior* PO1 . . . . .52 F6
Hobbs Ct **2** PO12 . . . . .52 E5
Hogan Cl PO30 . . . . .9 A3
Hogan Rd PO30 . . . . .9 A3
Holbein Lodge SO41 . . . . . . .49 B3
Holbrookes Cotts PO41 . . . .16 C7
Holbrook Rd PO1 . . . . .54 C3
Holford Rd PO33 . . . . .10 D6
Holgate La PO34 . . . . .13 D2
Holland Rd
Portsmouth PO4 . . . . .54 D2
Southampton SO19 . . . . . . .51 D2
Hollies The PO33 . . . . .12 D4
Hollis Dr PO30 . . . . .30 B3
Hollow Glade PO38 . . . . . . .41 D8
Hollow La
Chillerton PO30 . . . . .32 B4
Godshill PO38 . . . . .41 D8
Hollowood Rd PO36 . . . . . . .35 A7
Hollows The PO30 . . . . .19 F7
Holly Brooke Cl PO37 . . . . . .35 B3
Holly Ct SO41 . . . . .48 B2
Holly Ho SO19 . . . . .51 E2
Holly St PO12 . . . . .52 C5
Holly Tree Cl PO33 . . . . .12 D5
Hollywood Ct SO14 . . . . . . .48 D5
Hollywood La SO41 . . . . . . .48 D5
Holmbush Ct PO5 . . . . .54 B1
Holmes Ct **4** PO4 . . . . .15 D4
Holmewood Cl PO33 . . . . . .12 A2
Holmfield Ave PO41 . . . . . . .16 C6
Holm Oaks SO41 . . . . .48 C2
Holmsley Cl SO41 . . . . .48 B2
Holmwood Cl PO35 . . . . . . .25 E4
Holt Rd SO15 . . . . .50 F6
Holy Cross RC Fst Sch
PO32 . . . . .3 D4
Holy Rood Est SO14 . . . . . . .51 A3
Holyrood Ho **6** SO14 . . . . . .51 A3
Holy Rood Pl **11** SO14 . . . .51 A3
Holyrood St PO30 . . . . .20 D7
Home Farm Cl PO30 . . . . . . .20 E6
Homefort Ho **2** PO12 . . . . . .52 B5
Homegrove Ho PO5 . . . . . . .54 C1
Homeheights **8** PO5 . . . . . .53 C2
Homelands PO33 . . . . .7 D3
Home Meade PO30 . . . . .20 F6
Homerose Ho PO5 . . . . .54 B2
Homesea Ho PO5 . . . . .54 B2
Homewood Ho SO14 . . . . . .48 C2
Hooke Hill PO40 . . . . .15 A1
Hookes Way PO30 . . . . .20 D8
Hope Lodge Sch SO18 . . . . .51 E7
Hope Mead PO36 . . . . .34 D8
Hope Rd
Ryde PO33 . . . . .12 E4
Shanklin PO37 . . . . .43 D8
Hope Road App PO37 . . . . . .43 D8
Hope St PO1 . . . . .54 B4
Hopkins Wlk PO30 . . . . .22 A1
Hordle Walhampton Sch
SO41 . . . . .49 A6
Horestone Dr PO34 . . . . . . .13 D1
Horestone Rise PO34 . . . . . .13 D1
Hornbeam Cl PO30 . . . . .20 C8
Hornbeam Sq
RYDE PO33 . . . . .12 F2
Ryde PO33 . . . . .12 F2
Horndean Ho **6** PO1 . . . . . . .54 C4
Hornet Cl PO12 . . . . .52 C4
HORRINGFORD 34 A7
Horsebridge Hill PO30 . . . . . .9 A3
Horseshoe Bridge SO14 . . . .51 C8
Horseshoe Cl PO31 . . . . .8 F7
Hoskins Ho PO1 . . . . .53 B6
Hospital Rd PO32 . . . . .3 C3
Houndwell Pl SO14 . . . . . . .51 A4
Howard Cl
Newport PO30 . . . . .20 F8
Niton PO38 . . . . .45 B4
Howard Lo **20** PO5 . . . . . . .53 C2
Howard Rd
Shanklin PO37 . . . . .35 D1
Southampton SO15 . . . . . . .50 D6
Howard's Gr SO15 . . . . .50 C8
Howards Mead SO41 . . . . . .48 B2
Howell Cl SO14 . . . . .51 C5
Howgate Rd SO41 . . . . .25 C4
Howgate Rd PO35 . . . . .25 D3
Howlett Cl SO41 . . . . .48 C4
Hoxall La PO30 . . . . .29 D3
Hoy Cl PO38 . . . . .44 C7
Hudson Rd PO5 . . . . .54 C2
Hulse Lodge **6** SO15 . . . . . .50 F8
Hulse Rd SO15 . . . . .50 F8
Hulton Cl SO19 . . . . .51 D1
HULVERSTONE 29 B4
Hulverstone La PO30 . . . . . .29 B4
Hundred La SO41 . . . . .49 A7
Hungerberry Cl PO37 . . . . . .43 A7
Hunnycross Way PO30 . . . . .20 D7
HUNNY HILL 20 C7
Hunny Hill
Brighstone PO30 . . . . .29 F3
Newport PO30 . . . . .20 C8
Hunnyhill Prim Sch PO30 . .20 C8
Hunter Rd PO4 . . . . .53 F3
Huntly Way SO18 . . . . .51 F7
Hunts Rd PO38 . . . . .46 A3
Hurstake Rd PO30 . . . . .20 E8
Hurst Castle* SO41 . . . . . . .14 B6
Hurst Hill PO39 . . . . .26 G7
Hurst Point View PO39 . . . .14 D1
Hurst View PO39 . . . . .26 G8
Hutchinson Dr PO33 . . . . . . .13 B3
Hutfield Ct **1** PO12 . . . . . . .52 B6
Huxford PO30 . . . . .34 A8
Hyde Park Ho PO5 . . . . .54 B2
Hyde Park Rd PO5 . . . . .54 B2
Hyde Rd PO38 . . . . .43 B8
Hyde St PO5 . . . . .54 B2
Hynes Ct **1** SO17 . . . . .51 B8

I

Idsworth Ho PO1 . . . . .54 B4
Imperial Appartments **8**
SO14 . . . . .51 B3
Imperial Ave SO14 . . . . .51 B7
Imperial Ct SO14 . . . . .50 B7
Imperial Rd SO14 . . . . .51 A3
Imperial Way SO15 . . . . . . .51 C5
Ingledene Cl PO12 . . . . .52 B5
Inglewood Pk PO38 . . . . . . .46 C6
Inglis Rd PO5 . . . . .54 C1
Ingram Ct SO17 . . . . .51 C8
Inkerman Rd SO19 . . . . .51 D3
Institute Hill PO38 . . . . .45 B4

Inverness Rd
Gosport PO12 . . . . .52 A7
Portsmouth PO1 . . . . .53 E7
Irequois Ct E7 SO14 . . . . . . .51 B7
Ironside Ct E7 SO14 . . . . . . .50 F3
Irwin Hts PO12 . . . . .52 A9
Isambard Brunel Jun Sch
PO2 . . . . .53 EB
Isambard Brunel Rd PO1 . .54 B3
Isenhurst Ct PO35 . . . . .25 D4
Island Planetarium*
PO41 . . . . .14 F6
Island Point SO41 . . . . .48 F4
Island View Chalets PO39. .14 D2
Isle of Wight Airport
PO36 . . . . .35 B5
Isle of Wight Bus Mus*
PO30 . . . . .20 EB
Isle of Wight Coll PO30 . . .20 DB
Isle of Wight Donkey
Sanctuary* PO38 . . . . . . .42 B7
Isle of Wight Lavender*
PO33 . . . . .21 C6
Isle of Wight Military Mus*
PO31 . . . . .9 A6
Isle of Wight Natural History
Ctr* PO38 . . . . .41 DB
Isle of Wight Owl & Falconry
Ctr* PO38 . . . . .42 A4
Isle of Wight Pearl*
PO30 . . . . .29 E1
Isle of Wight Shipwreck Ctr
& Maritime Mus* PO30. .21 E2
Isle of Wight Steam
Railway* PO33. . . . . .22 EB
Isle of Wight Studio Glass*
PO38 . . . . .46 E4
Isle of Wight Zoo* PO36. .36 B4
ITCHEN 51 F4
Ivy Cl PO38 . . . . .46 B4
Ivy Ho E7 PO12 . . . . .52 B7
Ivy La PO1. . . . . .53 A6
Ivy Rd SO17 . . . . .51 C8

J

Jack Cockerill Way E7
PO5 . . . . .53 D1
Jackmans Cl SO19 . . . . .51 D3
Jacob's St PO1 . . . . .54 B4
Jago Rd PO12 . . . . .52 F7
Jamaica Pl PO12 . . . . .52 C5
Jamaica Rd PO12 . . . . .52 D6
James Ave PO36 . . . . .53 EB
James Butcher Ct E7 PO5 .53 D1
James Mews PO36 . . . . .35 D2
Jameson Gdns PO39 . . . . . .14 E1
Jameson Rd SO19 . . . . .51 F3
James St SO14 . . . . .51 B4
Janaway Gdns SO17 . . . . . .51 D8
Janson Rd SO15 . . . . .50 D8
Jarndyce Wlk PO2 . . . . .53 D7
Jessie Rd
Gosport PO12 . . . . .52 A5
Portsmouth PO4 . . . . .53 E4
Jessie Terr E7 SO14 . . . . . . .51 A3
Jireh Pl E7 PO41 . . . . .15 C6
Jo Benson Ct E7 PO4 . . . . . .53 F2
Jocelyn Ct PO36 . . . . .36 A5
John Nash Ave PO32 . . . . . .3 D3
Johnson Rd PO30 . . . . .9 A2
Johnson St E7 SO14 . . . . . . .51 A4
John's Rd SO19 . . . . .51 D3
John St
Newport PO30 . . . . .20 D7
Ryde PO33 . . . . .12 C5
Jonas Nichols Sq SO14. . . .51 B4
Jonathan Cl SO41 . . . . .48 E5
Jordan Cl PO31 . . . . .2 D4
Jordan Ho SO15 . . . . .50 C5
Jordans La SO41 . . . . .49 B8
Joseph Nye Ct E7 PO1 . . . .53 A5
Joseph St E7 PO12 . . . . .52 C5
Josephs Way PO37 . . . . . . .43 B8
Josian Wlk SO14 . . . . .51 B5
Joys La SO41 . . . . .49 EB
Jubilee Cl
Freshwater PO40. . . . . .27 C8
Godshill PO38 . . . . .41 C8
Jubilee Pl PO33 . . . . .12 D5
Jubilee Rd
Gosport PO12 . . . . .52 B6
Portsmouth PO4 . . . . .53 F3
Jubilee Terr E7 SO14 . . . . . .54 A1
Juniper Cl
Carisbrooke PO30 . . . . .20 B7
Lymington SO41 . . . . .48 B2
Juniper St E7 SO18 . . . . .51 E7
Juniper Rd SO18. . . . . .51 F7
Jupiter Ct PO1. . . . . .53 A4
Jurds Lake Way SO19 . . . . .51 E1
Justin Cl PO12. . . . . .52 D7

K

Kealy Rd PO12. . . . . .52 A7
Keats Mews PO12 . . . . .43 C7
Keats Retreat PO37 . . . . . . .43 C7
Keelan Ct PO5 . . . . .53 D2
Keel Gdns E7 SO41 . . . . . . .48 E4
Keith Cl PO12 . . . . .52 B7
Keith Ho E7 PO4 . . . . .53 A5
Kellett Rd SO15 . . . . .50 E8
Kelly Ct E7 SO18 . . . . .51 E8
Kelsey Ct PO32 . . . . .3 E3
Kelston Cl SO15 . . . . .50 A7
Kemming Rd PO38 . . . . . . .45 D6
Kemmin La PO38 . . . . .45 F7
Kempelt Ho E7 PO1 . . . . . . .53 A5
Kemps Quay Ind Pk SO18 .51 D7
Kendal Rd PO39 . . . . .26 H8
Kenilworth Ho E7 SO14. . . .51 C6
Kenilworth Rd
Portsmouth PO5 . . . . .53 D1
Southampton SO15 . . . . . . .50 F6
Kennedy Cl PO33 . . . . .10 E4
KENNERLEY HEATH. 33 B4
Kennet Cl PO12 . . . . .52 B2
Kensington Ct E7 PO12 . . . .52 C9
Kensington Rd PO12 . . . . . .52 C4
Kent Ave PO32. . . . . .3 D3
Kent Ho E7 SO14 . . . . .51 C5
Kentish Rd SO15 . . . . .50 C7
Kent Rd
Portsmouth PO5 . . . . .54 B1
Ventnor PO38 . . . . .47 B6
Kent St
Portsmouth PO1 . . . . .53 A5
Ryde PO33 . . . . .12 C4
Southampton SO14 . . . . . . .51 C6
Kerrigan Ct SO17 . . . . .51 A7
Kerry Cl SO41. . . . . .48 D3
Kerry Fields PO33 . . . . .13 D1
Kestrel Cl PO38 . . . . .35 C2
Kestrel Rd PO30 . . . . .20 A6
Keswick Rd SO19 . . . . .51 D2
Kettering Terr PO2 . . . . .53 C8
Keyes Ct E7 PO5 . . . . .54 C1
Key Haven Ct E7 PO39 . . . .14 D1
Kidson Ct PO12 . . . . .52 D5
Kilbride Path E7 PO2 . . . . . .53 D8
Kilmiston Ct PO3 . . . . .53 E7
Kilpatrick Cl E7 PO12 . . . . .53 D8
Kimberley Ct SO19 . . . . . . .51 E2
Kinchington Rd PO30 . . . . .20 B6
King Albert Ct PO1 . . . . . . .54 C4
King Albert St PO1 . . . . . . .54 C4
King Arthur Ct PO33 . . . . . .12 B5
Kingates La PO36 . . . . .45 C6
King Charles 1st Ct PO28 . .47 A6
King Charles St E7 PO1 . . . .53 A4
Kingcome Ho PO1 . . . . .54 B4
King Edward Ave SO16. . . .50 A8
King Edward Ct PO37 . . . . .35 C1
King Edward VI Sch SO15 .50 E8
Kingfisher Cl PO30 . . . . . . .20 A6
King George V Cl PO33 . . . .12 B4
King Henry 1 St PO1 . . . . . .54 A3
King James Ct PO31 . . . . . . .2 F4
King James Terr E7 PO1 . . .53 A3
King Richard 1 Rd PO1. . . .54 A3
Kings Bay Rd PO38 . . . . . . .47 C6
Kings Bench Alley E7 PO1 .53 A5
Kingsbury Rd SO14 . . . . . . .51 B7
Kings Cl
Bembridge PO35 . . . . .25 C6
Lymington SO41 . . . . .48 D4
Kingsclere Ct SO19 . . . . . . .51 F1
Kings Cote Villas E7 PO3 . .53 E1
Kings Cres SO41 . . . . .48 D4
Kingsdown Pl PO1 . . . . .54 D3
Kingsfield SO41 . . . . .49 A2
Kingsland Cl E7 SO14 . . . . .51 A4
Kingsland Rd E7 SO14 . . . . .51 A5
Kingsland Mkt SO14 . . . . . .51 A4
KINGSLAND PLACE 51 A5
Kingsland Sq E7 SO14 . . . . .51 A4
Kingslea 2 PO31 . . . . .3 A4
Kingslea Pk PO32 . . . . .3 D1
Kingsley Rd SO15 . . . . .50 B7
Kings Manor Rd PO40 . . . .15 B2
Kingsmere E7 PO31 . . . . .3 A4
Kings Mews PO5 . . . . .54 B1
Kings Park Rd SO15 . . . . . . .51 A6
Kings Rd
Bembridge PO35 . . . . .25 C6
Portsmouth PO5 . . . . .54 B1
Ryde PO33 . . . . .11 E5
King's Saltern Rd SO41 . . . .49 A2
King St
Gosport PO12 . . . . .52 B6
Portsmouth PO5 . . . . .54 B2
Southampton SO14 . . . . . . .51 A3
King's Terr PO1, PO5. . . . . .54 A1
KINGSTON
40 .47
Portsmouth 53 F7
Kingston Cres PO2 . . . . .53 D8
Kingston Cross PO2. . . . . . .53 D8
Kingston Pk SO41 . . . . .48 D2
Kingston Rd
East Cowes PO32 . . . . .3 C2
Portsmouth PO1, PO2 . . . . .53 EB
Southampton SO15 . . . . . . .50 D6

Kingsway
Cowes PO31 . . . . .3 A4
Southampton SO14 . . . . . . .51 A5
Kingswell Path PO1. . . . . . .54 B4
Kingswell St E7 PO1 . . . . . .54 B3
Kingswood
E7 Cowes PO31. . . . . .3 A4
Marchwood SO40 . . . . .50 A1
King William St PO1 . . . . . .53 A6
Kinterbury Ct E7 SO17 . . . .51 A8
Kipling Cl SO19 . . . . .51 F1
Kirkstall Rd PO4 . . . . .53 E1
Kitbridge Rd PO30 . . . . . . .20 C7
Kite Hill PO33 . . . . .11 A5
KNIGHTON. 22 E2
Knighton Rd SO19 . . . . .51 F4
Knighton Shute PO38 . . . . .22 F3
Knight's Cross PO33 . . . . . .21 F8
Knights Ct PO38 . . . . .47 B6
Kyngs Cl PO36. . . . . .24 C3
Kynon Cl E7 PO12 . . . . .52 C9

L

Laburnum Cl PO30 . . . . . . .20 E5
Laburnum Cl SO19 . . . . . . .51 B8
Lacey's La PO18 . . . . .45 B4
Lacon Ct SO18 . . . . .51 EB
Ladywood Ho PO5 . . . . .54 B2
Lake Common Rd PO36 . . .35 D4
Lake Green Rd PO36 . . . . . .35 D4
Lake Hill PO36 . . . . .35 E4
Lake Ho SO15 . . . . .50 C6
Lake Industrial Way PO36 .35 B3
Lakelands Dr SO15 . . . . . . .50 C6
Lake Mid Sch PO36 . . . . . .35 C3
Lake Rd
Portsmouth PO1 . . . . .54 B4
Southampton SO17 . . . . . . .51 D2
Laker Ho SO15 . . . . .50 F7
Lakeside Ct PO4 . . . . .53 F2
Lake Sta PO36 . . . . .35 E3
Lammas SO41 . . . . .2 E5
Lamorbey Rd PO36 . . . . . . .35 D3
Lamorbey Terr PO36 . . . . . .35 D3
Lamward Mans E7 SO14. . .51 A7
Lance's Hill SO19 . . . . .51 F7
Landguard Manor Rd
PO37. . . . . .35 C1
Landguard Rd
Shanklin PO37 . . . . .43 C8
Southampton SO15 . . . . . . .50 D6
London Ct PO12 . . . . .52 A3
LANDPORT. 53 C7
Landport St
Portsmouth PO1 . . . . .54 B4
Portsmouth, Southsea PO5. .54 A2
Landport Terr PO1 . . . . .54 A2
Landport View PO1. . . . . . .54 A2
Landscape La PO30 . . . . . . .21 B7
Landsdowne St PO5. . . . . . .54 A2
Lane Cl PO35 . . . . .25 E4
Lane End Cl PO35 . . . . .25 E4
Lane End Rd PO35 . . . . .25 E4
Lanes End PO39 . . . . .14 C1
Lane The
Gosport PO12 . . . . .52 A2
Portsmouth PO4 . . . . .53 F2
Sandown PO36 . . . . .36 A4
Langbar Cl SO19 . . . . .51 E6
Langford Rd PO2 . . . . .53 F7
Langley Ct PO30 . . . . .20 C7
Langley Rd
E7 Cowes PO31. . . . . .3 B4
Portsmouth PO2 . . . . .53 E8
Southampton SO15 . . . . . . .50 A6
Langton Farm Gdns PO1 . .53 E7
Langtry E7 PO31 . . . . .3 A5
LANSDOWNE HILL 50 F4
Lansdowne Hill E7 SO14. . .50 F3
Lansdowne Ho E7 PO12 . . .52 A7
Lansdowne Rd SO15 . . . . . .50 A7
Lansdown Gdns PO30 . . . . .32 B4
Lanterns The PO5 . . . . .25 C5
Lanyards Lea PO31 . . . . .3 A3
Lapwing Cl PO12 . . . . .52 B8
Larch Ct SO41 . . . . .54 C4
Lark Rise
Carisbrooke PO30 . . . . .20 A5
Shanklin PO37 . . . . .35 C1
Lasham Rd E7 SO16 . . . . . . .50 B8
Latham Ct SO15 . . . . .50 B7
Latimer Gate E7 PO12 . . . .51 A3
Latimer St E7 SO14 . . . . . . .51 A3
Latimer Rd PO33 . . . . .25 A6
Launceston Cl E7 PO12 . . .52 C8
Laundry La PO30 . . . . .20 C6
Laurel Cl
E7 Gosport PO12 . . . . .52 C8
Southampton SO19 . . . . . . .51 D3
Laurel Est PO41 . . . . .3 B3
Laurel Ho E7 PO30 . . . . . . .20 D6
Lavender Cl SO19 . . . . .51 F5
Lavender Glade PO33 . . . . .12 C5
Lavinia Rd
Gosport PO12 . . . . .52 B5
Portsmouth PO2 . . . . .52 B6
Lawn Ct SO17 . . . . .51 A7
Lawn Rd
Lymington SO41 . . . . .48 B3
Southampton SO17 . . . . . . .51 B8
Lawnside Rd SO15 . . . . .50 B8
Lawns The PO30 . . . . .9 D2
Lawrence Ct SO19 . . . . .51 F2
Lawrence Gr SO19 . . . . .51 F2
Lawrence Mans PO5 . . . . . .54 D1

Lawrence Rd PO5. . . . . .54 D1
Lawrence Sq E7 PO12 . . . . .52 D5
Lawson Rd PO5. . . . . .54 D2
Lea Ct PO36 . . . . .35 D4
Leamington Ho E7 PO5. . . .54 B2
Leander Dr E7 PO12 . . . . . .52 D5
Lear Rd PO12. . . . . .53 D4
Lear Rd PO12 . . . . .52 B6
Ledwell Ct PO12 . . . . .52 D7
Leed St PO36 . . . . .35 F5
Lee Lands SO41 . . . . .48 D1
Leep La PO12 . . . . .52 B3
Lee Rd PO12 . . . . .52 A7
Lees La PO12 . . . . .52 B6
Leesland CE Inf Sch PO12 .52 B6
Leesland CE Jun Sch
PO12 . . . . .52 A6
Leesland Rd PO12 . . . . .52 A6
Lees Lane N E7 PO12 . . . . . .52 B6
Leeson Rd PO38 . . . . .47 D7
Leigh Rd SO41 . . . . .48 C3
Leighton Ave E7 SO18 . . . . .50 B8
Leighton Mount PO37. . . . .43 A7
Leighton Rd SO19 . . . . .51 F3
Leighwood Cl PO33 . . . . . . .11 E3
Lemon Rd SO15. . . . . .50 B7
Lennox Cl PO12 . . . . .52 C2
Lennox Ct E7 PO5. . . . . .53 D2
Lennox Mans PO5 . . . . .53 D1
Lennox Road N PO5. . . . . . .53 D2
Lennox Road S PO5 . . . . . . .53 D2
Lentune Way SO41 . . . . . . .48 D4
Len Williams Terr PO2 . . . .53 E7
Leonard Rd PO12 . . . . .52 A7
Leopold St PO4 . . . . .53 E2
Leroux Cl SO14 . . . . .50 F5
Leslie Loader Ho SO19 . . . .51 E5
Lessland La PO38, PO36. . .34 B2
Le Tissier Ct E7 SO15. . . . . .50 E6
Leventhorpe Ct PO12 . . . . .52 C5
Leverett Cl PO12 . . . . .52 C9
Lewis Ho E7 SO14 . . . . .51 A5
Leyland Cl PO12 . . . . .52 B4
Leyton Rd SO14 . . . . .51 C6
Lichfield Dr PO12 . . . . .52 C8
Lift Rd PO37 . . . . .43 D7
Lighthouse The E7 PO1. . . .53 A4
Lilliput Antique Dolls & Toy
Mus* PO36 . . . . .24 B3
Lime Kiln Shute PO36. . . . .34 D5
LIMERSTONE. 30 E2
Limerstone Rd PO30 . . . . . .30 D2
Lime St SO14 . . . . .51 A3
Limes The
Marchwood SO40 . . . . .50 A1
Newport PO30. . . . . .20 C7
Shanklin PO37 . . . . .43 C6
Lime Tree Ct PO40 . . . . . . .27 B7
Lime Tree Ho E7 SO41 . . . . .48 E4
Lincoln Cl PO35. . . . . .25 D3
Lincoln Rd PO1. . . . . .53 E5
Lincoln Way PO35 . . . . .25 D3
Linden Gr PO12 . . . . .52 B4
Linden Rd PO30 . . . . .20 C5
Linden Terr PO36 . . . . .24 B2
Lind Ho SO14 . . . . .51 A7
Lind Hill E7 PO33 . . . . .12 C2
Lindon Ct PO4. . . . . .53 F4
Lind Pl PO33 . . . . .12 B6
Lind Rd PO12. . . . . .52 C2
Lindsay Ho E7 PO5 . . . . . . .53 D2
Lind St SO14 . . . . .12 C6
Liners Ind Est SO15 . . . . . . .50 C6
Lingdale Pl E7 SO17. . . . . . .51 A8
Lingfield Ct E7 PO1 . . . . . . .53 B3
Lington Ct E7 PO30 . . . . . . .20 C6
Linklater Path E7 PO1 . . . . .53 D7
Link Rd E7 PO32 . . . . .3 C4
Linkside PO33 . . . . .35 D5
Linnet Cl PO30. . . . . .20 A6
Linnet Rise PO33 . . . . .35 C3
Linstone Dr PO41. . . . . .15 A5
Lion Brewery The E7 PO2. .53 D8
Lion Rd PO12. . . . . .52 B8
Lion St PO1 . . . . .53 B5
Lion Terr PO1 . . . . .53 B5
Lisbon Rd SO15 . . . . .50 D6
Lisle Cl SO41 . . . . .48 D3
Lisle Ct SO41 . . . . .49 C3
Lisle Court Rd SO41 . . . . . . .49 C3
Liss Rd PO4 . . . . .53 F4
Little Anglesey PO12 . . . . . .52 B3
Little Anglesey Rd PO12. . .52 A3
Little Arthur St PO2 . . . . . . .53 E7
LITTLE ATHERFIELD. 39 C4
Little Coburg St PO1 . . . . . .54 C4
Little Dene Copse SO41 . . .48 B2
Little George St PO1 . . . . . .53 E7
Little Gn PO12 . . . . .52 A3
Little Green Orch PO12. . . .52 A3
Little Hambrook St E7
PO5 . . . . .54 A1
Little La PO12 . . . . .52 A3
Little Lance's Hill SO19 . . .51 F6
Little London PO30 . . . . . . .20 E8
Little Preston Rd PO33. . . .12 B3
Little Princelett Cross
PO36 . . . . .34 E2
Little Southsea St PO5 . . . .54 A1
Littlestairs Rd PO37. . . . . . .35 F1
Littleton Ct PO38 . . . . .46 F6
Littletown La PO33. . . . . . . .10 D2
LITTLE WHITEHOUSE 7 F5
Little Whitehouse Rd PO30,
PO31. . . . . .7 F5
Liverpool Rd PO1 . . . . .53 E5
Liverpool St SO14. . . . . .51 A7
Livesay Gdns PO1. . . . . .53 F6

Inv-Lym 61

Livingstone Rd
Portsmouth PO5 . . . . .54 C1
Southampton SO14 . . . . . . .51 A8
Loane Rd SO19 . . . . .51 F3
Lockerley Cl SO41 . . . . .48 E2
LOCKSGREEN. 7 C2
LOCKSLEY 27 B7
Locksley Cl PO40 . . . . .27 B7
Locksley Ct SO15 . . . . .50 F7
Locksley Mews E7 PO40 . . .15 D6
Lodge Arts Ctr The* PO1. .54 B3
Lodge Dr PO30 . . . . .30 A2
Lodge Gdns PO12. . . . . .52 A4
Lodge Rd
Lymington SO41 . . . . .48 B3
Southampton SO14 . . . . . . .51 A7
Lodgeside PO32 . . . . .3 D2
Lodge The SO15 . . . . .50 F7
Lodsworth Ho PO1 . . . . .54 C4
Lombard Ct E7 PO1 . . . . . . .53 A4
Lombard St PO1 . . . . .53 A3
Lomond Cl PO2. . . . . .53 D8
Londesborough Pl SO41. . .48 D2
Londesborough Rd PO4 . . .53 E3
London Rd SO15 . . . . .51 A6
Long Acre Ct PO1 . . . . .53 E7
Longbeach PO40 . . . . .14 C2
LONGBRIDGE. 34 D8
Longbridge Ho E7 PO5 . . . .54 B2
Longbridge Ind Pk SO14 . .51 C3
Long Cl SO41 . . . . .48 A3
Long Curtain Rd PO5 . . . . .53 A2
Longford Pl SO41 . . . . .48 D1
Long La
Downend PO30 . . . . .21 E4
Newport PO30 . . . . .21 B6
Longlands La PO36 . . . . . . .34 C6
Longlands Shute PO35. . . .24 E2
Long Lane Shute PO30. . . .21 D5
Longman Ct E7 PO5. . . . . . .53 C2
Longmead Rd PO33 . . . . . .12 C4
Longmore Ave SO19 . . . . . .51 D2
Longmore Cres SO19. . . . . .51 D2
Long Orch PO33 . . . . .12 E3
Longs Wlk PO1 . . . . .53 D7
Long Water Dr PO12 . . . . . .52 C2
Lonsdale Ave PO30. . . . . .9 A2
Lord Montgomery Way E7
PO1 . . . . .54 A2
Lords Ct PO1 . . . . .54 C4
Lords St PO1 . . . . .54 C4
Lorne Rd PO5 . . . . .54 D1
Louis Flagg Ho E7 PO5. . . .54 B2
Louis Rd PO36 . . . . .35 D4
Love La
Bembridge PO35 . . . . .25 D6
Cowes PO31 . . . . .3 A3
Ventnor PO38 . . . . .46 E4
Love Lane Prim Sch PO31. .3 A3
Lovett Way PO37. . . . . .35 C2
Lowcay Rd PO5. . . . . .53 E2
Lower Adgestone Rd
PO36 . . . . .23 F1
Lower Alfred St SO14 . . . . .51 B6
Lower Banister St E7
SO15 . . . . .50 F6
Lower Bettesworth Rd
PO33 . . . . .12 B3
Lower Brookfield Rd PO1 .53 E6
LOWER BUCKLAND. 48 E5
Lower Buckland Rd SO41 .48 D5
Lower Canal Wlk SO14 . . . .51 A3
Lower Church Path PO1. . .54 B3
Lower Church Rd PO31 . . . .2 D3
Lower Fields PO38. . . . . . . .45 C4
Lower Forbury Rd PO5 . . . .54 C2
Lower Furlongs PO36 . . . . .24 B3
Lower Green Rd PO33. . . . .24 F7
LOWER HAMSTEAD. 6 B2
Lower Highland Rd PO33. .12 C4
Lower Hill Rd PO41 . . . . . . .2 C3
LOWER HYDE 43 C8
Lower Hyde Est PO37. . . . .43 B8
Lower Mortimer Rd SO19 .51 D3
Lower Rd PO36 . . . . .35 D8
Lower Vicarage Rd SO19 . .51 D3
Lower William St Ind Est
SO14 . . . . .51 D6
Lower William St SO14. . . .51 D6
Lower Wingfield St PO1 . . .54 C4
Lower Woodside Rd PO33 .10 EB
Lower York St SO14 . . . . . . .51 D6
LOWTHERVILLE 46 E6
Lowtherville Rd PO38 . . . . .46 F7
Luccombe Ct PO37. . . . . . . .43 C6
Luccombe Rd PO37 . . . . . . .43 C5
LUCCOMBE VILLAGE 43 C4
Lucerne Rd PO37 . . . . .43 C8
Lucerne Villa PO37 . . . . . . .43 C8
Lucia Foster Welch Coll
Student Village E7 SO14. .51 B3
Lucknow St PO1. . . . . .54 D3
Ludbrook Way PO38 . . . . . .45 E7
Ludlow Inf Sch SO19 . . . . .51 E4
Ludlow Jun Sch SO19 . . . . .51 E4
Ludlow Rd SO19 . . . . .51 E4
Lugley St PO30 . . . . .20 C7
Lukely Ct PO30 . . . . .20 C6
Lukely Gdns PO30 . . . . .20 C6
Lumsden Ave SO15 . . . . . . .50 D7
Lumsden Mans E7 SO15 . . .50 C7
Lushington Hill PO33 . . . . .10 C4
LYMINGTON. 48 C5
Lymington CE Inf Sch
SO41 . . . . .48 D4

Lymington Jun Sch SO41 . .48 D4
Lymington New Forest Hospl
SO41 .48 D4
Lymington Pier Sta SO41 . .49 A3
Lymington Rehabilitation
Unit SO41 . . . . .48 E4
Lymington Town Sta
SO41 .48 F4
Lynchens CI PO35 . . . . .25 C4
Lynch La
Brighstone PO30 . . . . .30 A5
Calbourne PO30 . . . . .30 A7
Lyndhurst Rd PO12 . . . . .52 A5
Lyndock CI SO19 . . . . .51 E2
Lyndock PI SO19 . . . . .51 E2
Lynn Rd PO2 . . . . .53 F8
Lynwood Ct SO41 . . . . .48 D3
Lyon St SO14 . . . . .51 A6
Lysander Ct 21 PO1 . . . . . . .53 A4
Lyteltane Rd SO41 . . . . .48 D2

M

Mabey CI PO12 . . . . .52 C3
Machin CI PO30 . . . . .20 B6
Macketts La SO33 . . . . .34 B5
Macnaghten Rd SO18 . . . . . .51 D8
Macnamara Almshouses
PO31 .3 B5
Macrocarpa Rd 4 PO7 . . . . .47 A6
Maddison St 5 SO14 . . . . . .50 F4
Madeira CI PO38 . . . . .47 C6
Madeira Rd PO40 . . . . .14 D2
Madeira Rd
Seaview SO34 . . . . .13 D3
Totland PO39 . . . . .14 C1
Ventnor PO38 . . . . .47 C6
Madeira Vale PO38 . . . . .47 C6
Madrisa Ct SO41 . . . . .48 E4
Mafeking Rd PO4 . . . . .53 F3
Magazine La SO40 . . . . .50 A3
Magdalen Cres PO31 . . . . .2 F4
Magnolia Rd SO19 . . . . .51 F5
Magnum Mall PO17 . . . . . . .35 D1
Maida Vale Rd PO37 . . . . . . .35 D1
Maiden La SO41 . . . . .48 F1
Main Rd
Brighstone PO30 . . . . .30 B2
Newport PO30 . . . . .7 D3
Portmore SO41 . . . . .49 B7
Rookley PO38 . . . . .33 A4
Wellow PO41 . . . . .17 D4
Maitland St SO41 . . . . .48 E4
Maitland St PO1 . . . . .53 D7
Major Ct PO12 . . . . .52 A5
Malcolm CI PO40 . . . . .27 C7
Malcolm Dyer Ct 8 PO30 . .20 C6
Malcroft Mews SO40 . . . . . .50 A1
Maldon Rd SO19 . . . . .51 E4
Malins Rd PO2 . . . . .53 E8
Malins Road Apts 16 PO2 . .53 D7
Mallard Point PO31 . . . . .9 B8
Mallfield Terr PO36 . . . . .24 D2
Mall Marlands (Sh Ctr) The
SO14 .50 F4
Mall The
Brading PO36 . . . . .24 B2
Ryde PO33 . . . . .11 E4
Sandown PO36 . . . . .35 E4
Totland PO39 . . . . .14 D1
Malmesbury PI SO15 . . . . . . .50 D7
Malmesbury Rd SO15 . . . . . .50 D7
Malta Rd PO2 . . . . .53 E8
Malthouse Ct 2 PO30 . . . . .20 D7
Malthouse Gn PO41 . . . . . . .17 E4
Malthouse Rd PO2 . . . . .53 D8
Malvern Rd PO5 . . . . .53 D1
Manchester Rd PO1 . . . . .53 E5
Mandela Way SO15 . . . . .50 E5
Manna Rd PO35 . . . . .25 C4
Manners La PO4 . . . . .53 E4
Manners Rd PO4 . . . . .53 E4
Manners View PO30 . . . . .9 B1
Manor Cres
Newport PO30 . . . . .20 F7
Rookley PO38 . . . . .32 F4
Manor Ct PO30 . . . . .35 D4
Manor Gn PO30 . . . . .17 E7
Manor Inf Sch PO1 . . . . .53 E7
Manor Park Ho 1 SO18 . . . .51 C7
Manor Quay SO18 . . . . .51 D7
Manor Rd
Freshwater Bay PO40 . . . . .27 E7
Portsmouth PO1 . . . . .53 E7
Sandown PO36 . . . . .35 D4
Shanklin PO37 . . . . .43 B6
Wroxall PO38 . . . . .42 D3
Manor Road N SO19 . . . . . . .51 E4
Manor Road SO19 . . . . .51 E3
Manor Villas 4 PO36 . . . . . .14 D1
Manor Wharf SO18 . . . . .51 C7
Mansion Ct 6 PO4 . . . . .53 E1
Mansion Rd
Portsmouth PO4 . . . . .53 E1
Southampton SO15 . . . . . . .50 D6
Maple Ct
Lymington SO41 . . . . .48 E4
Southampton, Woolston
SO19 .51 E2
Maple Dr PO30 . . . . .20 C7
Maple Rd
Portsmouth PO2 . . . . .53 D2
Southampton SO18 . . . . . . .51 C5
Maples Dr PO38 . . . . .47 C7

Maples The PO36 . . . . .35 D2
Marchwood Ind Pk SO40 . . .50 A3
Marchwood Rd SO15 . . . . . . .50 B6
Maresfield Rd PO32 . . . . .3 C4
Margam Ave SO19 . . . . .51 F5
Margaret Rule Hall 6
PO1 .53 B3
Margate Rd PO5 . . . . .54 C2
Margery's Ct 31 PO1 . . . . . .53 A5
Marina Ave PO33 . . . . .12 F5
Marina Bldgs 3 PO12 . . . . .52 B5
Marina CI PO32 . . . . .3 A5
Marine Cotts 7 PO12 . . . . . .52 B6
Marine Cross Rd PO37 . . . . .43 C8
Marine Ct PO38 . . . . .47 A5
Marine Dr PO41 . . . . .16 C8
Marine Par
Southampton SO14 . . . . . . .51 B4
Ventnor PO38 . . . . .47 A5
Mariners Ct SO41 . . . . .48 F2
Mariners Way
Cowes PO31 . . . . .3 A2
Gosport PO12 . . . . .52 D4
Marine View PO32 . . . . .3 C2
Marion Rd PO4 . . . . .53 E2
Maritime Ave SO40 . . . . .50 A3
Maritime Chambers SO14 . . .51 B2
Maritime Wlk SO14 . . . . .51 A2
Maritime Wlk SO14 . . . . .51 B2
Mark CI SO15 . . . . .50 A7
Market Hill PO31 . . . . .3 B5
Market PI 9 SO14 . . . . .51 A3
Market Sq 1 PO41 . . . . .15 C6
Market St
Ryde PO33 . . . . .12 C6
Ventnor PO38 . . . . .47 A6
Marketway PO1 . . . . .54 B4
Marlborough Ct 3 PO30 . . . .20 B6
Marlborough Ct 15 PO12 . . .52 C9
Marlborough Ho SO15 . . . . . .50 F8
Marlborough Rd SO15 . . . . . .48 D5
Marlborough Rd
Carisbrooke PO30 . . . . .20 B6
Ryde PO33 . . . . .12 E3
Southampton SO15, SO16 . .50 B8
Ventnor PO38 . . . . .47 A6
Marlborough Row PO1 . . . . .53 A6
Marlowe Ct SO19 . . . . .51 F1
Marmion Ave PO5 . . . . .53 D2
Marmion Rd PO5 . . . . .53 C2
Marram CI SO41 . . . . .48 E5
Marshall Ct 10 SO15 . . . . . .50 F8
Marshall Sq SO14 . . . . .50 F8
Marsh CI
Freshwater Bay PO40 . . . . .27 C7
Sandown PO36 . . . . .36 A4
Marsh Ho 8 SO14 . . . . .51 A3
Marsh La
Lymington SO41 . . . . .48 E5
Southampton SO14 . . . . . . .51 B3
Marsh Rd
4 East Cowes PO32 . . . . . . .3 D2
Gurnard PO31 . . . . .2 C3
Martine CI PO40 . . . . .14 E2
Marvel La PO30 . . . . .20 E2
Marycourt Sch PO12 . . . . . . .52 A2
Mayfield SO14 . . . . .51 B4
Marymead CI PO33 . . . . .12 D6
Mary Rose* PO1 . . . . .52 F7
Mary Rose Ave PO33 . . . . . . .12 D4
Mary Rose Sch The PO1 . . . .54 B3
Matthews Way PO34 . . . . . . .13 D2
Maturin CI SO41 . . . . .48 D3
Mauretania Ho 13 SO14 . . .51 C6
Maxstoke CI PO5 . . . . .53 D3
Maxted CI PO31 . . . . .3 A3
May Ave SO41 . . . . .48 D5
Maybrick Rd SO19 . . . . .12 A5
May CI PO38 . . . . .33 C1
Maycroft Ct 4 SO15 . . . . . . .50 F8
Mayfair Gdns SO15 . . . . .50 F7
Mayfield CE Mid Sch
PO33 .12 A5
Mayfield Dr PO30 . . . . .21 A7
Mayfield Rd
East Cowes PO32 . . . . .3 D2
Gosport PO12 . . . . .52 C4
Ryde PO33 . . . . .12 A5
Mayflower CI SO41 . . . . .49 A2
Mayflower Ct
Cowes PO31 . . . . .3 B4
1 Southampton, Banister's Park
SO15 .50 F7
10 Southampton SO16 . . . . .50 B8
Mayflower Rd SO15 . . . . .50 B8
Mayo CI PO1 . . . . .53 D7
May Rd SO15 . . . . .50 C7
Maythorne Way PO37 . . . . . .43 C4
Maytree Inf Sch SO14 . . . . . .51 B6
Mayville High Sch 20 PO5 . .53 D2
Meaders Rd PO33 . . . . .12 D4
Meadow Barn CI PO39 . . . . .26 H8
Meadowbrook PO33 . . . . . . .11 F5
Meadow CI
Bembridge PO35 . . . . .25 D5
Sandown PO36 . . . . .35 D3
Whitwell PO38 . . . . .45 E7
Meadow Dr PO35 . . . . .25 D5
Meadow End PO35 . . . . .25 D5
Meadow Glade PO40 . . . . . . .27 C8
Meadow Gn PO30 . . . . .20 D5
Meadowlands SO41 . . . . .48 C4
Meadow Rd
East Cowes PO32 . . . . .3 D2
Lymington SO41 . . . . .48 C2
Meadows CI PO30 . . . . .30 B2

Meadowside PO30 . . . . .21 A7
Meadow St PO5 . . . . .54 A2
Meadow View CI PO33 . . . . .12 B3
Meadow Way PO36 . . . . .36 C5
Meadow Wlk PO1 . . . . .54 B4
Mead Rd SO41 . . . . .48 B2
Medeway PO36 . . . . .35 D4
Medham Farm La PO31 . . . . . .9 A8
Medina Ave PO30 . . . . .20 E6
Medina Court Ind Est PO31 . .3 B2
Medina High Sch PO30 . . . . . .9 D1
Medina House Sch PO30 . . .20 F7
Medina L Ctr PO30 . . . . .9 D1
Medina Pk PO32 . . . . .9 E6
Medina Rd PO31 . . . . .3 B4
Medina View PO32 . . . . .3 C2
Medina Village Ind Est
PO31 .3 B4
Medley PI SO15 . . . . .50 A7
Melbourne Ho PO1 . . . . .54 B3
Melbourne PI
Cowes PO31 . . . . .3 A6
Portsmouth PO5 . . . . .54 B2
Melbourne St
Newport PO30 . . . . .20 C6
Southampton SO14 . . . . . . .51 B4
Melbury CI SO41 . . . . .48 D3
Melcombe Ho PO31 . . . . .2 F6
Melton Hall PO33 . . . . .12 D5
Melville Gdns PO36 . . . . .35 F5
Melville Rd PO12 . . . . .52 B8
Melville St
Ryde PO33 . . . . .12 D6
Sandown PO36 . . . . .35 F5
Merchants Row 6 PO1 . . . . .53 A3
Merchants Wlk 16 SO14 . . .50 F3
Meredith Inf Sch PO2 . . . . . .53 E8
Merganser CI PO12 . . . . .52 B8
Meriden Rd PO5 . . . . .54 A2
Merlin Lodge SO14 . . . . .51 D3
Mermaid Way SO14 . . . . .51 A2
Merridale Rd SO19 . . . . .51 E5
Merrie Gdns PO36 . . . . .35 C3
Merryl La PO38 . . . . .41 C7
MERRY OAK 51 F5
Merryoak Gn SO19 . . . . .51 F5
Merryoak Rd SO19 . . . . .51 F5
MERSTONE 33 D6
Merstone La PO30, PO38 . . .33 D6
Merton Ct 3 PO5 . . . . .54 C1
Merton Rd PO5 . . . . .54 C1
Methuen St SO14 . . . . .51 A7
Mews La
Fairlee PO30 . . . . .9 D1
Newport, Staplers PO30 . . .21 B8
Mews The
7 Gosport PO12 . . . . .52 E5
Newport PO30 . . . . .20 D7
Micawber Ho 22 PO1 . . . . . .53 D7
Midanbury CI 6 SO18 . . . . .51 E8
Midanbury Wlk SO18 . . . . . .51 F8
Middle Barn La PO38 . . . . . .42 E3
Middle Common Rd SO41 . .48 A3
Middle Ct PO1 . . . . .53 E7
Middle Rd SO41 . . . . .48 D3
Middle St
Portsmouth PO5 . . . . .54 B2
Southampton SO14 . . . . . . .51 A7
MIDDLETON 27 A7
Middleton Terr PO31 . . . . .3 B5
Midhurst Rd PO30 . . . . .54 C4
Mile End Rd PO2 . . . . .53 C7
Milestone Cres PO36 . . . . . .34 F7
Milford CI
Lymington SO41 . . . . .48 C1
Shanklin PO37 . . . . .43 C8
Milford Rd SO41 . . . . .48 C2
Mill Gate Ho 30 PO1 . . . . . .53 A5
Mill Hill PO33 . . . . .3 A3
Mill House Bsns Ctr SO19 . .51 D4
Milligan Ho PO33 . . . . .12 B4
Milligan Rd PO33 . . . . .12 B4
Mill La
Brighstone PO30 . . . . .30 B1
Brighstone PO30 . . . . .30 F1
Gosport PO12 . . . . .52 B7
Lymington SO41 . . . . .48 F4
Newport PO30 . . . . .7 C6
Portsmouth, Landport PO1 . .53 C7
South Baddesley SO41 . . . . .49 F4
Mill Pond Rd PO12 . . . . .52 B7
Mill Rd
Bembridge PO35 . . . . .25 C4
Gosport PO12 . . . . .52 A7
Shalfleet PO30 . . . . .17 E7

Mill Rd continued
Southampton SO15 . . . . . . .50 A7
St Helens PO33 . . . . .25 A6
Yarmouth PO41 . . . . .15 D5
Mill Sq PO33 . . . . .10 F4
Mill St PO30 . . . . .20 D7
Millstream Ct PO30 . . . . . . .20 C7
Millward PI PO23 . . . . .12 C4
Millward Rd PO33 . . . . .12 C4
Millways PO40 . . . . .14 F2
Milne Ct PO30 . . . . .20 D8
Milner Ct SO15 . . . . .50 C8
Milne Way PO30 . . . . .20 E5
Milton Rd
Cowes PO31 . . . . .3 B2
Southampton SO15 . . . . . . .50 F6
Milverton Ho PO5 . . . . .54 B2
Mimosa CI PO30 . . . . .20 C7
Mimosa St PO37 . . . . .43 C8
Minerva Cres 20 PO1 . . . . . .53 A4
Minerva Ct 2 PO4 . . . . .53 E1
Minerva Dr 9 PO12 . . . . . . .52 C8
Minerva Rd PO32 . . . . .3 C2
Minnitt Rd PO12 . . . . .52 E5
Minstead Ct 44 SO17 . . . . . .51 A8
Minster Ct 37 SO15 . . . . . . .50 C6
Mirabella CI SO19 . . . . .51 D2
Mistral 1 SO19 . . . . .51 B3
Mitchell Ave PO38 . . . . .47 A6
Mitchell CI SO19 . . . . .51 D3
Mitchell's Rd PO33 . . . . .12 A3
Mitten Rd PO35 . . . . .25 D4
Moira Ho PO31 . . . . .3 B5
Molesworth Rd PO12 . . . . . .52 C4
Monastery Rd SO18 . . . . . . .51 E7
Monckton Rd PO32 . . . . .52 B2
Monks Brook PO30 . . . . .9 B2
Monks Ct 4 SO41 . . . . .48 F2
Monks La PO40 . . . . .14 E4
Monkton St PO33 . . . . .12 D5
Monmouth Ct SO41 . . . . . . .48 E3
Montagu CI PO12 . . . . .52 C9
Montague Wallis Ct 40
PO1 .53 A5
Monterey Rd PO33 . . . . .12 A3
Montgomerie Rd PO5 . . . . . .54 C2
Monument Rd SO14 . . . . . . .51 A2
Monument La SO41 . . . . .49 A5
Moon CI PO32 . . . . .3 D3
Mooms Hill PO3, PO40 . . . . .26 H6
Moorgreen Rd PO33 . . . . .3 A4
Moorhead Ct SO14 . . . . .51 C2
Moorings The PO31 . . . . .3 A3
Moor La PO30 . . . . .30 A3
Moorland Rd PO1 . . . . .53 E6
MOORTOWN 30 B3
Moortown La PO30 . . . . .30 A3
Moor View PO30 . . . . .33 D1
Moray Ct PO33 . . . . .12 C9
Mordaunt Rd SO14 . . . . .51 A7
Morecombe Ct 4 PO5 . . . . .54 C2
Moreland Rd PO12 . . . . .52 B6
Morey Ct PO33 . . . . .12 C4
Morley CI SO19 . . . . .51 F6
Mornington Rd PO31 . . . . .2 F6
Morris Rd SO15 . . . . .50 E5
Mortimer Rd SO19 . . . . .51 E4
MORTON 24 B1
Mortonbrook PO36 . . . . .35 F7
Morton Comm PO36 . . . . . . .36 A5
Morton Lodge PO36 . . . . . . .36 A5
Morton Manor* PO36 . . . . . .24 A1
Morton Manor Rd PO36 . . . .24 A1
Morton Mews PO36 . . . . . . .24 A1
Morton Old Rd PO36 . . . . . .24 A1
Morton Rd PO36 . . . . .24 A1
Mosbach PI 8 SO41 . . . . . . .48 E4
Moselle Ct SO15 . . . . .50 C5
Mottisfont CI 1 SO15 . . . . . .50 A6
MOTTISTONE 29 D4
Mottistone Manor Gdn*
PO30 .29 D4
Moulin Ave PO5 . . . . .53 E2
Mound CI PO12 . . . . .52 A4
Mountbatten Ave PO31 . . . . . .2 F5
Mountbatten Bsns Ctr
SO15 .50 E5
Mountbatten Dr
Carisbrooke PO30 . . . . .20 B7
Ryde PO33 . . . . .12 A4
Mountbatten Way
Portsmouth PO1 . . . . .53 B7
Southampton SO15 . . . . . . .51 A6
Mountfield 8 PO40 . . . . .13 D6
Mountfield Rd PO38 . . . . . . .42 B3
Mountjoy Ct 4 PO1 . . . . . . .53 A3
Mount Pleasant Ho PO30 . . .20 E6
Mount Pleasant Ind Pk
SO14 .51 B7
Mount Pleasant Jun Sch
SO14 .51 B7
Mount Pleasant La SO41 . . .48 A7
Mount Pleasant Rd
Gosport PO12 . . . . .52 B4
Newport PO30 . . . . .20 D6
Southampton SO14 . . . . . . .51 B6
Mount Rd
East Cowes PO32 . . . . .4 A1
Wootton PO33 . . . . .10 A8
Mount St PO33 . . . . .12 C5
Mount The PO41 . . . . .15 D6
Mousehole La SO18 . . . . . . .51 E8
Muggleton La PO30 . . . . .30 E1
Muira Est SO14 . . . . .51 C5
Mulberry CI
Gosport PO12 . . . . .52 B5
Newport PO30 . . . . .20 C7
Mulberry Way PO33 . . . . . . .12 F2

Mulberry Wlk SO15 . . . . . . .50 C8
Mullen CI SO19 . . . . .51 E4
Mumby Rd PO12 . . . . .52 D6
Murefield Rd PO1 . . . . .54 C3
Murray's La PO1 . . . . .52 F7
Museum Rd PO1 . . . . .53 B4
Mus of Archaeology*
SO14 .51 A2
Mus of Island History*
PO30 .20 E7

N

Nancy Rd PO1 . . . . .54 D3
Nansen Rd PO35 . . . . .25 D3
Napier Rd PO5 . . . . .53 D2
Napier The PO37 . . . . .43 D7
Napoleons Landing PO36 . . .35 F4
Nat Gonella Sq 4 PO12 . . . .52 D5
Navy Rd PO1 . . . . .53 A6
Needlemakers 3 PO39 . . . . .14 E1
Needles Old Battery The*
PO39 .26 B4
Needles Pk The* PO39 . . . . .26 D5
Nelson CI PO32 . . . . .3 A3
Nelson Cres PO33 . . . . .11 F4
Nelson Ct
Cowes PO31 . . . . .3 B2
6 Portsmouth PO1 . . . . . . .53 D7
Nelson Dr PO31 . . . . .3 B2
Nelson Ho 3 PO12 . . . . .52 E5
Nelson La PO33 . . . . .12 D6
Nelson Pl
Lymington SO41 . . . . .48 F3
Ryde PO33 . . . . .12 D6
Nelson Rd
Gosport PO12 . . . . .52 B5
Newport PO30 . . . . .20 C6
Portsmouth, Landport PO1 . .53 D7
Portsmouth PO5 . . . . .54 C1
Nelson's Quay PO33 . . . . . . .24 F6
Nelson St
Ryde PO33 . . . . .12 C6
12 Southampton SO14 . . . .51 B3
Nepean CI PO12 . . . . .52 B2
Neptune Ct 16 PO1 . . . . . . .53 A4
Neptune Ho 14 PO1 . . . . . . .51 B2
Neptune Way SO14 . . . . .51 B2
Nessus St PO2 . . . . .53 D8
Netley Ct 8 PO12 . . . . .52 C9
Netley Mans 19 PO5 . . . . . .53 D1
Netley Rd PO33 . . . . .53 C1
Netley Terr 14 PO5 . . . . .53 C2
NETTLECOMBE 41 D1
Nettlecombe Ave PO4 . . . . . .53 F1
Nettlecombe La PO38 . . . . . .45 E7
NETTLESTONE 13 C2
Nettlestone Gn PO34 . . . . . .13 C2
Nettlestone Hill PO33,
PO34 .13 C2
Nettlestone Prim Sch
PO34 .13 C2
Neva Rd SO18 . . . . .51 F8
NEW BARN. 3 E4
New Barn Bsns Pk PO30 . . .21 C1
New Barn La PO30 . . . . .31 C3
New Barn Rd PO32 . . . . .3 E3
NEWBRIDGE 17 D3
Newbridge Jun Sch PO12 . . .53 F7
Newbridge Way SO41 . . . . . .48 C1
NEWCHURCH 34 D7
Newchurch Prim Sch
PO36 .34 E7
New Cliff Ho SO19 . . . . .51 E1
Newcombe Rd SO15 . . . . . . .50 E6
Newcomen Rd PO36 . . . . . . .35 E4
Newcome Rd PO1 . . . . .53 E6
Newenham Rd SO41 . . . . . . .48 E2
Newland Ave PO12 . . . . .52 A5
Newlands
Merstone PO30 . . . . .33 D5
St Helens PO33 . . . . .25 A6
Newlands Ave SO15 . . . . . . .50 D7
Newman La PO38 . . . . .40 A3
Newman St 2 SO16 . . . . . . .50 B8
Newnham La PO33 . . . . .11 C3
Newnham Rd PO33 . . . . .11 E3
NEWPORT 20 B7
Newport CE Prim Sch
PO30 .20 C7
Newport Rd
Cowes PO31 . . . . .8 F8
Freshwater Bay PO40 . . . . .27 E7
Godshill PO38 . . . . .33 C1
Niton PO38 . . . . .45 B4
Sandown PO36 . . . . .35 C3
Ventnor PO38 . . . . .46 F6
Newport Roman Villa*
PO30 .20 E6
Newport St PO33 . . . . .12 C5
New Rd
Brading PO36 . . . . .24 B2
Brighstone PO30 . . . . .30 A1
Porchfield PO30 . . . . .7 D2
Portsmouth PO2 . . . . .53 F7
Sandown PO36 . . . . .35 D4
Southampton SO14 . . . . . . .51 A5
Wootton PO33 . . . . .10 F5
Whitwell PO38 . . . . .39 A7
New Road E PO2 . . . . .53 F8
New St
Lymington SO41 . . . . .48 E4
Newport PO30 . . . . .20 D6
New Street Mews SO41 . . . .48 E4
New Theatre Royal* PO1 . . .54 A3

NEWTOWN
Gosport 52 D5
Newport 6 E2
Southampton 51 B6
Newtown CE Prim Sch
PO12 . . . . 52 C6
Newtown Harbour National
Nature Reserve* PO30 . . 6 D2
Newtown Marshes Nature
Reserve* PO30 . . . . 6 F4
Newtown Old Town Hall*
PO30 . . . . 6 E2
NEW VILLAGE 27 C8
Nicholas Ct PO36 . . . . 24 A1
Nicholson Gdns 1 PO4 . . 54 C3
Nicholson Rd PO33 . . . . . 12 D3
Nicholson St PO31 . . . . 9 A3
Nichols Rd SO14 . . . . 51 B5
Nickel St 4 PO5 . . . . 54 A1
Nickleby Ho 10 PO1 . . . . . 53 D7
Nightingale Cl PO35 . . . . . 25 D5
Nightingale Gr SO15 . . . . 50 C7
Nightingale Rd
Carisbrooke PO30 . . . . . . 20 A6
Portsmouth PO5 . . . . 54 D1
Nightingale Ct 3 SO15 . . 50 C6
Nine Acres Prim Sch
PO30 . . . . 20 D6
NINGWOOD 17 C6
Ningwood Hill PO41 . . . . . 17 A7
Ninham Ct PO37 . . . . 35 C2
Nippert Ct 2 PO30 . . . . . 20 D6
Nirvana Mans 12 PO5 . . . 53 D1
NITON 45 A4
Niton Prim Sch PO38 . . . . 45 B4
Niton Rd PO38 . . . . 32 F4
Niton Shute PO38 . . . . 45 A4
Nobbs La PO1 . . . . 53 A4
Node Cl PO33 . . . . 12 B3
Nodehill Mid Sch PO30 . . 20 D6
Nodes Rd PO31 . . . . 8 F8
Nodgham La PO30 . . . . . . 20 A5
Nokie Comm PO30 . . . . . . 8 E4
Norcliffe Rd SO17 . . . . 51 A8
Norcott Dr PO35 . . . . 25 D4
Norfolk Cl SO15 . . . . 50 D7
Norfolk St PO5 . . . . 54 B2
Norland Rd PO4 . . . . 54 D1
NORLEYWOOD 49 E8
Norleywood Rd SO41 . . . 49 E8
Norman Ct
Camp Hill PO30 . . . . 8 F1
4 Portsmouth PO4 . . . . 53 E2
Normandy La SO41 . . . . . 49 A5
Normandy Way SO40 . . . 50 A1
Norman Ho 16 SO14 . . . . 51 C6
Norman Way PO33 . . . . . 10 E6
Norrish Ct 2 . . . . 53 E7
NORTHAM 51 C6
SO14 . . . . 51 C6
Northam Bsns Ctr 21
SO14 . . . . 51 C6
Northam Mews PO1 . . . . 54 C3
Northam Rd SO14 . . . . . . 51 B5
Northam St PO1 . . . . 54 C3
Northbourne Ave PO37 . . 43 B8
Northbrook Cl PO1 . . . . . 53 D7
Northbrook Rd SO14 . . . . 51 B5
North Cl SO41 . . . . 49 A5
Northcliff Gdns PO37 . . . 35 C1
Northcliff Hts PO37 . . . . . 35 C1
Northclose Rd PO35 . . . . 25 D5
North Court Cl PO30 . . . . 31 B2
North Cross St PO12 . . . . 52 D5
North Ct PO1 . . . . 53 E7
Northern Anchorage
SO19 . . . . 51 D3
Northern Way PO1 . . . . . 52 F8
Northesk Ho PO1 . . . . 54 C4
North Fairlee Rd PO30 . . . 9 E3
Northgate Ave PO2 . . . . . 53 F8
North Greenlands SO41 . 48 C2
Northlands Gdns SO15 . . 50 E8
Northlands Rd SO15 . . . . 50 E8
Northover Rd SO41 . . . . . 48 A4
North Rd
Shanklin PO37 . . . . 43 C8
Southampton SO17 . . . . 51 C8
North St
Brighstone PO30 . . . . . . 30 B2
Gosport PO12 . . . . 52 D6
Lymington SO41 . . . . . . 48 C2
Portsmouth PO1 . . . . . . 54 A4
Portsmouth, Portsea PO1 53 A4
Sandown PO36 . . . . 36 A4
Ventnor PO38 . . . . 47 B6
Northumberland Rd
Newport PO30 . . . . 9 A1
Portsmouth PO5 . . . . . . 53 D1
Southampton SO14 . . . . 51 B6
North View
Newchurch PO36 . . . . . . 34 D6
Thorley PO41 . . . . 16 D6
North Wlk PO33 . . . . 12 E6
NORTHWOOD 8 E8
Northwood Dr 1 SO41 . . 48 C2
Northwood Prim Sch PO31 8 E7
NORTON 15 A5
Norton Cl SO19 . . . . 51 E3
Norton Grange Village
PO41 . . . . 15 A6
NORTON GREEN 15 A3

Norton Green Ind Pk
PO40 . . . . 14 F3
Nostalgia Toy Mus*
PO38 . . . . 41 D8
Nubia Ct PO31 . . . . 2 F5
Nunnery La PO30 . . . . 20 C4
Nunwell House & Gdns*
PO36 . . . . 23 F3
Nunwell Rd PO36 . . . . . . 35 E5
Nurseries The PO40 . . . . . 14 F1
Nursery Gdns PO32 . . . . . . 3 C3
Nursery La PO33 . . . . 12 A5
Nutfield Pl PO1 . . . . 54 C4
Nyria Way PO12 . . . . 52 D5

O

Oakbank Rd SO19 . . . . . . 51 D3
Oak Ct SO41 . . . . 48 C2
Oakfield CE Prim Sch
PO33 . . . . 12 E4
Oakfield Ct PO33 . . . . 12 D4
Oakfield Rd PO32 . . . . 3 D3
Oakfield Rd PO33, PO34 . 13 B4
Oak Hills PO37 . . . . 43 B7
Oaklands SO41 . . . . 48 F2
Oaklands Cl PO33 . . . . . . 11 B5
Oakleigh Ct PO33 . . . . . . 12 E5
Oakley Ct 11 SO16 . . . . . 50 B8
Oakley Ho
Portsmouth PO5 . . . . . . 54 D1
3 Southampton, Banister's Pk
SO15 . . . . 50 F7
16 Southampton SO15 . 50 B8
Oakley Rd SO16 . . . . 50 B8
OAKLFIELD 12 D4
Oaklyn Gdns PO37 . . . . . 35 C1
Oak Rd
Newport PO30 . . . . 20 F8
Southampton SO19 . . . . 51 E2
Oaks Cl PO32 . . . . 3 C4
Oakside Gdns PO35 . . . . 25 C5
Oak St PO12 . . . . 52 C5
Oaks The SO19 . . . . 51 F5
Oaktree Cl PO36 . . . . 35 D3
Oak Tree Way PO32 . . . . . . 3 C4
Oakville Mans 11 SO15 . 50 F6
Oakwood Cl PO33 . . . . . . 12 B3
Oakwood Ct PO30 . . . . . . 20 C7
Oakwood Rd PO33 . . . . . 12 B3
Oasis Acad Mayfield SO19 51 F2
Obelisk Ct SO19 . . . . 51 D2
Obelisk Rd SO19 . . . . 51 D2
Oberland Ct SO41 . . . . . . 48 D4
Oceana Ho SO15 . . . . 50 E5
Oceanic Way SO40 . . . . . 50 B3
Ocean Ho SO14 . . . . 51 A1
Ocean View Rd PO36 . . . 35 E4
Ocean Way SO14 . . . . . . 51 B2
Ochiltree Ho PO37 . . . . . 43 B7
Ockendon Cl PO5 . . . . . . 54 B2
Officers Quarters The
PO12 . . . . 52 D6
Ogle Rd SO14 . . . . 50 F4
Old Auction Ho 18 PO12 . 52 E5
Old Bembridge Rd PO35 . 25 C6
Old Blackgang Rd PO38 . 44 F2
Old Bridge Rd PO4 . . . . . 54 B2
Oldbury Ho 4 PO5 . . . . . 54 B2
Old Chapel La PO33 . . . . 24 F7
Old Coastguard Cotts
PO40 . . . . 27 D6
Old Commercial Rd PO1 . 53 C7
Old Cricket Mews SO15 . 50 F8
Old Farmhouse Mews
SO14 . . . . 48 E5
Old Farm Wlk SO41 . . . . 48 D3
Old Forge Cl The PO33 . . 11 F5
Old Forge Ct SO41 . . . . . 48 D2
Old Infirmary Ho 13 PO1 53 A4
Old Maltings The SO41 . . 48 D3
Old Oak View PO30 . . . . . 8 F1
Old Orchards SO41 . . . . . 48 E2
Old Park Rd PO38 . . . . . . 46 A3
Old Rd
East Cowes PO32 . . . . . . 3 D4
Gosport PO12 . . . . 52 C4
Southampton SO14 . . . . 51 B2
Old Reservoir La PO36 . . 35 E4
Old Salterns Gate PO34 . 13 D4
Old School Ct PO38 . . . . 42 B5
Old School La PO30 . . . . 22 D1
Old Seaview La PO34 . . . 13 D4
Old Smithy & Gdns The*
PO38 . . . . 41 D8
Old Star Pl 2 PO1 . . . . . 53 A5
Old Station Rd PO38 . . . . 47 A6
Old Town Ct PO31 . . . . 3 B5
Old Town Hall PO37 . . . . 47 B6
Old Vicarage La PO30 . . . 7 A1
Old Westminster La 7
PO30 . . . . 20 D7
Olinda St PO1 . . . . 53 E6
Oliver Rd SO41 . . . . 48 C3
Olivers Ct PO5 . . . . 53 E8
Olivia Ct 3 PO30 . . . . . . 20 D7
Omega Ho PO5 . . . . 54 C3
Omega St PO5 . . . . 54 C3
Ommanney Rd 1 PO41 . 15 F6
Onslow Rd
4 Portsmouth PO5 . . . . 53 D1
Southampton SO14 . . . . 51 A6
Orchard Cl
Freshwater PO40 . . . . . . 15 A1
Wroxall PO38 . . . . 42 B5
Orchard Ct PO37 . . . . 35 C1

Orchard Ho 4 SO14 . . . . . 51 A3
Orchard La SO14 . . . . 51 A3
Orchardleigh Rd PO37 . . . 43 C7
Orchard Mews PO30 . . . . 20 E7
Orchard Pl
Cowes PO31 . . . . 3 A4
Southampton SO14 . . . . 51 A3
Orchard Rd
East Cowes PO32 . . . . . . 3 D3
Portsmouth PO4 . . . . . . 53 E4
Seaview PO34 . . . . 13 D2
Shanklin PO37 . . . . 43 D8
Orchard St PO30 . . . . 20 D6
Orchards Way PO30 . . . . 31 B2
Orchard The PO30 . . . . . . 30 B2
Orchid Lodge PO37 . . . . . 35 C1
Ordnance Rd
Gosport PO12 . . . . 52 D5
Southampton SO15 . . . . 51 A6
Ordnance Row PO1 . . . . . 53 A5
Ordnance Way SO40 . . . . 50 A3
Orion Ave PO12 . . . . 52 C8
Ormsby Rd PO5 . . . . 54 B1
Orwell Cl PO12 . . . . 52 A8
Osborne Chase PO31 . . . . 3 A3
Osborne Cl PO33 . . . . 12 C4
Osborne Ct PO31 . . . . 3 A5
Osborne Ho* PO32 . . . . . . 3 F2
Osborne Hts PO37 . . . . . . 3 E4
Osborne Mid Sch PO32 . . 3 E1
Osborne Rd
East Cowes PO32 . . . . . . 3 C3
Gosport PO12 . . . . 52 D6
Portsmouth PO5 . . . . . . 54 D1
Ryde PO33 . . . . 12 B4
Shanklin PO37 . . . . 43 C7
Osborne Road S SO17 . . 51 C8
Osterley Rd SO19 . . . . . . 51 E5
Our Lady & St Joseph RC
Prim Sch SO14 . . . . 48 A4
Outram Rd PO5 . . . . 54 C1
Overdell Ct 8 SO15 . . . . 50 E7
Oxford Ave SO14 . . . . . . 51 A7
Oxford Rd
Portsmouth PO5 . . . . . . 54 D1
Southampton SO14 . . . . 51 A7
Oxford St
Cowes PO31 . . . . 8 F7
Southampton SO14 . . . . 51 A3
Oyster Mews 7 PO4 . . . . 53 A3
Oyster St PO1 . . . . 53 A3

P

Pacific Cl SO14 . . . . 51 C2
Packsfield La PO33 . . . . . 10 D3
Paddock Cl
Godshill PO38 . . . . 41 D8
Shorwell PO30 . . . . 31 B2
Paddock Dr PO35 . . . . . . 25 F4
Paddock Gdns SO41 . . . . 48 D5
Paddock Rd PO37 . . . . . . 43 B7
Paddock The
Gosport PO12 . . . . 52 A4
Winford PO36 . . . . 34 F4
Padwell Rd SO14 . . . . . . 51 A7
Paget Rd PO12 . . . . 52 A4
Paget St SO14 . . . . 51 B4
Pagham PO38 . . . . 33 B4
Pain's Rd PO5 . . . . 54 C2
PALLANCEGATE 8 D5
Pallance La PO31 . . . . 8 D7
Pallance Rd PO31 . . . . 8 D8
Palm Ct 17 PO5 . . . . 54 B1
Palmer's La PO36 . . . . . . 34 E7
Palmers Rd PO33 . . . . . . 10 D6
Palmerston Ct 2 PO5 . . . 53 C2
Palmerston Mans 3 PO5 53 C2
Palmerston Rd
Portsmouth PO5 . . . . . . 53 C2
Shanklin PO37 . . . . 43 C7
Southampton SO14 . . . . 51 A4
Palmerston Road Prec 4
PO5 . . . . 53 C2
Palmyra Rd PO12 . . . . . . 52 A8
Pamplyn Cl SO41 . . . . . . 48 C4
Pan Cl PO30 . . . . 20 E6
Pan La
Newport PO30 . . . . 20 F6
Niton PO38 . . . . 45 B4
Pannall Rd PO12 . . . . 52 A8
Pan St PO1 . . . . 54 B4
Parade The
Cowes PO31 . . . . 3 B5
Portsmouth PO1 . . . . . . 53 A6
Paradise Cotts PO38 . . . . 45 D8
Paradise St PO1 . . . . 54 B4
Parham Rd PO12 . . . . 52 C7
Parish Ct SO41 . . . . 48 E4
Park Ave
Lymington SO41 . . . . . . 48 D4
Ventnor PO38 . . . . 47 B6
Park Cl PO30 . . . . 19 F7
Park Court Flats 7 SO15 . 50 C6
Park Ct
Cowes PO31 . . . . 3 A5
Portsmouth PO5 . . . . . . 54 B1
Parkers Hill PO40 . . . . . . 14 F1
Park Gate PO32 . . . . 3 E1
Park Ho Rd PO5 . . . . 53 C2
PARKHURST 9 A3
Parkhurst Rd PO30 . . . . . . 9 A2
Park La
Nettlestone PO34 . . . . . . 13 C1
Shorwell PO30 . . . . 39 B8
1 Southampton SO15 . . 50 F5
Parkland Pl 15 SO17 . . . . 51 A8

Parklands Ave PO31 . . . . . 2 F4
Parklands Cl PO12 . . . . . . 52 B7
Parkmead Ct PO33 . . . . . 12 D5
Park Mews PO36 . . . . 35 E6
Park Rd
Brading PO36 . . . . 24 A3
Cowes PO31 . . . . 2 F3
Gosport PO12 . . . . 52 B6
Lymington SO41 . . . . . . 48 D4
Portsmouth PO1 . . . . . . 53 B5
Ryde PO33 . . . . 12 C5
Shanklin PO37 . . . . 43 D8
Southampton SO15 . . . . 50 D6
Wootton Bridge PO33 . . 10 B3
Park Rise PO36 . . . . 35 E5
Park Rd SO16 . . . . 50 C6
Parkside The SO16 . . . . . 50 A8
Park St
Gosport PO12 . . . . 52 B6
Portsmouth PO5 . . . . . . 54 A2
Parkstone Ave PO4 . . . . . 53 E2
Park Terrs 11 PO12 . . . . . 52 C5
Park View PO33 . . . . 10 C3
Park View PO38 . . . . 42 B5
Parkwater Farm Ind Unit
PO30 . . . . 19 B7
Parkway
Freshwater PO40 . . . . . . 15 A2
Ryde PO33 . . . . 11 E4
Park Way SO14 . . . . 34 F4
Park Wlk SO14 . . . . 51 A5
Parsonage Rd
Sandown PO36 . . . . 35 F7
Southampton SO14 . . . . 51 C8
Partlands Ave PO33 . . . . 12 B4
Partlands Cl PO33 . . . . . . 12 B4
Partridge Rd PO30 . . . . . . 9 A3
Paulsgrove Rd PO2 . . . . . 53 F8
Pavilion Ct 4 SO15 . . . . . 50 E7
Pavilion Rise PO12 . . . . . 12 E5
Pavilion Way PO12 . . . . . 52 D6
Peacock Cl PO37 . . . . 43 A7
Peacock Hill PO35 . . . . . 25 A1
Peacock La PO1 . . . . 53 A3
Pearce Ct PO12 . . . . 52 D6
Pearmain Dr 6 SO41 . . . 48 E2
Pearman Ct SO41 . . . . . . 48 C2
Peartree Ave SO19 . . . . . 51 E5
Peartree Cl SO19 . . . . . . 51 D4
Pear Tree Cl PO33 . . . . . . 12 A3
Peartree Ct
7 Lymington SO41 . . . . 48 E2
Southampton SO19 . . . . 51 E4
PEARTREE GREEN 51 D4
Peartree Rd SO19 . . . . . . 51 D4
Peel Pl PO5 . . . . 54 B2
Peel Rd PO12 . . . . 52 C5
Peel St SO14 . . . . 51 C5
Peggotty Ho 22 PO1 . . . . 53 D7
Pelham Ct PO35 . . . . 25 C4
PELHAMFIELD 12 B6
Pelham Rd
Cowes PO31 . . . . 3 B3
Gosport PO12 . . . . 52 B6
Portsmouth PO5 . . . . . . 54 B1
Ventnor PO38 . . . . 46 D5
Pelhurst Rd PO33 . . . . . . 12 B4
Pell La PO33 . . . . 11 F4
Pellview Ct PO33 . . . . 11 F4
Pemberley Cl PO36 . . . . . 35 D4
Pembroke Cl PO36 . . . . . 53 A3
Pembroke Rd PO1 . . . . . . 53 A3
Penhale Inf Sch PO1 . . . . 53 E5
Penhale Rd PO1 . . . . 53 E5
PENNINGTON 48 B3
Pennington Cl SO41 . . . . 48 C2
Pennington Cross SO41 . 48 D2
Pennington Inf Sch SO41 48 C3
Pennington Jun Sch
SO41 . . . . 48 C3
Pennington Oval SO41 . . 48 B3
Penny Ct 2 PO12 . . . . . . 52 C6
Penny St PO1 . . . . 53 A3
Pepys Cl
Gosport PO12 . . . . 52 B2
Portsmouth PO5 . . . . . . 53 F3
Percival Rd PO2 . . . . 53 F8
Percy Chandler St PO1 . . 54 C4
Percy Rd
Gosport PO12 . . . . 52 C6
Portsmouth PO4 . . . . . . 53 C5
Sandown PO36 . . . . 35 D4
Southampton SO18 . . . . 50 A8
Perkins Ho 13 PO1 . . . . . 53 B5
Perowne Way PO36 . . . . 35 E7
Perseus Terr 15 PO1 . . . . 53 A5
Perth Ho PO1 . . . . 54 C3
Peterborough Rd PO4 . . . 51 A7
Petersfield Ho PO1 . . . . . 54 C4
Petersham Ho 5 PO5 . . . 53 D1
Petticoat La PO30 . . . . . . 30 B2
Pettinger Gdns SO17 . . . 51 D8
Peveril Rd SO19 . . . . 51 E4
Phoenix Flats PO32 . . . . . 3 C3
Pickwick Ho 12 PO1 . . . . 53 D7
Picton Ho 10 PO5 . . . . . . 54 B2
Pierhead Rd PO2 . . . . 53 A8
Pier Rd
East Cowes PO32 . . . . . . 3 F3
Portsmouth PO1 . . . . . . 53 B3
Seaview PO34 . . . . 13 E3
Pier St
Sandown PO36 . . . . 35 F5
Ventnor PO38 . . . . 47 A6
Yarmouth PO41 . . . . . . 15 C6
Pilgrim Pl SO41 . . . . 48 E3

Pinegrove Rd SO19 . . . . . 51 F4
Pine Ridge Ct PO31 . . . . . 14 C1
Pinetops Cl SO41 . . . . . . 48 B3
Pine Tree Cl PO31 . . . . 2 E5
Pineview Dr PO30 . . . . . . 19 F6
Pink Rd PO2 . . . . 53 E8
Pipit Cl PO12 . . . . 52 B8
Pippin Cl 8 SO41 . . . . . . 48 E2
Pippins Cl PO30 . . . . 30 A2
Pippins The PO31 . . . . 3 A3
Pirelli St SO15 . . . . 50 F4
Pitt Place La PO30 . . . . . 29 E3
Pitt Rd SO15 . . . . 50 C6
Pitts La PO33 . . . . 11 F6
Pitt St PO33 . . . . 12 B4
Pitt Rd SO15 . . . . 47 D7
Pixley Hill PO40 . . . . 15 A4
Place Rd PO31 . . . . 2 F2
Place Side PO31 . . . . 2 F2
Plaish La PO30 . . . . 19 E3
Planet Ice PO33 . . . . 12 D7
Plantation Ct SO41 . . . . . 48 E2
Platform Rd SO14 . . . . . . 51 A2
Player St PO33 . . . . 12 C5
Playfair Rd PO5 . . . . 54 C2
Play La PO33 . . . . 12 A4
Playstreet La PO33 . . . . . 12 A4
Plover Cl PO36 . . . . 35 C3
Plymouth St PO5 . . . . . . 54 B2
Polecloise La PO30 . . . . . 19 E7
Poles La SO41 . . . . 48 E1
POLYGON 50 E6
Polygon Ct SO15 . . . . . . 50 E6
Polygon Sch SO15 . . . . . 50 E6
Polygon The SO15 . . . . . 50 E5
Pomona Rd PO37 . . . . . . 43 C7
Pompey Ctr PO4 . . . . 53 F5
Pompey Ctr Trad Pk The
. . . . 53 F5
Poncast La PO33 . . . . 11 C1
Pond La PO34 . . . . 13 C3
PONDWELL 13 A3
Pondwell Cl PO33 . . . . . . 13 B3
Pondwell Hill PO33 . . . . . 13 B3
Ponsonby Ho PO5 . . . . . . 54 B2
Poole Rd SO19 . . . . 51 E4
Popham Rd PO37 . . . . . . 43 C6
Poplar Ct PO35 . . . . 25 F4
Poplar St SO19 . . . . 51 F6
Poplars The
Bembridge PO35 . . . . . . 25 D4
Fishbourne PO33 . . . . . 11 B6
Porchester Rd SO19 . . . . 51 E3
PORCHFIELD 7 B1
Porchfield Bsns Pk PO30 . 7 B1
Porchester Rd PO2 . . . . . 53 E8
Porter Ave PO36 . . . . 35 D3
Porter Ct PO36 . . . . 35 D3
Porter's La PO1 . . . . 53 A3
Portland Bldgs 5 PO12 . . 52 C5
Portland Ho 7 PO12 . . . . 52 D5
Portland Rd PO5 . . . . 53 C2
Portland St
Newport PO30 . . . . 20 D6
Portsmouth PO1 . . . . . . 53 B5
Southampton SO14 . . . . 50 F4
Port La Salle PO41 . . . . . 15 F6
PORTMORE 49 A7
Port Royal St PO5 . . . . . . 54 C3
PORTSEA 53 B6
PORTSEA ISLAND 53 F6
Portside Ct SO40 . . . . . . 50 A3
PORTSMOUTH 54 A4
Portsmouth City Mus &
Gallery* PO1 . . . . 53 B3
Portsmouth Gram Jun Sch 1
PO1 . . . . 53 B4
Portsmouth Gram Sch 5
PO1 . . . . 53 B3
Portsmouth Harbour Sta
PO1 . . . . 52 F6
Portsmouth High Sch
27 Portsmouth PO5 . . . 53 C2
Portsmouth PO5 . . . . . . 54 A1
Portsmouth & Southsea Sta
PO1 . . . . 54 B3
Portswood Ave SO17 . . . 51 B8
PORTSWOOD PARK 51 B8
Portswood Rd SO17 . . . . 51 B8
Postern Cl 3 PO36 . . . . . 50 F3
Postern Rd PO30 . . . . 8 F1
POUND GREEN 27 B8
Pound La
Calbourne PO30 . . . . . . 18 B5
Shanklin PO37 . . . . 31 A1
Ventnor PO38 . . . . 47 A6
Pound Mead PO33 . . . . . 11 A4
Pound Rd SO41 . . . . 48 B2
Pound Tree Rd SO14 . . . . 51 A4
Powell Cl PO30 . . . . 21 B7
Powell Ho PO30 . . . . 20 E7
Powell Rd PO1 . . . . 53 E6
Powerscourt Rd PO2 . . . 53 E8
Powlett Rd SO41 . . . . 48 E3
Poynings Pl PO1 . . . . 53 A4
Presidents Ct 12 PO12 . . 52 C9
Preston Cl PO33 . . . . 12 D3
Preston Rd
Bembridge PO35 . . . . . . 25 D4

Preston Rd continued
Portsmouth PO1 ....53 F8
Pretoria Rd PO4 ....53 F3
PRIDDY'S HARD 52 C8
Priestlands La SO41 ......48 C3
Priestlands Pl SO41 ......48 D3
Priestlands Rd SO41 ......48 C3
Priestlands Sch SO41 .....48 D2
Prince Alfred St PO12 ....52 B4
Prince George St PO1 .....53 A5
Princelett Shute PO36 ....34 D3
Prince of Wales Ave SO15 .50 A8
Prince of Wales Entrance
  PO32 ....3 E2
Prince of Wales Rd 3
  PO12 ....52 C5
Prince Regent Ct PO5 .....54 B2
Princes Cl PO29 ....14 E1
Princes Ct 2 SO14 ....11 C6
Prince's Ct 4 PO1 ....53 D7
Prince's Espl 2 ....2 D5
Princes Ho
  Portsmouth PO5 ....54 A1
  8 Southampton SO14 ......11 C6
Prince's Pl 1 PO1 ....53 D7
Princes Rd
  Freshwater PO40 ....14 E1
  Southampton SO15 ....50 D6
Princess Cl PO32 ....33 D3
Princess Royal Cl SO41 ...48 D4
Princes St PO31 ....3 A4
Prince's St
  Portsmouth PO1 ....53 D7
  Southampton SO14 ....11 C6
Prince St PO33 ....12 C5
Princes Way PO37 ....35 C2
Prior Cres PO30 ....9 A3
Priors Wlk PO30 ....20 B7
Priory Coll PO4 ....53 F5
Priory Ct
  Portsmouth PO5 ....54 D2
  Ventnor PO38 ....46 F6
Priory Dr PO34 ....13 D1
Priory Farm La PO30 ......20 B5
Priory Ho 6 SO14 ....51 A5
Priory Rd
  Carisbrooke PO30 ....20 A5
  Gosport PO12 ....52 B9
  Gosport PO12 ....52 C9
  Shanklin PO37 ....43 C6
  Southampton, St Denys
    SO17 ....51 C8
Priory Sch PO37 ....43 C3
Priory Wlk SO14 ....45 C4
Pritchetts Way PO38 ......33 A5
Private Rd SO41 ....48 E5
Privett Ho PO1 ....53 A6
Proctor La PO1 ....53 F5
Prospect Bsns Ctr The
  PO31 ....2 F2
Prospect Rd
  Cowes PO31 ....2 F2
  Newport PO30 ....20 E6
  Portsmouth PO1 ....53 C7
  Shanklin PO37 ....43 C6
Providence Ct 2 PO1 .....53 C7
Puckaster La PO38 ....45 B2
Puckpool Cl PO33 ....13 A4
Puckpool Hill PO33, PO34 .13 A4
Puckwell La PO38 ....45 B4
Pump House La PO32 ....3 D2
Pump La PO35 ....25 C6
Purbrook Rd PO1 ....53 E5
Purgle Rd PO30 ....20 B6
Pursley Cl PO34 ....35 C2
Pycroft Cl SO19 ....51 F5
Pye St PO1 ....54 B4
PYLE 44 C7
Pyle Shute PO38 ....39 F2
Pyle St PO30 ....20 D7
Pylewell Park Gdns*
  SO41 ....49 E4
Pyramids L Ctr PO5 ....53 D1
Pyrford Gdns 8 SO41 .....48 E2
Pyrford Mews SO41 ....48 E2

Q

Quarr Abbey* PO33 ....11 C6
Quarr Cl PO33 ....11 E5
Quarr Hill PO33 ....11 D5
Quarr Pl PO33 ....11 E5
Quarr Rd PO33 ....11 B6
Quarry La PO30 ....17 F4
Quarryside PO30 ....20 D5
Quarry View PO30 ....8 F1
Quarry View PO30 ....8 F1
Quarterdeck The PO1 ......52 E6
Quay 2000 SO14 ....51 C8
Quay Arts Ctr* PO30 .....20 E7
Quay Hill SO41 ....48 F4
Quay La PO36 ....24 B3
Quays 'Eddie Read'
  Swimming & Diving
  Complex The SO15 ....50 F3
Quayside Rd SO18 ....51 D7
Quay St
  Lymington SO41 ....48 F4
  Newport PO30 ....20 E7
  5 Yarmouth PO41 ....15 C6

R

Racecourse PO32 ....10 A4
Radcliffe Ct SO14 ....51 B5
Radcliffe Rd SO14 ....51 B6
Radnor St PO5 ....53 B2
Radstock Rd SO19 ....51 E3
Radway Cres SO15 ....50 D8
Raglan Ct PO12 ....52 A5
Raglan St PO5 ....54 C3
Railway Flats PO1 ....53 E5
Railway View PO1 ....53 A6
Railway View Rd SO17 .....51 C8
Rainbow Pl SO15 ....50 C6
Raleigh Ho 37 PO1 ....51 A5
Ramilies Ho 16 PO12 .....52 C5
Ramley Rd SO41 ....48 B3
Rampart Rd SO18 ....51 D7
Rampart Row PO12 ....52 E4
Rampart The SO41 ....48 D5
Ranalagh Dr PO30 ....11 B6
Randolph St SO15 ....50 C7
Ranelagh Ct 4 SO17 ......51 A8
Ranelagh Gdns SO15 ....50 C6
Ranelagh Rd PO36 ....35 E4
Ranger Cl SO41 ....51 B2
Rashley Mews SO41 ....48 E3
Ratcliffe Ave PO33 ....12 B4
Raven Croft PO5 ....54 B1
Raven Rd SO14 ....51 A8
Ravenscourt Rd SO41 ......48 D2
Ravenswood Gdns 12
  PO5 ....54 B1
Rawlinson Terr PO1 ....53 A6
Raymond Rd SO15 ....50 D7
Rayners PO38 ....46 E7
Rebecca Ct 16 PO30 ......20 D6
Recreation Ground Rd
  PO30 ....20 C6
Rectory Cl
  Gosport PO12 ....52 A3
  Wootton PO33 ....10 E5
Rectory Dr PO33 ....10 E5
Rectory La
  Brighstone PO30 ....30 B2
  Gatcombe PO30 ....32 C8
  Niton PO38 ....45 B4
Rectory Rd
  Niton PO38 ....45 B4
  Shanklin PO37 ....43 C6
Redan The PO12 ....52 C2
Redcliff Cl PO36 ....36 C5
Redhill Ho PO1 ....54 C4
Redhill La PO38 ....42 A6
Red House Mews SO41 ......48 E3
Redlake Rd PO40 ....15 B2
Redlands Dr SO19 ....51 F6
Redmoor Cl SO19 ....51 F6
Rednal Ho PO5 ....54 C3
Red Rd PO33 ....10 F5
Redshank Way PO30 ....9 E4
Redstart Cl PO30 ....20 B7
Redstone Bsns Ctr PO36 ...36 A4
Redver Gdns PO30 ....20 D8
Redvers Cl SO41 ....48 D2
Redwing Cl PO30 ....20 B6
Redwing Quay SO15 ....25 C5
Redwood Cl
  Carisbrooke PO30 ....20 B7
  Lymington SO41 ....48 D5
Reed's Pl PO12 ....52 B7
Reeds Rd PO33 ....52 B8
Reed St PO33 ....12 D4

Reeth Flats PO38 ....45 B2
Regency Ct 12 PO1 ....53 A4
Regent Ct 2 PO1 ....53 D7
Regent Pl PO5 ....54 A1
Regents Ct 8 SO16 ....50 B8
Regent's Gr 1 SO16 ......50 B8
Regents Park Com Coll 3
  SO16 ....50 A8
Regent's Park Gdns SO15 ..50 B7
Regent's Park Rd SO15 ....50 A7
Regents Pl PO12 ....52 D7
Regent St
  Portsmouth PO1 ....53 C7
  Shanklin PO37 ....43 C8
  Southampton SO14 ....11 A1
Regina Rd PO40 ....15 A1
Reigate Ho PO1 ....54 C4
Reldas The 9 PO1 ....53 A3
Renny Rd PO1 ....53 F5
Renouf Cl SO41 ....48 C3
Renown Ho 15 PO12 ....52 C5
Resolution Ho 14 PO12 ...52 C5
Retreat The PO5 ....54 B1
Revenge Ho 13 PO12 ......52 C5
Rew Cl PO38 ....40 A6
Rew Down Nature Reserve*
  PO38 ....46 E5
Rew La PO38 ....46 D7
Rew St
  Cowes PO31 ....2 D1
  Gurnard PO31 ....2 C2
REW STREET 2 C2
Rew Valley Sp Ctr PO38 ...46 E7
Reynolds Ct PO30 ....12 F4
Reynolds Rd
  Gosport PO12 ....52 C3
  Southampton SO15 ....51 A8
Rhododendron Wlk PO32 ....4 B2
Riboleau St PO33 ....12 C5
Ricardo Way SO41 ....48 D7
Richmond Ho 1 SO15 .....51 A8
Richmond Meade PO40 ......14 E1
Richmond Pl
  Portsmouth, Portsea PO1 ..53 A7
  Portsmouth, Southsea PO5 .53 C2
Richmond Rd
  Gosport PO12 ....52 A5
  Portsmouth PO5 ....53 D2
  Southampton SO15 ....50 C6
Richmond St SO14 ....51 B3
Richmond Terr 28 PO5 ....53 C2
Richville Rd SO16 ....50 A8
Ridge The PO31 ....9 B8
Ridget La PO30 ....29 C3
Ridgeway La SO41 ....48 D1
Ridgeway The PO36 ....35 F7
Rigby Rd SO17 ....51 B8
Ringbury SO41 ....48 D6
Ringwood Rd PO33 ....12 D5
Rink Rd PO33 ....12 D5
Rink Rd Ind Est PO33 ....12 E5
Ripplewood SO40 ....50 A1
Riverbourne Ct SO18 ......51 D8
River Ct SO41 ....48 F4
Riverdene Pl SO18 ....51 D8
River Rd PO41 ....15 C6
Riverside Bsns Pk SO41 ...48 F4
Riverside Cl
  Southampton, Bitterne Manor
    SO18 ....51 C7
  Southampton, Bitterne
    SO18 ....51 D8
Rivers Reach SO41 ....48 F3
River's St PO5 ....54 C2
River View PO32 ....9 F8
River View Ho SO19 ....51 D3
Riverview Pk PO30 ....9 C3
River Way PO30 ....20 C6
RN Submarine Mus & HMS
  Alliance* PO12 ....52 E4
Road View PO1 ....53 C8
Robere Ho SO19 ....51 E5
Robert Mack Ct 30 PO1 ...53 A5
Roberts Rd SO15 ....50 E5
Robin Ct SO15 ....50 F8
Robin Hill Countryside
  Adventure Pk* PO30 ...21 F4
Robin Hood St PO30 ....20 E7
Rochester Rd PO4 ....53 F3
Rochester St SO14 ....51 C5
ROCK 30 A4
Rockstone Ct 2 SO14 .....51 A6
Rockstone La SO14 ....51 A6
Rockstone Pl SO15 ....50 F6
Rodney Ho 9 PO12 ....52 D5
Roebuck Dr PO12 ....52 C8
Rogate Ho 1 PO1 ....54 C4
Rogers Cl PO12 ....52 B7
Rogers The PO37 ....35 C2
Rolfs Cl PO35 ....25 E4
Rolla Ct 8 PO30 ....20 D6
Rollesbrook Gdns SO15 ....50 F6
Rolls Cl PO31 ....8 A6
Rolls Hill Rd PO31 ....8 A7
Roman Ho SO18 ....51 C7
Romsey Cl SO15 ....50 D6
Ronsons Cl PO31 ....3 A3
Ronstan Gdns PO40 ....15 B2
Rooke Ho 17 PO1 ....53 A5
Rookes La SO41 ....48 E2
Rooke St PO30 ....9 E4
ROOKLEY 32 F5
Rookley Ctry Pk* PO38 ...33 A4
ROOKLEY GREEN 32 F4
Rope Quays PO12 ....52 D6
Rope Walk 4 PO31 ....3 B4
Rope Wlk PO34 ....13 D4

Rosalind Ct PO33 ....12 C4
Roseberry Ct PO36 ....35 E5
Rosebrook Ct 4 SO18 ....51 A7
Rose Cl PO36 ....24 A3
Rose Ct PO36 ....34 E4
Rosemary La
  20 Portsmouth PO1 ....53 A5
  Ryde PO33 ....12 C3
Rosemary Vineyard*
  PO33 ....12 C2
Rosemead PO36 ....35 D3
Rosemount PO36 ....35 E4
Rose Rd SO14 ....51 A8
Rosery The PO12 ....52 B2
Rosetta Dr PO32 ....3 C3
Roseway PO36 ....35 D5
Rosewood Gdns SO40 ......50 A1
Rosida Gdns SO15 ....50 E6
ROSLIN 32 C1
Roslyn Ho PO5 ....54 B1
Rosoman Cl SO19 ....51 F4
Rosoman Ho SO19 ....51 F4
Rosoman Rd SO19 ....51 F4
Rossington Ave SO18 .....51 F8
Rossington Way SO18 .....51 F7
Rostrevor La 8 PO4 .....53 E1
Rostrevor Mans 8 PO4 ...53 E1
Rosyth Rd SO18 ....51 F7
Rotary Ct PO33 ....12 B3
Rotary Ho SO15 ....50 D8
Rothesay Rd PO12 ....52 A8
Rothschild Cl SO19 ......51 E1
ROUD 41 B5
Roud La PO38 ....41 B5
Rougemont PO33 ....12 E4
Roundhouse Ct SO41 ......48 D3
Rowan Cl
  Portsmouth PO4 ....53 F4
  Southampton SO19 ....51 F3
Rowan Gdns PO30 ....20 C7
Rowans Pk SO41 ....48 D5
Rowans The PO33 ....12 D4
Rowantree Dr PO34 ....13 D2
Rowborough La PO30 .....24 B4
Rowborough Rd SO18 .....51 F8
Rowena Ct PO5 ....54 C2
Rowlands Cross PO33 .....11 D2
Rowlands La PO33 ....22 E6
Rowridge La PO30 ....19 A2
Roxan Ct 8 SO15 ....50 F7
Royal Cl PO37 ....35 C2
Royal Cres PO36 ....35 F5
Royal Crescent Rd 10
  SO14 ....51 B3
Royal Entrance PO32 ......3 E3
Royal Exchange PO30 .....20 F7
Royal Mews 15 PO5 ......53 D2
Royal Naval Mus* PO1 ...52 F7
Royal South Hants Hospl
  SO14 ....51 A6
Royal St PO30 ....35 F5
Royal Wlk PO33 ....12 F5
Rudd Way 18 SO14 ....51 B3
Rudmore Rd PO2 ....53 C8
Rudmore Sq PO2 ....53 C8
Rufflers Way PO33 ....11 F5
Rugby Rd PO5 ....54 D1
Ruskins The PO35 ....25 C5
Russell Ho PO30 ....20 F8
Russell Rd PO30 ....31 B2
Russell St
  Gosport PO12 ....52 A7
  11 Southampton SO14 ....51 A3
Russet Cl 3 SO41 ....48 F2
Rustington Ho 3 PO1 ....54 B3
Rychris Ct PO37 ....43 C3
Rydal Rd PO12 ....52 A9
RYDE 12 E6
Ryde Bsns Pk PO33 ......12 D3
Ryde Ct 3 SO14 ....51 A3
Ryde Esplanade Sta PO33 .12 C6
Ryde High Sch PO33 .....12 A4
Ryde House Dr PO33 .....12 A6
Ryde Pier Head Sta PO33 .12 C8
Ryde Rd PO34 ....13 D4
Ryde Sch with Upper Chine
  PO33 ....12 B5
Ryde Terr SO14 ....51 B3

S

Sackville St PO5 ....54 B2
Sadlers Cl PO33 ....12 E4
Sainsbury Lodge PO1 .....54 D3
St Agathas Way PO1 ......54 B4
St Alban's Gdns PO36 ....46 F6
St Albans Rd PO4 ....53 F3
St Alban's Rd
  Southampton SO14 ....51 B5
  Ventnor PO38 ....46 F6
St Andrews Ho 8 SO17 ...51 B8
St Andrews Rd SO41 ......51 A5
St Andrew's Rd
  Gosport PO12 ....52 B5
  Portsmouth PO5 ....54 C2
St Andrew's St 7 PO1 ...53 B4
St Andrews Way PO40 .....14 F2
St Annes Gdns SO41 ......48 D3
St Anne's Gdns SO19 .....51 A8
St Annes Mews 8 SO14 ...51 A8
St Anne's RC Sch SO15 ...50 F6
St Anne's Rd SO19 ....51 E2
St Ann's Cres PO12 ......52 A7
St Ann's Rd PO4 ....53 F3
St Augustine Rd PO4 .....53 F3
St Augustines Rd PO30 ...20 B7
St Barbara PO40 ....14 E3

St Barbe Mus & Art Gall*
  SO41 ....48 E4
St Bartholomew's Gdns
  PO5 ....54 C1
St Bernard Ho 18 SO14 ..51 A3
St Boniface CE Prim Sch
  PO38 ....47 B6
St Boniface Cliff Rd PO37 .35 D1
St Boniface Gdns PO38 ...47 B6
St Boniface Rd PO38 .....47 B6
St Boniface Terr PO38 ....47 B6
St Catherine's Lighthouse*
  PO38 ....44 F1
St Catherine's Oratory*
  PO38 ....44 E5
St Catherine's Rd SO18 ...51 E8
St Catherines Rd SO18 ...51 E8
St Catherine's Rd PO38 ...45 A2
St Catherine's Sch PO38 ..47 A6
St Catherine View
  Portsmouth PO5 ....53 D1
  Ventnor PO38 ....47 B6
St Catherines View
  Godshill PO38 ....41 C8
  Ventnor PO38 ....47 B6
St Christopher Ct 1 PO5 .53 E1
St Cross Bsns Pk PO30 ....9 B2
St Cross Ct 1 PO30 ......20 D7
St Cross La PO30 ....20 D7
St Cyres Memorial Cotts
  SO41 ....48 F5
St David's Rd
  East Cowes PO32 ....3 C3
  Portsmouth PO5 ....54 C2
ST DENYS 51 C8
St Denys Sta SO17 ....51 C8
St Edmunds PO38 ....40 A4
St Edmunds Cotts PO33 ...10 E6
St Edmunds RC Sec Sch
  PO1 ....54 C3
St Edmund's Rd SO16 .....50 B8
St Edmunds Wlk PO33 .....10 E5
St Edward's Rd
  Gosport PO12 ....52 B5
  Portsmouth PO5 ....54 B1
St Edward's Terr 6 PO12 .52 A7
St Faith's Cl PO12 ......52 A6
St Faith's Rd
  Cowes PO31 ....3 A3
  Southampton SO14 ....54 B4
St Francis Rd PO12 ......52 C2
St Georges App PO30 .....20 E6
St George's Beneficial CE
  Prim Sch 45 PO1 ......53 A5
St George's Bsns Ctr 44
  PO1 ....53 A5
St George's Cl PO33 .....12 D8
St George's La PO5 ......54 A1
St Georges Ho 47 SO17 ..51 B8
St Georges La PO30 .....20 F4
St George's Rd
  Portsmouth, Old Portsmouth
    PO1 ....53 A4
  Ryde PO33 ....12 B6
  Shanklin PO37 ....43 C8
St Georges Sq PO1 ......53 A5
St George's St SO14 .....51 A4
St Georges Way PO1 .....53 A5
St George's Way PO1 .....53 A5
St Georges Wlk PO12 ....52 A6
ST HELENS 24 F6
St Helens Cl PO4 ....53 F2
St Helen's Mans 7 PO4 ..53 E1
St Helen's Par PO4 ......53 E1
St Helen's Prim Sch PO33 .24 F7
St Helier Rd PO12 ....52 C9
St James Cl
  East Cowes PO32 ....3 D4
  Yarmouth PO41 ....15 C6
St James Ct 4 SO30 .....20 D6
St James Ho 14 SO14 ....51 A3
St James' Sq 5 PO30 ....20 D7
St James' Sq 2 PO41 ....15 C6
St James's Rd
  Portsmouth PO5 ....54 B2
  Southampton SO15 ....50 D8
St James's St
  Newport PO30 ....20 D7
  Portsmouth PO1 ....53 B5
St James' St
  Newport PO30 ....20 D6
  8 Ryde PO33 ....12 C6
  Yarmouth PO41 ....15 C6
St James's Rd SO41 .....12 C4
St John's CE Prim Sch
  Gosport PO12 ....52 B8
  Sandown PO36 ....35 F6
St Johns Cl PO12 ....20 D5
St John's Coll PO5 ......54 C1
St John's Cres PO36 ....34 A4
St John's Hill PO33 .....12 D4
St Johns Inf Sch 13 SO14 .50 F3
St Johns Mews PO5 ......54 C1
ST JOHN'S PARK 12 E4
St John's Pl PO14 ....20 D6
St John's RC Cath* PO1 ..54 A4
St Johns RC Prim Sch
  PO1 ....54 C3
St John's Rd
  Newport PO30 ....20 D6
  Ryde PO33 ....12 D5
  Sandown PO36 ....35 F5
  Shanklin PO37 ....43 C7
  Wroxall PO38 ....42 B5
St John's Road Sta PO33 ..12 D4
St Johns Sq 6 PO12 .....52 B6
St John's Wood Rd PO33 ..12 D5

St Joseph's Cl PO32 .... 3 E2
St Josephs Mews PO5 ...... 54 C1
St Jude's CE (Controlled)
   Prim Sch PO1 .... 53 B3
St Judes Cl PO5 .... 54 B1
ST LAWRENCE 46 A3
St Lawrence Rd PO38 ...... 46 E7
St Lawrence Shute PO38 .. 46 B4
St Luke's CE Sec Sch PO5 54 B3
St Lukes Dr PO35 .... 24 D3
St Luke's Rd PO12 .... 52 A7
St Margarets PO38 .... 46 F7
St Margarets CE Prim Sch
   PO38 .... 46 E7
St Margarets Glade PO38 .. 46 E7
St Mark's CE Jun Sch
   SO15 .... 50 D7
St Mark's Cl PO12 .... 52 B2
St Marks Cl ▮ PO12 ...... 52 A1
St Mark's Rd PO12 .... 52 B3
St Marks Rd
   Lymington SO41 .... 48 D3
   Southampton SO14 ...... 51 B5
St Mark's Rd PO12 .... 52 A4
St Martin's Ave PO37 ...... 53 D1
St Martin's Ho ▮ PO5 .... 53 D1
St Martins Rd PO38 .... 42 C4
St Mary's Ave PO12 ...... 52 A3
St Mary's CE Prim Sch
   SO14 .... 51 B4
St Mary's Cl PO33 .... 12 B3
St Mary's Coll SO18 ...... 51 F8
St Mary's Ct PO36 .... 24 B3
St Mary's Hospl (Newport)
   PO30 .... 9 A1
St Mary's Hospl
   (Portsmouth) PO1 ...... 53 F6
St Mary's L Ctr SO14 ...... 51 B4
St Mary's Pas ▮ PO33 .... 12 C5
St Mary's Pl SO14 .... 51 A4
St Mary's RC Prim Sch
   Gosport PO12 .... 52 A6
   Ryde PO33 .... 12 E5
St Mary's Rd
   Brading PO36 .... 24 A3
   Cowes PO31 .... 3 A4
   Portsmouth PO1 .... 53 F6
   Southampton SO14 ...... 51 A6
St Mary's Stad
   (Southampton FC) SO14 . 51 B5
St Mary St SO14 .... 51 B4
St Matthews Cl ▮ SO14 .. 51 A5
St Matthews Ct PO12 ...... 52 D6
St Michael's Ave PO33 .... 12 B3
St Michaels Cl PO30 ...... 17 F7
St Michaels Rd PO33 ...... 24 A4
St Michael's Rd PO1 ...... 54 A2
St Michael's Sq ▮ SO14 .. 50 F3
St Michael's St ▮ SO14 .. 50 F3
St Nicholas Ct PO30 ...... 20 D5
St Nicholas St PO1 .... 53 A3
St Patrick's RC Prim Sch
   SO19 .... 51 E3
St Paul's Ave PO37 .... 43 C8
St Paul's Cres PO37 ...... 43 C8
St Paul Rd PO5 .... 54 A2
St Paul's Sq PO5 .... 54 A2
St Paul's View Rd PO30 .. 20 E8
St Peter's Gr PO5 .... 54 C1
St Pete Way PO30 .... 35 F6
St Ronan's Ave PO4 ...... 53 E2
St Ronan's Rd PO4 ...... 53 E2
St Saviours RC Prim Sch
   PO39 .... 26 H7
St Saviour's Rd PO39 .... 26 H8
St Simons Rd PO33 ...... 53 B2
St Stephens Rd PO2 ...... 53 C8
St Swithins Cres PO41 .... 15 F6
St Swithuns Ct ▮ SO14 .. 51 A5
St Swithun's RC Prim Sch ▮
   PO5 .... 53 D2
St Thomas of Canterbury RC
   Prim Sch PO30 .... 20 B5
St Thomas Pk SO41 ...... 48 D3
St Thomas Rd PO32 ...... 3 D4
St Thomas's Cl ▮ PO33 .. 12 C6
St Thomas's Sq PO33 .... 12 C6
St Thomas's Rd PO12 .... 52 B8
St Thomas's Sq ▮ PO30 . 20 D7
St Thomas's St
   Lymington SO41 .... 48 D3
   Portsmouth PO1 .... 53 A3
St Thomas' St PO33 ...... 12 C6
St Urians PO36 .... 35 D4
St Ursula Gr PO5 .... 54 C1
St Valerie Rd PO12 ...... 52 B4
St Vincent Coll PO12 .... 52 B6
St Vincent Rd
   Gosport PO12 .... 52 B7
   Portsmouth PO5 .... 53 D2
St Vincents Cl PO33 ...... 12 A5
St Vincent's Rd PO33 .... 12 A5
St Vincent St PO5 .... 54 A2
St Wilfrids Prim Sch
   PO38 .... 47 B6
Salcombe Rd SO15 ...... 50 C7
Salem Rd PO37 .... 43 C7
Salisbury Rd
   Portsmouth PO4 .... 53 F2
   Ryde PO33 .... 12 E3
Salisbury St ▮ SO15 .... 50 F6
Salisbury Way PO36 ...... 35 F6
Salsette Ct PO33 .... 12 E6
Salterne Ho ▮ SO41 .... 48 E2
Salterns's Rd PO34 ...... 13 D4

Salter's Rd PO33 .... 12 A3
Saltmarsh Rd SO14 ...... 51 B3
Samantha Ct PO37 ...... 43 D8
Samber Cl SO41 .... 48 C4
Samber Mill PO30 .... 39 A8
Samphire Cl SO41 .... 48 E5
Sampson Rd PO1 .... 52 F7
Samuel Rd PO1 .... 53 F6
Sandcove Rise PO34 .... 13 D3
Sandcroft Ave PO33 ...... 12 C4
SANDFORD 42 A8
Sandford Barns PO38 .... 41 F8
Sandford Cotts PO38 .... 41 F8
Sandham Cl PO36 .... 35 E7
Sandham Gdns PO36 .... 35 C3
Sandham Mid Sch PO36 .. 35 D6
Sandhurst Cl PO5 .... 54 C1
Sandhurst Rd SO15 ...... 50 E6
San Diego Rd PO12 ...... 52 B7
Sandlands PO34 .... 13 D3
Sandon Ct PO36 .... 35 E5
SANDOWN 35 E5
Sandown CE Prim Sch
   PO36 .... 35 F6
Sandown High School
   PO36 .... 35 D6
Sandown Rd
   Bembridge PO35 .... 25 B2
   Brading PO35 .... 24 D1
   Sandown PO36 .... 35 D2
   Sandown Sta PO36 ...... 35 E5
Sandpath SO31 .... 11 E5
Sandpiper PO34 .... 13 D3
Sandpipers PO35 .... 25 A4
Sandringham Ct
   ▮ Gosport PO12 .... 52 C9
   ▮ Southampton, Millbrook
      SO15 .... 50 A6
Sandringham La PO1 .... 54 D3
Sandrock Rd PO38 ...... 45 A2
Sandy Cl PO30 .... 20 F1
Sandy La
   Blackwater PO30 .... 20 D1
   Shanklin PO37 .... 35 C1
Sandy Way PO30 .... 35 D7
Sapphire Cl ▮ PO12 .... 52 C8
Saracen Cl SO41 .... 48 C1
Sarah Robinson Ho ▮▮
   PO1 .... 53 A5
Sarum Wlk SO41 .... 48 D6
Saunders Dr PO31 ...... 3 A2
Savoy Country Club PO41 . 15 A3
Savoy Ct
   Newport PO30 .... 20 E7
   Sandown PO36 .... 36 A3
   Shanklin PO37 .... 43 C7
Saxon Ho ▮▮ SO14 ...... 51 C6
Saxon Pl SO41 .... 48 D6
Saxon Rd SO15 .... 50 D5
Scarrots La PO30 .... 20 D7
School Cl PO36 .... 34 E7
School Cres PO38 ...... 33 E1
SCHOOL GREEN 14 F1
School Green Rd PO40 .. 14 F1
School Hill Rd PO32 .... 3 C3
School La
   Arreton PO30 .... 21 F2
   Calbourne PO30 .... 18 A2
   Carisbrooke PO30 ...... 20 A5
   Lymington SO41 .... 48 E6
   Lymington, Warborne SO41 . 48 F4
   Newchurch PO36 ...... 34 E7
   Newport PO30 .... 20 D7
   Niton PO38 .... 45 B4
   Wootton PO33 .... 10 F5
School Pl SO19 .... 51 E4
School Rd PO38 .... 41 D8
School St PO33 .... 12 C4
Scinde Cres PO37 ...... 43 C8
Sconce Rd PO41 .... 15 A6
Scotchells Brook La PO36 35 B4
Scotchell's Cl PO37 .... 35 C2
Scott Rd
   Portsmouth, Portsea Island
      PO1 .... 52 F7
Scotts Cl PO30 .... 20 D7
Scullards La ▮ SO14 .. 50 F4
Sea Breeze Cotts PO30 .. 29 F1
Sea Cl
   Ryde PO33 .... 12 B6
   Sandown PO36 .... 35 D2
SEAFIELD 52 D4
Seafield Rd PO34 ...... 13 D4
Seafield Terr PO12 ...... 52 C9
Seager's Ct PO1 .... 53 A4
Seagrove Cl PO34 ...... 13 D3
Seagrove Dr PO36 ...... 35 F6
Seagrove Farm Rd PO34 . 13 D3
Seagrove Manor PO34 .. 13 D3
Seagrove Manor Rd PO34 13 D3
Seahorse Wlk PO12 ...... 52 D6
Sealark Rd PO12 .... 52 B8
Sea Mill Gdns ▮▮ PO1 .. 53 A5
Sea Rd SO19 .... 51 D4
Searle Cl PO12 .... 52 C4
Seaton Cl SO41 .... 48 E5
SEAVIEW 13 C3
Seaview Cotts ▮ PO39 .. 14 D1
Seaview Ho PO33 ...... 13 E3
Seaview Rd PO31 ...... 3 A3
Sea View Rd
   Cranmore PO41 .... 5 E2
   Totland PO40 .... 14 D2

Seaview Wildlife Encounter*
   PO34 .... 13 B4
Seaward Gdns SO19 .... 51 E4
Seaward Rd SO19 ...... 51 E4
Seaward Twr ▮▮ PO12 .. 52 E5
Sedgeley Gr PO12 ...... 52 A8
Sedgley Cl PO5 .... 54 C2
Selborne Gdns PO12 .... 52 A5
Selborne Terr PO1 ...... 54 D3
Seldon Ave PO33 .... 12 F4
Selhurst Ho PO1 .... 54 C3
Sellwood Rd PO40 ...... 27 C7
Selma Cl ▮ PO5 .... 53 D2
Selman Gdns PO31 ...... 8 F8
Selsey Ave PO12 .... 52 A9
Selsey View PO37 ...... 35 D1
Selwyn Ct PO33 .... 25 A6
Senator Ind Est PO36 .... 36 A5
Serpentine Rd ▮ PO5 .. 53 C2
Settle Cl SO41 .... 50 B8
Settlers Cl PO1 .... 54 C4
Seven Sisters Cl PO38 .. 46 A3
Seven Sisters Rd PO38 .. 46 A4
Seymour Cl PO2 .... 53 D7
Seymour Ct ▮ PO32 .... 3 C4
Seymour Pl PO5 .... 25 C6
Shaftesbury Rd
   Gosport PO12 .... 52 C4
   Portsmouth, Southsea PO5 53 C2
Shaftsbury Rd PO12 .... 52 C4
Shakespeare Ave SO17 . 51 B8
Shakespeare Rd PO1 .... 53 E7
Shakespeare Terr ▮▮ PO12 53 A3
Shalbourne Rd PO12 .... 52 A8
SHALCOMBE 29 A8
SHALFLEET 17 D7
Shalfleet CE Prim Sch
   PO41 .... 17 B7
Shallow La SO41 .... 48 E8
Shamblers Rd PO31 .... 3 B3
Shamrock Cl PO12 ...... 52 D8
Shamrock Quay SO14 .. 51 D5
Shamrock Rd SO19 .... 51 D5
SHANKLIN 43 D7
Shanklin CE Prim Sch
   PO37 .... 43 B7
Shanklin Chine* PO37 .. 43 C7
Shanklin Rd
   Godshill PO38 .... 41 F8
   Shanklin PO37 .... 42 F4
Shanklin Sta PO37 ...... 43 C8
Shanklin Twrs PO37 .... 43 C7
Shannon Ct ▮ PO12 .... 52 C9
Shannon Rd ▮ SO14 .. 51 C5
Shaplands Mews ▮ PO33 12 C6
Sharon Ct
   Cowes PO31 .... 3 A6
   ▮ Gosport PO12 ...... 52 E5
Sharon Orchard* PO33 . 12 C2
Shearer Rd PO1 .... 53 E7
Sheat Farm Ind Est PO30 32 C6
Sheffield Rd PO1 .... 54 D3
Sheilings The PO30 ...... 14 E2
Shelley Ct SO15 .... 50 E5
Shepheard's Way PO12 . 52 C3
Shepherd Mews ▮ PO33 12 C6
Shepherds' La PO30 .... 34 B8
Sherborne St PO33 ...... 25 C5
Sherbourne Ave PO33 .. 22 A5
Sherfield Ho SO14 ...... 50 E7
Sherwin Wlk PO12 ...... 52 A4
Sherwood Rd
   Gosport PO12 .... 52 A5
   Newport PO30 .... 9 A1
Shide Chalk Pit Nature
   Reserve* PO30 .... 20 F5
Shide Cross PO30 ...... 20 D5
Shide Cl PO30 .... 20 E5
Shide Rd PO30 .... 20 E5
Shide Villa PO30 .... 20 E5
Shiner Cl PO34 .... 13 C2
Shipbuilding Rd PO1 .... 52 F8
Ship Leopard St ▮▮ PO1 53 A5
Shippards Rd PO30 ...... 30 A2
SHIRLEY 50 C8
Shirley Ave SO15 ...... 50 C8
Shirley Bsns Pk SO15 .. 50 C6
Shirley High St SO15 ..
   SO16 .... 50 B8
Shirley Rd
   Portsmouth PO5 .... 53 E2
   Southampton SO15 ...... 50 C7
Shirley Twrs SO15 ...... 50 C7
Sholing Rd SO19 .... 51 F4
Sholing Sta SO19 ...... 51 F2
Shooters Hill PO3 ...... 3 B4
Shore Hill PO38 .... 47 A5
Shore Path PO12 .... 2 D4
Shore Rd
   Gurnard PO31 .... 2 D4
   Ventnor PO38 .... 47 C5
Short Row PO1 .... 53 A6
SHORWELL 31 B3
Shorwell Shute PO30 .. 31 B4
Shotts La SO41 .... 49 C4
Shrewsbury Ct PO34 .... 13 D3
Shrubbery Dr PO33 .... 11 E5
Shrubb's Ave SO41 .... 48 E4
Shute The PO36 .... 34 E8
Sibden Hill & Batts Copse
   Nature Reserve* PO37 43 A7
Sibden Mews SO19 .... 43 C7
Sibden Rd PO37 .... 43 B7
Sidings The PO31 ...... 3 B3
Silcombe La PO40 ...... 14 E1

Silver Birch Dr PO30 .... 20 B7
Silverdale Ct ▮ SO15 .. 50 E7
Silverdale Rd SO15 .... 50 E7
Silver St ▮ PO5 .... 54 A1
Silver Trees PO37 ...... 43 A7
Simeon St PO33 .... 12 D6
Simmonds Cl PO40 .... 27 C7
Simnel St ▮ SO14 ...... 50 F3
Sirenia Cl PO30 .... 30 A2
Sir George's Rd SO15 .. 50 D6
Sirius Cl PO34 .... 13 D2
Sirius Ct PO5 .... 54 B2
Sirius Ho ▮▮ PO5 ...... 53 D2
Sir Max Aitken Mus* PO31 3 B5
Six Cotts PO32 .... 10 A7
Six Dials SO14 .... 51 A5
Skinner's Hill PO36 .... 34 F6
Skipper Cl SO40 .... 50 A3
Slade Rd PO33 .... 12 D4
Slay La PO38 .... 45 D7
Slindon St PO1 .... 54 B3
Slingsby Cl PO1 .... 54 A1
Slipway The PO31 ...... 2 F3
Sloane Stanley Ct PO12 52 B7
Slocum Rd ▮▮ PO12 .... 52 C5
Sloop La PO33 .... 10 F5
Smallbrook Junction*
   PO33 .... 12 D2
Smallbrook La PO33 .... 12 D2
Smallbrook Stadium
   PO33 .... 12 C1
Smart's Cross PO38 .... 41 C4
Smithards La PO31 .... 3 B3
Smith St PO12 .... 52 A6
Snook's Hill PO30 ...... 20 C7
Snooks La SO41 .... 49 B6
Snowberry Rd PO30 .... 20 C7
Snowdrop La PO30 .... 32 A8
Soberton Ho PO1 ...... 54 C4
Solent Ave SO41 .... 49 A3
Solent Bsns Ctr SO15 .. 50 B6
Solent Cl
   Lymington SO41 .... 48 F3
   Ryde PO33 .... 12 F5
Solent Gate ▮▮ PO5 .... 53 E1
Solent Gdns
   Freshwater PO40 ...... 14 C2
   Ryde PO33 .... 11 F5
Solent Hill PO40 ...... 14 F3
Solent Ind Ctr SO15 .... 50 C6
Solent Landing PO35 .. 25 B4
Solent Mead SO41 .... 48 E3
Solent Mid Sch PO31 .. 2 F7
Solent Rd
   Cranmore PO41 .... 5 E1
   Southampton SO15 .... 50 E4
Solent View
   Bembridge PO35 ...... 25 D5
   Totland PO40 .... 14 D2
   Walhampton SO41 .... 49 B3
Solent View Ct PO34 .. 13 D3
Solent View Rd
   Gurnard PO31 .... 2 D3
   Seaview PO34 .... 13 D2
Solihull Ho PO5 .... 54 A2
Solway Ho ▮▮ SO14 .... 51 C6
Somborne Ho PO1 .... 54 C4
Somerset Ct ▮ SO15 .. 50 C6
Somerset Rd
   Portsmouth PO5 .... 53 D1
   Ryde PO33 .... 12 E3
   Seaview PO34 .... 13 D3
Somerset Terr SO15 .... 50 C6
Somers Park Prim Sch
   PO5 .... 54 C3
Somers Rd
   Portsmouth PO5 .... 53 D1
   Portsmouth PO5 .... 54 C3
Somers Road N PO1 .... 54 C3
Somerton Ind Pk PO31 . 3 A2
Somerton Mid Sch PO31 . 3 A2
Somervell Cl PO12 ...... 52 A3
Sommers Ct SO19 ...... 51 C3
SOUTHAMPTON 50 D3
Southampton Central Sta
   SO15 .... 50 E5
Southampton City Art Gall*
   SO15 .... 50 F5
Southampton City Coll
   SO14 .... 51 B4
Southampton Maritime
   Mus* SO14 .... 50 F3
Southampton Oceanography
   Ctr SO14 .... 51 B2
Southampton Rd SO40 .. 50 A5
Southampton Solent Univ ▮▮
   SO14 .... 51 A5
Southampton Solent Univ
   Marine Operations Ctr
   SO40 .... 50 A6
Southampton St ▮ SO15 50 F6
Southampton Wr Activity Ctr
   SO14 .... 51 C3
South Baddesley Rd SO41 49 F6
South Baddesley Prim Sch
   SO41 .... 49 E6
South Bank Rd PO32 .... 3 D2
Southbourne Rd SO41 .. 48 C3
Southbrook Rd ▮ SO15 . 50 E5
Southcliffe Ho ▮▮ SO14 . 51 A6
Southcliff Rd SO14 ...... 51 A7
South Cross St PO12 .. 52 D5

Southdown PO38 .... 39 E2
Southdown Mews PO40 . 27 E7
Southdown Rd PO40 .. 27 E7
Southern Rd
   Lymington SO41 ...... 48 D3
   Southampton SO15 .... 50 E4
Southfield Gdns PO33 .. 12 B3
SOUTHFORD 41 B2
Southford La PO38 .... 45 C8
South Front SO14 ...... 51 A4
South Gr SO41 .... 48 F3
Southgrove Rd PO38 .. 47 A6
Southgrove Terr PO38 .. 47 A6
Southlands SO41 ...... 48 C2
Southlands Sch & The Wing
   SO41 .... 48 F1
South Mill Rd SO15 .... 50 A4
South Normandy ▮ PO1 53 A4
South Parade PO5 ...... 53 D1
South Parade Pier* PO4 53 E1
South Quay PO33 ...... 25 A6
South Rd
   Cowes PO31 .... 3 B3
   Portsmouth, Portsea Island
      PO1 .... 53 E7
   Southampton SO17 .... 51 C8
SOUTHSEA 53 C1
Southsea Castle* PO5 .. 53 C1
Southsea Inf Sch ▮ PO33 53 E2
Southsea Model Village*
   PO4 .... 53 F1
Southsea Terr PO5 ...... 54 A1
South St
   Gosport PO12 .... 52 D5
   Lymington SO41 ...... 48 C2
   Newport PO30 .... 20 E7
   Portsmouth PO5 ...... 54 A1
   ▮▮ Ryde PO33 .... 12 C5
   Ventnor PO38 .... 47 B6
   Yarmouth PO41 ...... 15 D6
South Terr PO1 .... 53 A5
Southview ▮ PO4 ...... 53 F2
South View ▮ PO4 ...... 20 D6
South View Cotts PO38 . 40 A4
South View Rd SO15 .... 50 D8
Southwick Ho ▮ PO1 .. 54 C4
South Wight Sports Ctr
   PO36 .... 35 D5
Sovereign Ave PO12 .... 52 C8
Sovereign Way PO33 .. 12 B4
Spanners Cl PO38 ...... 40 A4
Spartina Dr SO41 ...... 48 F5
Spear Rd SO14 .... 51 A8
Speeds La PO33 .... 11 B1
Spencer Cl PO33 ...... 12 A6
Spencer Ct ▮ PO5 .... 53 D2
Spencer Glade PO33 .. 12 A6
Spencer Rd
   Portsmouth PO4 ...... 53 F2
   Ryde PO33 .... 12 B6
Spenlow Cl PO2 .... 53 D8
Spice Quay ▮ PO1 .... 53 A4
Spicer Ho PO1 .... 53 B6
Spicer St PO1 .... 54 B4
Spindleberry Cl PO30 .. 20 C7
Spindlers Rd PO38 .... 46 A3
Spinnaker Cl PO31 .... 2 F3
Spinnaker La PO30 .... 32 A3
Spinnaker Ct ▮▮ PO1 .. 53 A5
Spinnaker Quay PO12 .. 52 F4
Spinnaker Twr* PO1 .... 53 A4
Spitfire Ct SO19 ...... 51 D3
Spitfire Quay SO19 .... 51 C4
Spithead Ave PO12 .... 52 C2
Spithead Bsns Ctr PO36 35 C3
Spithead Cl PO34 ...... 13 D3
Spring Cl SO19 .... 51 F4
Spring Cres SO17 ...... 51 B8
Spring Ct ▮ SO15 ...... 50 E5
Springfield Cl SO41 .... 49 A3
Springfield Rd SO19 .. 51 F2
Springfield Mews PO36 . 35 F5
Spring Firs SO19 ...... 51 F3
Spring Garden La PO12 . 52 C6
Spring Gdns
   Portsmouth PO1 ...... 54 A3
   Shanklin PO37 .... 43 C8
   Ventnor PO38 .... 47 C6
Springhead PO38 ...... 45 A4
SPRINGHILL 3 E4
Spring Hill PO38 ...... 47 B6
Spring Hill Ct PO38 .... 47 B6
Springhill RC Prim Sch
   SO15 .... 50 E6
Spring La PO30 .... 20 B5
Spring Rd
   Lymington SO41 ...... 49 A2
   Southampton, Itchen SO19 . 51 F4
   Southampton, Merry Oak
      SO19 .... 51 F6
Spring St PO1 .... 54 B3
SPRING VALE 13 B4
Springvale Rd PO34 .. 13 B5
Spring Wlk
   Newport PO30 .... 19 F6
   Portsmouth PO1 ...... 54 B4
Square The
   Freshwater Bay PO40 . 27 C7
   Gosport PO12 .... 52 C9
   Lymington SO41 ...... 48 C3
Squires Wlk SO19 ...... 51 E1
Stacey Ct PO5 .... 53 C1
Stafford Rd
   Portsmouth PO5 ...... 54 C1
   Southampton SO15 .... 50 D6
Stag La PO30 .... 9 B4

Stag Rd PO36...........35 E3
Stainers Cl PO33.........12 C5
Stamford St PO1.........54 D4
Standford St PO14........51 B4
Stanford Gdns SO41......48 D2
Stanford Hill SO41........48 D3
Stanford Rd SO41........48 D3
Stanhope Dr PO31.........3 A6
Stanhope Gate 1 PO5....53 C2
Stanhope Lodge PO31.....2 F5
Stanhope Rd PO1.........54 B3
Stanley La PO5..........53 C2
Stanley Rd
  Cowes PO31............3 B3
  Lymington SO41........49 A2
Stanley St PO5...........54 A2
Stansted Rd PO5.........54 A7
Stanton Bldgs SO15......50 A7
Stanton Rd SO15.........50 A7
Stanton Rd Ind Est SO15...50 A7
STAPLERS..............21 A7
Staplers Ct PO30.........20 F7
Staplers Rd PO30........21 B7
Starkes Ho PO40.........27 C7
Starks Cl PO30...........31 B2
Star St PO33............12 C5
Station App
  Portsmouth PO1.......53 A5
  Sandown PO36.........35 E5
Station Ave PO36.........35 E5
Station Gdns PO36.......24 B2
Station La PO36..........35 E5
Station Rd
  Ashey PO33...........23 B7
  Bembridge PO35.......25 C6
  Brading PO36..........24 B3
  Newbridge PO41........17 C4
  Ningwood PO30, PO41...17 C6
  Sandown PO36.........35 E5
  Southampton, Sholing SO19..51 F3
  St Helens PO33........24 F6
  Wootton Bridge PO33...10 D3
  Wroxall PO38..........42 C4
  Yarmouth PO41........15 D5
Station St
  Lymington SO41........48 F4
  Portsmouth PO1.......54 B3
  Ryde PO33.............12 C5
Staunton St PO1.........54 B4
Steel St PO5.............54 A1
STEEPHILL..............46 E5
Steephill Court Rd PO38...46 D5
Steephill Down PO38.....46 F6
Steephill Rd
  Shanklin PO37.........43 C7
  Ventnor PO38..........46 E5
Steerforth Cl PO2.........53 D8
Stenbury View PO38......42 C3
Stephen Lodge PO5.......54 B1
Stephenson Cl PO2........52 A3
Stephenson Rd PO31.......3 A3
Steuart Rd SO18.........51 D7
Stewart Ct PO40.........15 A1
Stewart Pl PO1...........53 E7
Steyne Cross PO35.......25 C3
Steyne Rd
  Bembridge PO35........25 D4
  Seaview PO34.........13 D3
Stickworth Hall PO30......33 F7
Stirling Cl SO19..........51 F6
Stockpart Ave SO19......51 F6
Stoke Gdns PO12........52 C5
Stoke Rd PO12...........52 C5
Stokes Cl PO33..........50 E6
Stokeway 4 PO12........52 C5
Stonechat Cl PO30........20 B6
Stoneham Cotts PO33....11 E5
Stone La
  Gosport PO12..........52 B4
  25 Portsmouth PO1....52 B5
Stonelands Bsns PO33....11 F5
Stonelands Pk PO33......11 F5
Stonepitts Cl PO33.......12 A6
Stones Cl PO31...........3 A4
Stone St PO5............54 A1
Stony La PO1............53 A6
Stower PO36.............35 F7
Strand SO14............51 A4
Strand The PO33.........12 D6
Stratford Ho PO5........54 B2
Stratford Pl SO41........48 D5
Strathmore Rd PO12.....52 C5
Strathwell Cres PO38.....45 D6
Strawberry La PO30......29 E5
Stroud PO40.............27 C8
Stroud Wood Rd PO33....11 F2
Suffolk Ave SO15........50 D7
Sultan Rd PO1, PO2......53 D7
Summerfields Prim Sch
  PO30................20 F8
Summers Ct PO40........27 A8
Summers La PO39........26 H7
Summers St SO14........51 C6
Sunbeam Way PO12......52 B4
Sun Ct PO5.............54 C2
Sunderland SO14........51 B2
Sun Hill
  Calbourne PO30........18 B2
  Cowes PO31...........3 B5
Sunningdale Rd PO30....20 C6
Sunnyhill Cl PO33........35 C3
Sunnyside Gdns PO36....35 E4
Sunnyvale PO37.........43 C8
Sunny Wlk PO1..........53 A6
Sun Pl PO33............12 C5

Sunset Bgwls PO40......14 D2
Sunset Cl PO40..........14 F1
Sunset Dr PO36.........35 F6
Sun St PO1.............53 A5
Surbiton Gr PO33........12 D4
Surrey Cl SO15..........50 C6
Surrey Rd SO19.........51 D2
Surrey St
  Portsmouth PO1.......54 B3
  Ryde PO33............12 C4
Sussex Ct
  6 Gosport PO12......52 C9
Sussex Pl
  Portsmouth, Landport PO1..54 B4
  Portsmouth PO5.......54 B1
SUSSEX PLACE..........51 A4
Sussex Rd
  Portsmouth PO5.......54 B1
  Southampton SO14....51 A4
Sussex Terr PO5.........54 B1
Sutherland Rd PO4.......53 E4
Sutton Cl PO33..........12 D3
Suvretta Ho PO37........43 C7
Swains La PO35..........25 E5
Swains Rd PO35.........25 D5
Swallow Cl PO30.........20 A6
Swanage Cl SO19........51 E3
SWANMORE.............12 B8
Swanmore Mid Sch PO33..12 B3
Swanmore Rd SO19......12 B4
Swan Quay SO18.........51 D8
Sway Rd SO41...........48 B6
Swedish Hos SO41.......49 E8
Swift Gdns SO19.........51 D1
Swift Hollow SO19.......51 D1
Swift St SO19...........51 D1
Swiss Cottage Mus* PO32..4 B2
Swiss Cottage Rd PO32....4 A2
Sycamore Cl PO30.......20 C7
Sycamores The PO33....12 D4
Sydenham Ct PO1........54 D3
Sydenham Terr PO1......54 D3
Sydney Cl PO30.........20 C5
Sydney Cotts PO36......24 B3
Sydney Ho PO1..........54 B4
Sydney Rd PO12.........52 B5
Sylvan Ave PO32..........3 D3
Sylvan Dr
  Carisbrooke PO30.....20 B7
  Newport PO30.........20 C7
Synor Ho 12 SO15.......51 A6

Tadhurst Ho 4 PO1......54 C3
Talbot Ct 21 SO14.......51 A3
Talbot Rd
  Portsmouth PO4.......53 E4
  Sandown PO36........35 E4
Tamar Cl PO30...........35 F7
Tamarisk Gdns SO18.....51 E8
Tamworth St 3 PO12....52 A4
Tandy Cl PO33..........12 A4
Tanglewood SO40........50 A1
Tankerville Rd SO19......51 D3
Tapnell Cotts PO41.......16 C1
Tasman Cl SO14.........51 B2
Tasman Ct SO14.........51 B2
Taswell Rd PO5.........53 D2
Tattels La PO41.........16 C6
Taylor Cl SO19..........51 D1
Taylor Rd PO12.........52 C3
Tebourba Dr PO12........52 A4
Ted Bates Ct 7 SO15....50 E6
Ted Bates Rd 9 SO14....51 B3
Ted Kelly Ct 13 PO1.....53 A5
Telephone Rd PO4........53 E4
Temeraire 11 SO15.......50 F8
Templar Ct 2 SO14......51 A7
Temple Gdns SO19.......51 F2
Temple Rd SO19.........51 F2
Temple St PO1..........54 B4
Tennyson Cl
  Ryde PO33............12 C5
  Yarmouth PO41........15 D6
Tennyson Ho 6 PO3......53 E1
Tennyson Mon The*
  PO39.................26 H5
Tennyson Rd
  Cowes PO31............3 B3
  Freshwater PO40......14 E1
  Portsmouth PO2.......53 F8
  Yarmouth PO41........15 E6
Tennysons View PO40....27 C6
Tennyson View PO30.....18 A3
Terence Gdns PO4.......53 E2
Terminus Rd PO31........3 A5
Terminus Terr SO14......51 B3
Ternal Mead PO38.......33 D1
Terrace La PO41.........27 C6
Terrace Rd PO30........20 D6
Terrace The PO38.......44 C5
Testcombe Rd PO12.....52 B4
Testwood Rd SO15.......50 B6
Teviot Ho 9 SO14.......51 C6
Tewkesbury Ave PO12...52 B8
Thackeray Rd SO17......51 D8
Thatchers La SO41......49 F8
Theatre Mews 17 PO5...53 D2
Thetis Rd PO31...........3 B4
Thicket The PO35.......54 C1
Thomas Grant Ave PO12..52 D7
THORLEY..............16 C6
Thorley Rd PO41........15 E6
THORLEY STREET.......16 D5
Thornbrake Rd PO12.....52 C4

Thornbrough Cl PO33....12 A5
THORNCROSS...........38 F8
Thorncross La PO40......38 G7
Thorners Ct 8 SO15.....50 B8
Thorner's Homes, Centre Ct
  16 SO15..............50 B8
Thorner's Homes, North Ct
  14 SO15..............50 B8
Thorner's Homes, South Ct
  18 SO15..............50 B8
Thorner's Homes, West Ct 18
  SO15..................7 E5
Thorness La PO31........12 F4
Thorngate Ct 5 PO12....52 D5
Thorngate Way 8 PO12..52 D5
Thornhill Flats PO31......3 A5
Thornleigh Rd SO19......51 E2
Thornton Cl PO33.........12 F4
Thornton Manor Dr PO33..12 F4
Thornton Rd PO12.......52 B9
Thornycroft Ave SO19....51 D2
Threefield La SO14.......51 A3
Three Gates Rd PO30.....2 F2
Three Tun Cl PO1.........53 A5
Thruxton Ct SO19........51 E3
Ticonderoga Gdns SO19...51 E1
Tides Reach
  Cowes PO31............3 B4
  Southampton SO18....51 D8
  Yarmouth PO41........15 D5
Tiger Rd PO1............52 F8
Tilbrook Rd SO15........50 A8
Tilbury Rd PO31..........2 D3
Timberley Ho 2 PO1.....54 C3
Timpson Ho PO34........13 D3
Timson Cl SO19..........51 D1
Timsbury Ct SO19........51 F4
Tinkers Hill PO30.........20 F7
Tintern Gr 2 SO15......50 E5
Tintern Rd PO33.........12 F4
Tipton Ho PO5...........54 B2
Tithe Barn SO41.........48 E5
Tivoli Ct PO2............53 F8
Toby St PO1.............54 B4
Tonbridge St PO5........53 C2
Torcross Cl SO19.........51 E2
Toronto Pl PO12.........52 B6
Toronto Rd PO2.........53 E7
Torquay Ave
  Gosport PO12.........52 A9
  Southampton SO15....50 D8
TOTLAND..............26 H8
Tottenham Rd PO1.......54 D4
Tower Ho SO19...........51 E1
Tower Rd PO4...........53 F3
Tower St PO1............52 F4
Town End PO41..........45 B4
Town La
  Chale Green PO38.....40 A5
  Newport PO30.........20 E7
  Sandown PO36........35 F5
Town Mews PO36.......35 F5
Town Quay
  Cowes PO31............3 B5
  Portsmouth PO1.......52 F4
  Southampton SO15....50 F2
Trafalgar Ct
  Cowes PO31............3 A5
  12 Newport PO30.....20 D6
  6 Portsmouth PO5....53 D2
Trafalgar Dr PO33........11 F4
Trafalgar Pl
  Lymington SO41.......48 F4
  Portsmouth PO1......54 D4
Trafalgar Rd
  Newport PO30.........20 D6
  Southampton, Freemantle
    SO15................51 A5
  Southampton SO14....51 A2
Trafalgar Sq PO12.......52 B6
Tranby Rd SO19.........51 E4
Tranmere Cl SO41.......48 F2
Treefields PO33.........12 A5
Treeside Rd SO15........50 C8
Tregantle Mews PO35....25 D5
Trelawny Way PO39......31 C5
Trent Ho 8 SO14........51 C5
Trevanions Way PO39....27 A8
Trevor Rd
  Newport PO30.........20 C6
  Portsmouth PO4.......53 E3
Tribe Rd PO12...........52 A6
Trimmer's Ct PO33.......20 C7
Trinity Church La PO31....3 A6
Trinity Cl PO12..........52 E5
Trinity Ct
  Ryde PO33.............12 C6
  8 Southampton SO15..50 C6
Trinity Gn PO12..........52 E5
Trinity Rd
  Southampton SO14....51 A5
  Ventnor PO38.........47 B6
Trinity St PO33..........12 C5
Troubridge Ct 7 PO1....53 D7
Troughton Ct PO36......35 F5
Tudor Ct 3 PO5.........53 D1
Tulse Hill PO38..........47 A6
Tupman Ho 21 PO1......53 D7
Turf Wlk PO39..........14 C1
Turner Rd PO1..........53 D7
Tuttons Hill PO31........12 B8
Tweed La SO41..........48 D8
Twin Oaks SO19.........51 F3

Two Firs PO36...........34 D6
Twyford Ho SO15........50 F7
Tylers Cl SO41...........48 D5
Tyne Wlk PO35...........25 D5
Tyseley Rd PO5..........54 B2

U

Uffa Fox Pl PO31..........3 B3
Ulster Cres PO30..........9 A1
Undercliff Dr PO38.......45 D3
Undercliff Gdns PO38.....46 E5
Undermount PO38........47 D7
Undershore SO41.........48 E6
Undershore Rd SO41......49 A4
Unicorn Rd PO1..........54 B4
Unicorn Training Ctr The
  PO1..................54 A4
Union Pl
  7 Lymington SO41....48 F4
  Portsmouth PO1......54 C4
Union Rd
  Cowes PO31............3 A5
  Ryde PO33............12 C6
  Sandown PO36........35 F5
  Southampton SO14....51 C6
Union St
  Newport PO30.........20 D6
  10 Portsmouth PO1...53 A5
  Ryde PO33............12 C6
University of Portsmouth 6
  PO1..................54 A2
Univ of Portsmouth (Eldon
  Bldg) PO1............54 B2
Unwin Cl SO19..........51 D1
Uplands Rd
  Cowes PO31............8 F8
  Totland PO39..........14 D1
Upper Adgestone Rd
  PO36.................23 E1
Upper Arundel St PO1....54 B3
Upper Ash Dr PO38......45 E6
Upper Banister St 1
  SO15................50 F6
UPPER BONCHURCH......47 D7
Upper Bugle St SO14.....50 F3
Upper Comm Rd SO41...48 A4
Upper Green Rd PO33...24 F7
Upper Highland Rd PO33..12 D4
Upper Horn Hill PO31.....2 C3
Upper House La PO38....44 D6
UPPER HYDE...........42 F7
Upper Hyde Farm La
  PO37.................43 A8
Upper Hyde La PO37.....43 A8
Upper La PO30..........30 B2
Upper Moorgreen Rd PO31..46 E7
UPPER PENNINGTON.....48 A3
Upper Rd PO36..........23 D1
Upper Woodside Rd PO33..10 F7
Upper Yarborough Rd
  PO32...................3 D2
UPTON................12 A2
Upton Rd PO33.........12 A3

V

Vadne Gdns PO12........52 B7
Vale Gr PO12...........52 A8
Vale The PO5...........53 C2
Valley Wlk PO32...........4 A3
Vancouver Wharf SO19...51 C4
Vanguard Rd 5 PO12....52 C9
Varna Rd SO15..........50 C6
Varos Ct PO12..........52 A7
Vaughan Way PO37......43 C6
Vectis Cotts PO30.........9 B4
Vectis Rd PO32...........3 D2
Velsheda Ct PO39........11 E4
Velsheda View PO31......2 F3
Venner Ave PO31..........8 F8
Ventnor PO30............20 D6
VENTNOR.............47 B5
Ventnor Rd
  Portsmouth PO4.......53 E4
  Shanklin PO37.........34 E2
  Whitwell PO38........45 E5
Vereker Dr PO32.........3 D4
Verlands Cl PO38........45 B3
Vernon Cl PO12.........52 A6
Vernon Rd PO12........52 A6
Vernon Sq PO33.........12 C5
Vernon Wlk 5 SO15....50 F6
Verulam Rd SO14.......51 B7
Verwood Dr PO33.......11 E4
Vespasian Ct SO18......51 D7
Vespasian Rd SO18......51 D7
Vicarage La PO36.......24 B4
Vicarage Wlk PO30......20 D7
Victoria & Albert Almshouses
  PO32...................9 E8
Victoria Ave
  Portsmouth PO1.......53 B3
  Shanklin PO37.........43 B7
Victoria Cres PO33......12 E3
Victoria Ct
  East Cowes PO32.......3 D3
  Freshwater Bay PO40..27 C7
  Newport PO30.........20 D6
  6 Portsmouth PO1....53 D7

Victoria Ct continued
  Shanklin PO37.........43 C7
Victoria Gr
  East Cowes PO32.......3 D2
  Portsmouth PO5......54 C1
Victoria Mews PO31.......3 A4
Victoria Pl
  6 Gosport PO12......52 B5
  4 Lymington SO41....48 E2
  Ryde PO33............12 C5
Victoria Rd
  Bouldnor PO41........16 C8
  Cowes PO31............3 A4
  Freshwater Bay PO40..27 C7
  Newport PO30.........20 E8
  Portsmouth PO1.......53 A6
  Sandown PO36........36 A3
  Southampton SO19....51 D2
  Yarmouth PO41........15 D5
Victoria Road N PO5.....54 C2
Victoria Road S PO5.....53 D2
Victoria St
  Gosport PO12.........52 C6
  Portsmouth PO1......53 D7
  Ryde PO33............12 C5
  Southampton SO14....51 C5
  Ventnor PO38.........47 B6
Victor Rd PO1...........53 F7
Victory Cl PO33.........11 F4
Victory Cres SO15......50 B6
Victory Rd
  27 Portsmouth PO1...53 A5
  Southampton SO15....50 B6
Victory Ret Pk PO2......53 C7
Victory Sq SO15.........50 B6
Village Rd PO12..........52 A3
Villiers Ct 8 PO5........53 C2
Villiers Rd
  Portsmouth PO5.......53 C2
  Southampton SO15....50 C8
Vincent Rd SO15........50 C8
Vincent's Gr SO15.......50 B8
Vincent St SO15.........50 C8
Vincent's Wlk SO14.....51 A4
Vineyard Ct SO19........51 D3
Viney Rd SO41..........48 F1
Vinings Gdns PO36......35 F6
Vinings Rd PO36.........35 F6
Vinyard The PO41.......15 F6
Vitre Gdns SO41.........48 E2
Vittlefield Cross PO33....19 C7
Vittlefields Ind Est PO30..19 B7
Vivash Rd PO1..........54 B3
Vulcan The 11 PO1.....53 A4
Vyse La 13 SO14........50 F3

W

WACKLAND............34 C7
Wackland La PO36......34 D7
Wainsford Cl SO41......48 B2
Wainsford Rd SO41......48 C2
Wakefield Pl PO12.......52 A3
Waldegrave Cl SO19.....51 D1
WALHAMPTON.........49 A4
Walhampton Hill SO41...48 F5
Walker's La PO30.........31 B2
Wallace Ct PO30.........20 F7
Wallace Rd
  Portsmouth PO2.......53 F8
  Southampton SO19....51 F1
Wallis Cl PO38..........42 C4
Walls Rd PO35...........25 E4
Walmer Rd PO1.........53 E4
Walpole Rd PO12.......52 D5
Walpole Terr 2 PO12...52 B4
Waltham St PO5.........54 A2
Walton Cl PO12..........52 A5
Walton Ct 10 PO1......53 A4
Walton Lodge PO33.....12 E5
Walton Rd PO12........52 A5
Waltzing Waters Aqua
  Theatre* PO39.......12 F1
Warblington Ct 2 PO1...53 A4
Warblington St PO1......53 A4
WARBORNE............48 F8
Warborne La SO41......48 F8
Ward Ave PO31...........3 A5
Ward Cl PO30............20 B7
Warden Rd PO39........14 E1
Warders Ct 2 PO12.....52 B6
Ward Ho PO1............53 A6
Ward Rd PO39..........14 C1
Wards Cotts PO31........3 B5
Warlands La PO30........17 D6
Warnes La PO30.........30 B2
Warnford Cl PO12.......52 A5
Warnford Ct SO15.......50 F7
Warren Ct PO36.........35 D4
Warren Point PO31........9 B8
Warren The PO36.......35 F7
Warrior Ave PO31.........3 B3
Warwick Cres PO5......54 B2
Warwick Pl 16 SO14....51 C6
Warwick Pl 4 PO33.....12 C5
Warwick St PO33........12 C5
Washington Rd PO2.....53 D8
WATERFORD...........49 B1
Waterford Cl SO41......48 F3
Waterford La SO41......48 F2
Watergate 12 PO12....52 D5
Watergate Rd PO30.....20 D4
Waterhouse La SO15....50 B7
Waterhouse Way SO15..50 B7
Water La 2 SO15.......50 F5
Waterloo Cres PO33.....11 F4

Waterloo Rd
Gosport PO12 . . . . . . 52 C2
Lymington SO41 . . . . . 48 F4
Southampton SO15 . . . 50 D6
Waterloo St PO5 . . . . . 54 B2
Waterloo Terr SO15 . . . 50 F6
Waterman Terr PO5 . . . 54 D1
Waters Edge PO41 . . . . 15 F6
Waterside Rd PO33 . . . 12 C6
Watery La PO36 . . . . . 34 D5
Watts Rd PO1 . . . . . . 53 D7
Wavecrest Cl SO40 . . . 50 A3
Waverley Ct PO37 . . . . 43 D7
Waverley Gr PO4 . . . . . 53 E2
Waverley Rd
Portsmouth PO4 . . . . . 53 E2
Southampton SO15 . . . 50 D5
Wayside Dr PO38 . . . . 20 D8
Weavers Yd PO35 . . . . 25 E4
Webbers Way PO12 . . . 52 C3
Webster Way PO36 . . . 35 A8
WEEKE 54 B8
Week La PO38 . . . . . . 46 A6
WEEKS 12 C4
Weeks Rd
Ryde, Swanmore PO33 . 12 C3
Ryde, Weeks PO33 . . . 12 C4
Weevil La PO12 . . . . . 52 D7
Welch Rd
Gosport PO12 . . . . . . 52 A8
Portsmouth PO4 . . . . . 53 E2
Weller Ho **18** PO1 . . . 53 D7
Wellington Ct
East Cowes PO32 . . . . . 3 E2
1 Gosport PO12 . . . . 52 C9
Ryde PO33 . . . . 12 B6
Southampton SO15 . . . 50 D6
Wellington Lodge PO33 . 12 B6
Wellington Rd
Carisbrooke PO30 . . . . 20 B6
Lymington SO41 . . . . . 11 F4
Wellington Sq PO41 . . . 15 F5
Wellington St PO5 . . . . 54 B2
WELLOW 16 F5
Wellow Ct **18** SO18 . . . 51 E8
Wellow Top Rd PO41 . . 17 B4
Well Rd PO32 . . . . 3 C4
Well St PO33 . . . . 12 C4
Wellwood Ho PO33 . . . 11 E5
Wellworthy Rd SO41 . . . 48 D6
Wentworth Ct PO37 . . . 43 A7
Wesley Ct
Portsmouth PO1 . . . . . 54 D3
Ventnor PO38 . . . . . . 46 F6
Wessex Ct **8** SO17 . . . 51 A8
Wessex Gate **2** SO15 . . 50 E7
West Ashey Farm Cotts
PO33 . . . . 23 A5
West Ave PO36 . . . . . . 35 D3
West Bargate **2** SO14 . . 50 F4
West Bay Rd SO15 . . . . 50 C5
Westbourne Rd PO2 . . . 53 F8
West Cl
Portsmouth, Buckland
PO1 . . . . 53 E7
Southampton SO19 . . . 51 F1
Western Ave SO15 . . . . 50 D5
Western District Cut
SO15 . . . . 50 D7
Western Esplanade SO14,
SO15 . . . . 50 F3
Western Par PO5 . . . . . 53 B2
Western Rd
Lymington SO41 . . . . . 48 D4
Shanklin PO37 . . . . . . 43 C7
Western Way PO1 . . . . 52 F8
Westfield Bglws PO38 . . 47 C6
Westfield Ind Est PO12 . 52 A5
Westfield Mans PO38 . . 47 C6
Westfield Pk PO33 . . . . 12 B6
Westfield Rd
Lymington SO41 . . . . . 49 A2
Southampton SO15 . . . 50 A7
St Helens PO33 . . . . . 24 F7
Westgate St **14** SO14 . . 50 F3
West Gn PO33 . . . . . . 24 F7
West Hayes SO41 . . . . 48 F3
West Hill St SO15 . . . . 50 E5
Westhill Dr PO37 . . . . . 43 B7
West Hill Gr **2** PO31 . . . 3 B4
Westhill La PO41 . . . . . 15 B4
Westhill Rd
Cowes PO31 . . . . 3 B4
Shanklin PO37 . . . . . . 43 B6
West Hill Rd PO33 . . . . 12 E5

West La PO33, PO36 . . . 23 F5
Westlake Ave PO36 . . . 35 D2
Westland Gdns PO12 . . . 52 A4
Westlands PO39 . . . . . 14 E1
West Marlands Rd SO14 . 50 F5
Westmill PO30 . . . . . . 20 C6
Westmill Rd PO30 . . . . 20 B7
Westminster La PO30 . . 20 C7
Westminster Pl PO1 . . . 53 D7
WESTON 51 E1
Weston Cl SO19 . . . . . 51 F1
Weston Com Sch PO39 . 26 G8
Weston Grove Rd SO19 . 51 D2
Weston La
Southampton SO19 . . . 51 F1
Totland PO39 . . . . 26 G7
Weston Rd
Cowes PO31 . . . . 3 A4
Totland PO39 . . . . 26 G8
West Park Rd SO15 . . . 50 F5
West Quay SO14 . . . . . 50 F4
West Quay Rd SO15 . . . 50 E4
West Rd SO19 . . . . . . 51 E2
Westridge Cross PO33 . . 12 E2
Westridge Ctr PO33 . . . 12 E2
Westridge Rd SO17 . . . 51 B8
Westrow Gdns SO15 . . . 50 F7
Westrow Rd SO15 . . . . 50 E7
West Side La PO38 . . . 24 A3
Westside La PO38 . . . . 39 F2
West St
Brading PO36 . . . . . . 24 B3
Godshill PO38 . . . . . . 41 C8
Newport PO30 . . . . . . 20 D6
Portsmouth PO1 . . . . . 52 F4
Ryde PO33 . . . . 12 B6
Seaview PO34 . . . . . . 13 D4
Southampton SO14 . . . 50 F3
Ventnor PO38 . . . . . . 47 B6
Wroxall PO38 . . . . . . 42 B4
West View PO30 . . . . . 20 D6
Westview Cotts PO38 . . 44 C7
Westview Rd PO31 . . . . 2 C1
Westview Terr PO33 . . . 12 D5
Westway PO31 . . . . . . 8 E8
West Way SO41 . . . . . 48 C2
West Wight Mid Sch
PO40 . . . . 27 B8
West Wight Sp Ctr PO40 . 27 B8
Westwood Cl PO31 . . . . 2 F4
Westwood Ct **12** SO17 . . 51 A8
Westwood Dr PO33 . . . 12 B5
Westwood Rd
Ryde PO33 . . . . 12 B5
Southampton SO17 . . . 51 A8
Wharf Rd
Portsmouth PO2 . . . . . 53 C8
Southampton SO19 . . . 51 D3
Wharncliffe Ho SO19 . . . 51 D3
Wharncliffe Rd SO19 . . . 51 D3
Wheatear Cl PO30 . . . . 20 A6
Wheatstone Rd PO4 . . . 53 F3
Wheeler Cl PO12 . . . . . 52 B7
Wheelers Bay Rd PO38 . 47 B5
Wheeler Way PO37 . . . 35 D2
Whinscot Cl PO38 . . . . 45 D7
WHIPPINGHAM 9 E8
Whippingham Cty Prim Sch
PO32 . . . . 9 F8
Whippingham Rd PO32 . . 9 F7
Whitaker Cres SO41 . . . 48 C3
Whitchurch Ct SO19 . . . 51 F3
Whitcombe Cross PO30 . 20 B3
Whitcombe Gdns PO31 . 53 F6
Whitcombe Rd PO30 . . . 20 B3
Whiteacres Cl **4** PO12 . . 52 B6
Whitecliff Cl PO36 . . . . 36 C5
White Cloud Pk PO4 . . . 53 F3
White Cloud Pl PO4 . . . 53 F3
WHITECROSS 35 D3
Whitecross Ave PO37 . . 35 C2
Whitecross Bsns Ctr
PO37 . . . . 35 C2
Whitecross Farm La PO36 . 35 C2
Whitecross La
Apse Heath PO37 . . . . 34 F2
Shanklin SO36, SO37 . . 35 C2
Whitefield Terr PO33 . . . 12 D4
White Hart La
4 Gosport PO12 . . . . 52 B5
Portsmouth PO1 . . . . . 53 A3
Whitehead Cres PO33 . . 10 E5
Whitehouse Gdns SO15 . 50 A6
Whitehouse Rd PO30 . . . 7 F3
Whitelaw Rd SO15 . . . . 50 B7
WHITELEY BANK 42 C8
White Lion Wlk PO12 . . 52 D6
White Oaks Cl **9** SO16 . . 50 B8
Whitepit La PO30 . . . . . 20 C5
Whiterails Rd PO33 . . . . 10 C2

White's Mead PO36 . . . 35 D4
Whitesmith Rd PO30 . . . 9 A1
Whitestar Pl **14** SO14 . . 51 B3
White Swan Rd PO1 . . . 54 A3
Whitethorns Ct PO36 . . 35 F5
Whitehedowed Ave SO15 . 50 D8
WHITWELL 45 E6
Whitwell Rd
Godshill PO38 . . . . . . 41 C6
Portsmouth PO4 . . . . . 53 E1
Ventnor PO38 . . . . . . 46 C5
Whitworth Cl PO12 . . . . 52 B5
Whitworth Cres SO18 . . 51 D8
Whitworth Ct SO18 . . . . 51 D7
Whitworth Rd
Gosport PO12 . . . . . . 52 A6
Portsmouth PO2 . . . . . 53 F8
Southampton SO18 . . . 51 D8
Wicken Hill La PO30 . . . 38 E8
Wickham St PO1 . . . . . 53 A5
Wicks Cl PO33 . . . . . . 12 D2
Widbury Rd SO41 . . . . 48 C2
Widgeon Cl PO12 . . . . 52 B8
Wight Hall La PO33 . . . 12 E6
Wigmore Ho PO1 . . . . . 54 C4
Wilberforce Rd
Brighstone PO30 . . . . . 30 B2
Gosport PO12 . . . . . . 52 C2
Portsmouth PO5 . . . . . 54 B1
Wilkes Rd PO36 . . . . . 35 F5
Willet's Cross PO30 . . . 31 B1
William Booth Ho **1** PO1 . 53 B5
William Rd SO41 . . . . . 48 E5
William St
Ryde PO33 . . . . 12 B3
Southampton SO14 . . . 51 C5
Willis Rd
Gosport PO12 . . . . . . 52 C5
Portsmouth PO1 . . . . . 54 C4
Willment Marine & Bsns Pk
SO19 . . . . 51 D5
Willments Ind Est SO19 . 51 D4
Willow Cl PO38 . . . . . . 46 E7
Willow Ct **5** PO20 . . . . 20 D6
Willowdene Ct PO35 . . . 25 E4
Willow Pl PO12 . . . . . . 52 B6
Willows The
Newport PO30 . . . . . . 20 C7
Ryde PO33 . . . . 12 D4
Willow Tree Cl PO30 . . . 20 C4
Willow Tree Dr PO31 . . . 8 F7
Willow Tree Ho PO33 . . . 48 C2
Willow Way PO36 . . . . 35 F7
Wilmar Lodge PO36 . . . 35 D3
Wilmcote Gdns **5** PO5 . . 54 C3
Wilmcote Ho PO5 . . . . 54 C3
Wilmingham La PO41 . . 15 E2
Wilson Gr PO5 . . . . . . 54 C1
Wilson St SO14 . . . . . . 51 C5
Wilton Ave SO15 . . . . . 50 F6
Wilton Cl SO15 . . . . . . 50 D8
Wilton Park Rd PO37 . . . 35 C1
Wilton Pl PO5 . . . . . . 53 D2
Wilton Rd PO37 . . . . . 35 C1
Wilton Terr PO5 . . . . . 53 D2
Wiltshire St PO5 . . . . . 54 A2
Wilverley Cl SO41 . . . . 48 B2
Wilver Rd PO30 . . . . . 20 C6
Wimbledon Park Rd PO5 . 53 D2
Wimpole Ct PO5 . . . . . 54 C4
Wimpole St PO1 . . . . . 54 C4
Winchat Cl PO30 . . . . . 20 B6
Winchester Cl
Newport PO30 . . . . . . 20 C5
Sandown PO36 . . . . . 35 E6
Winchester Cnr PO30 . . 17 F7
Winchester Mews
Ryde PO33 . . . . 12 D5
19 Southampton SO17 . . 51 A8
Winchester Park Ct PO36 . 35 F5
Winchester Park Rd PO36 . 35 F6
Winchester Rd PO2 . . . 53 E8
Winchester St **4** SO15 . . 50 F6
Winchfield Ho **4** PO12 . . 52 E5
Winding Way PO31 . . . . 35 D1
Windmill Ct
Cowes PO31 . . . . 3 A3
Ryde PO33 . . . . 12 A2
Windmill Cotts PO35 . . . 25 D4
Windmill La PO39 . . . . 26 H8
Windsor Ct
10 Portsmouth PO5 . . 53 C2
16 Southampton, Bevois Mount
SO17 . . . . 51 A8
2 Southampton, Bitterne
SO18 . . . . 51 E7
3 Southampton, Millbrook
SO15 . . . . 50 A6

Windsor Ct continued
6 Southampton, Westwood Pk
SO17 . . . . 51 A8
Windsor Dr PO37 . . . . . 43 A7
Windsor Ho **3** PO1 . . . . 54 C3
Windsor La **12** PO5 . . . . 54 B2
Windsor Mews **9** PO33 . . 12 C5
Windsor Rd PO12 . . . . . 52 A5
Windward Ct **12** PO12 . . 52 C5
WINFORD 34 E5
Winford Cross PO36 . . . 34 D5
Winford Ct PO36 . . . . . 34 E4
Winford Rd
Newchurch PO36 . . . . 34 D7
Winford PO36 . . . . . . 34 D4
Winford Way PO1 . . . . . 34 F5
Wingfield St PO1 . . . . . 53 D7
Winkle St
Calbourne PO30 . . . . . 18 A2
Southampton SO14 . . . 51 A2
Winn Ct SO17 . . . . . . 50 E7
Winston Ave PO33 . . . . 12 A4
Winston Churchill Ave
PO5 . . . . 54 B2
Winston Rd
Cowes PO31 . . . . 2 F4
Newport PO30 . . . . . . 20 C5
Winton Cl SO41 . . . . . 48 F3
Winton Cr PO33 . . . . . 12 D5
Winton St
Ryde PO33 . . . . 12 D5
8 Southampton SO14 . . 51 B3
Wisborough Rd PO5 . . . 53 E2
Wises Ct **1** PO12 . . . . 52 E5
Wish Pl PO5 . . . . 54 D1
Witbank Cl PO37 . . . . . 35 C1
Witbank Gdns PO37 . . . 35 C1
Withers Rd PO38 . . . . . 46 A4
Withewood Mans 2
SO15 . . . . 50 C7
Withybed Cl PO30 . . . . 20 B6
Withyfields PO30 . . . . . 17 E7
Wodehouse Rd SO19 . . . 51 E4
Wolfe Cl PO30 . . . . . . 20 B6
Wolseley Rd SO15 . . . . 50 C7
Wolverton Rd SO14 . . . 51 B5
Woodbine Cl PO30 . . . . 20 B6
Woodbine Cotts PO36 . . 24 B2
Woodhall Dr PO36 . . . . 35 C3
Woodhill Cl PO33 . . . . . 12 D4
Woodland Cl PO33 . . . . 13 A4
Woodland Ct PO40 . . . . 15 A1
Woodland Dr PO33 . . . . 12 C5
Woodland Ho PO37 . . . 43 B7
Woodland Mews PO33 . . 12 E5
Woodland Pl **1** SO15 . . . 50 E7
Woodlands PO35 . . . . . 25 D4
Woodlands Cres PO33 . . 10 E5
Woodland St PO1 . . . . . 54 D4
Woodlands Way SO18 . . 50 F8
Woodland View PO33 . . 12 B3
Woodley Gdns SO41 . . . 48 D5
Woodley Rd
Gosport PO12 . . . . . . 52 C5
Southampton SO19 . . . 51 D3
Woodmoor Cl SO40 . . . 50 A1
Woodnutt Cl PO40 . . . . 15 A1
Woodpath PO5 . . . . . . 54 B1
Woodpath Ho PO5 . . . . 54 B1
Woods Dr PO36 . . . . . 34 E4
WOODSIDE 48 E1
Woodside Ave
Alverstone Garden Village
PO36 . . . . 35 A7
Lymington SO41 . . . . . 48 E1
Woodside Cl
Cowes PO31 . . . . 8 E8
10 Lymington SO41 . . . 48 E2
Woodside Ct **8** SO17 . . . 51 B8
Woodside La SO41 . . . . 48 E1
WOODSIDE (NR
WOOTTON) 11 A7
Woodside Rd
Southampton SO17 . . . 51 B8
Wootton PO33 . . . . . . 11 A7
Wood St PO33 . . . . . . 12 D5
Woodstock Rd PO12 . . . 52 C4
Woodvale Ho PO31 . . . . 2 E4
Woodvale Rd PO31 . . . . 2 E4
Woodville Dr **4** PO1 . . . 53 B3
Woolcombe Rd PO30 . . . 9 A2
WOOLSTON 51 E2
Woolston Inf Sch SO19 . 51 E2
Woolston Sta SO19 . . . . 51 D3
Woolverton Rd PO38 . . . 46 A3
Wooton Lodge PO33 . . . 10 E5
WOOTTON 10 D5
WOOTTON BRIDGE 10 E4

Wootton Bsns Pk PO33 . 10 B2
Wootton Prim Sch PO33 . 10 D5
Wootton Sta* PO33 . . . 10 D3
Worcester Cl
5 Portsmouth PO5 . . . 54 C2
Sandown PO36 . . . . . 35 E6
11 Southsea PO5 . . . . 54 B2
Worcester Pl **6** SO41 . . . 48 F2
Worcester Rd PO30 . . . . 8 F1
Worsley Ct PO38 . . . . . 42 C4
Worsley Dr PO38 . . . . . 42 B5
Worsley La PO31 . . . . . 2 D4
Worsley Rd
Godshill PO38 . . . . . . 33 D1
Gurnard PO31 . . . . . . 2 D3
Newport PO30 . . . . . . 20 C8
Norton PO41 . . . . 15 A6
Portsmouth PO5 . . . . . 54 B1
Worth Apts PO5 . . . . . 53 D1
Worthing Rd PO5 . . . . . 53 D2
Wrax Rd PO36 . . . . . . 24 B2
Wray St PO33 . . . . 12 B3
Wrexham Ave PO33 . . . 12 A3
WROXALL 42 C4
Wroxall Cl PO31 . . . . . 8 F8
Wroxall Ho PO38 . . . . . 42 C4
Wroxall Prim Sch PO38 . 42 C4
Wyatts Cl PO31 . . . . . . 8 E8
Wyatts La PO31 . . . . . . 8 F8
Wychwood Cl PO34 . . . 13 D2
Wykeham Cl PO33 . . . . 11 E5
Wykeham Pl SO41 . . . . 48 E3
Wykeham Rd PO30 . . . . 20 C6
Wymering Rd PO2 . . . . 53 E8
Wyndcliffe Rd PO4 . . . . 53 E3
Wyndham Ct SO15 . . . . 50 E5
Wyndham Mews PO1 . . 53 D4
Wyndham Pl **4** SO15 . . . 50 E5

Y

YAFFORD 38 H8
Yaldhurst La SO41 . . . . 48 B3
Yapton St PO1 . . . . . . 54 B3
Yarborough Cl PO38 . . . 33 C1
Yarborough Ct PO38 . . . 47 A5
Yarborough Ho PO36 . . 36 A4
Yarborough Rd
East Cowes PO32 . . . . . 3 C3
1 Gosport PO12 . . . . 54 B1
Wroxall PO38 . . . . . . 42 C5
Yarborough Terr PO38 . . 42 C4
YARBRIDGE 24 A1
YARMOUTH 15 D6
Yarmouth Castle* PO41 . 15 C6
Yarmouth CE Prim Sch
PO41 . . . . 15 C5
Yarmouth Rd PO30 . . . . 19 B7
Yar Quay PO33 . . . . . . 25 A6
Yarrell Croft SO41 . . . . 48 B3
Yarrell Mead SO41 . . . . 48 B3
YAVERLAND 36 C6
Yaverland Cl PO36 . . . . 36 C5
Yaverland Rd PO36 . . . . 36 C5
Yelfs Rd **7** PO33 . . . . . 12 C6
York Ave PO32 . . . . . . 3 D3
York Bldgs SO14 . . . . . 51 A4
York Cl SO14 . . . . 51 C6
Yorke St PO5 . . . . 54 A2
York Ho
9 Gosport PO12 . . . . 52 D5
7 Southampton SO14 . . 51 C6
York La PO39 . . . . 26 G7
York Pl PO1 . . . . 53 B6
York Rd
Newport PO30 . . . . . . 20 E6
Sandown PO36 . . . . . 35 F5
Southampton SO15 . . . 50 C7
Totland PO39 . . . . 26 G7
Ventnor PO38 . . . . . . 46 F6
York St PO31 . . . . 3 B4
York Villas PO38 . . . . . 46 E6
York Wlk **6** SO14 . . . . . 51 A4
Youngwoods Copse PO36 . 35 A7
Youngwoods Way PO36 . 35 A7
Yves Mews PO5 . . . . . 53 D2

Z

Zetland Rd PO12 . . . . . 52 B6
Zig Zag Rd PO38 . . . . . 46 F6
Zille Est PO33 . . . . 12 D6